Numeric Data Types

Data Type	Description	Length
int	Stores integer values ranging from −2,147,483,648 to 2,147,483,647	4 bytes
tinyint	Stores integer values ranging from 0 to 255	1 byte
smallint	Stores integer values ranging from −32,768 to 32,767	2 bytes
bigint	Stores integer values ranging from -2^{63} to $2^{63}-1$	8 bytes
money	Stores monetary values ranging from −922,337,203,685,477.5808 to 922,337,203,685,477.5807	8 bytes
smallmoney	Stores monetary values ranging from −214,748.3648 to 214,748.3647	4 bytes
decimal(p,s)	Stores decimal values of precision p and scale s. The maximum precision is 38 digits	5–17 bytes
numeric(p,s)	Functionally equivalent to decimal	
float(n)	Stores floating point values with precision of 7 digits (when n=24) or 15 digits (when n=53)	4 bytes (when n=24) or 8 bytes (when n=53)
real	Functionally equivalent to float(24)	

Date and Time Data Types

Data Type	Description	Length	Example
date	Stores dates between January 1, 0001, and December 31, 9999	3 bytes	2008-01-15
datetime	Stores dates and times between January 1, 1753, and December 31, 9999, with an accuracy of 3.33 milliseconds	8 bytes	2008-01-15 09:42:16.142
datetime2	Stores date and times between January 1, 0001, and December 31, 9999, with an accuracy of 100 nanoseconds	6–8 bytes	2008-01-15 09:42:16.1420221
datetimeoffset	Stores date and times with the same precision as datetime2 and also includes an offset from Universal Time Coordinated (UTC) (also known as Greenwich Mean Time)	8–10 bytes	2008-01-15 09:42:16.1420221 +05:00
smalldatetime	Stores dates and times between January 1, 1900, and June 6, 2079, with an accuracy of 1 minute (the seconds are always listed as ":00")	4 bytes	2008-01-15 09:42:00
time	Stores times with an accuracy of 100 nanoseconds	3–5 bytes	09:42:16.1420221

(continued)

Microsoft® SQL Server® 2008 For Dummies®

Cheat Sheet

Numeric Data Types *(continued)*

Character String Data Types

Data Type	Description	Length
char(n)	Stores *n* characters	*n* bytes (where *n* is in the range of 1–8,000)
nchar(n)	Stores *n* Unicode characters	2*n* bytes (where n is in the range of 1–4,000)
varchar(n)	Stores approximately *n* characters	Actual string length+2 bytes (where *n* is in the range of 1–8,000)
varchar(max)	Stores up to $2^{31}-1$ characters	Actual string length+2 bytes
nvarchar(n)	Stores approximately *n* characters	2*(actual string length)+2 bytes (where *n* is in the range of 1–4,000)
nvarchar(max)	Stores up to $((2^{31}-1)/2)-2$ characters	2*(actual string length)+2 bytes

Binary Data Types

Data Type	Description	Length
bit	Stores a single bit of data	1 byte per 8 bit columns in a table
binary(n)	Stores *n* bytes of binary data	*n* bytes (where n is in the range of 1-8,000)
varbinary(n)	Stores approximately *n* bytes of binary data	Actual length+2 bytes (where *n* is in the range of 1–8,000)
varbinary(max)	Stores up to $2^{31}-1$ bytes of binary data	Actual length+2 bytes
cursor	Stores a reference to a cursor	N/A (cannot be used in a table)
sql_variant	May store any data type other than sql_variant, text, ntext, image, and timestamp	Up to 8,000 bytes
table	Stores a temporary table (such as a query result)	N/A (cannot be used in a table)
rowversion	Stores a value of the database time (a relative number that increments each time you insert or update data in a database. It is not related to calendar/clock time)	8 bytes
uniqueidentifier	Stores a globally unique identifier	2 bytes
xml	Stores formatted XML documents	Up to 2GB

For Dummies: Bestselling Book Series for Beginners

Microsoft® SQL Server® 2008

FOR

DUMMIES®

Microsoft® SQL Server® 2008

FOR DUMMIES®

by Mike Chapple

WILEY

Wiley Publishing, Inc.

Microsoft® SQL Server® 2008 For Dummies®

Published by
Wiley Publishing, Inc.
111 River Street
Hoboken, NJ 07030-5774
www.wiley.com

Copyright © 2008 by Wiley Publishing, Inc., Indianapolis, Indiana

Published by Wiley Publishing, Inc., Indianapolis, Indiana

Published simultaneously in Canada

For general information on our other products and services, please contact our Customer Care Department within the U.S. at 800-762-2974, outside the U.S. at 317-572-3993, or fax 317-572-4002.

For technical support, please visit www.wiley.com/techsupport.

Wiley also publishes its books in a variety of electronic formats. Some content that appears in print may not be available in electronic books.

Library of Congress Control Number: 2008933745

ISBN: 978-0-470-22465-6

Manufactured in the United States of America

10 9 8 7 6 5 4 3 2 1

About the Author

Mike Chapple, MCDBA, CISA, CISSP is an IT professional with over ten years' experience with SQL Server. He currently serves as an IT professional with the University of Notre Dame, where he also teaches an undergraduate computer applications course. Mike actively participates as a subject matter expert in the SQL Server community and writes extensively on SQL Server at the About.com Guide to Databases. He also serves on the Center for Internet Security SQL Server security standard development team.

Mike is a technical editor for *Information Security Magazine* and is author of several books, including *Information Security Illuminated* and the *CISSP Prep Guide*. Mike holds a BS in computer science from the University of Notre Dame, an MS in computer science from the University of Idaho, and an MBA from Auburn University.

Dedication

To my family: Renee, Richard, Matthew, and Christopher who lovingly put up with me during the hours I spent buried in my laptop writing this book.

Author's Acknowledgments

I would like to thank Kyle Looper and Susan Christophersen, my editors at Wiley, who provided me with invaluable assistance throughout the book development process. I also owe a debt of gratitude to my literary agent, Carole Jelen of Waterside Productions. Doug Couch served as technical editor for this title and was a great source of advice as we worked through some of the more difficult portions of the book. I'd also like to thank the many people who participated in the production of this book but I never had the chance to meet: the graphics team, production staff, and all those involved in bringing this book to press.

Publisher's Acknowledgments

We're proud of this book; please send us your comments through our online registration form located at www.dummies.com/register/.

Some of the people who helped bring this book to market include the following:

Acquisitions, Editorial, and Media Development

Project Editor: Susan Christophersen

Acquisitions Editor: Kyle Looper

Copy Editor: Susan Christophersen

Technical Editor: Doug Couch

Editorial Manager: Jodi Jensen

Editorial Assistant: Amanda Foxworth

Sr. Editorial Assistant: Cherie Case

Cartoons: Rich Tennant
(www.the5thwave.com)

Composition Services

Project Coordinator: Katherine Key

Layout and Graphics: Carl Byers, Reuben W. Davis

Proofreader: Toni Settle

Indexer: Broccoli Information Management

Publishing and Editorial for Technology Dummies

Richard Swadley, Vice President and Executive Group Publisher

Andy Cummings, Vice President and Publisher

Mary Bednarek, Executive Acquisitions Director

Mary C. Corder, Editorial Director

Publishing for Consumer Dummies

Diane Graves Steele, Vice President and Publisher

Joyce Pepple, Acquisitions Director

Composition Services

Gerry Fahey, Vice President of Production Services

Debbie Stailey, Director of Composition Services

Contents at a Glance

Table of Contents

Introduction

I've been using SQL Server for longer than I care to admit. Let's just say that I remember the days when Microsoft first released its own version of SQL Server after obtaining the rights to it from Sybase Corporation. That was a long time ago!

Why have I been using SQL Server for such a long time? Quite simply, I believe in its power as a user- and business-friendly database platform that's readily accessible to users in most modern enterprises. It's much more powerful than desktop databases such as Microsoft Access, and it's rapidly gaining market share over the industry leader, Oracle.

SQL Server is unique in that it easily accommodates users with a wide range of experience. If you're upgrading from Microsoft Access, you'll find many of SQL Server's graphical user interfaces friendly and familiar. On the other hand, if you're a database professional moving from another platform, you'll find that the ability to directly issue commands to the database accelerates your learning curve.

About This Book

This book provides you with an introduction to many of the commonly used features of SQL Server 2008. You'll find that it's an excellent starting point for anyone beginning to use SQL Server and offers a great foundation for your database career. Some of the important issues I cover in this book include:

- Choosing the appropriate edition of SQL Server for your needs
- Orienting yourself to the SQL Server database management tools
- Installing and configuring your first SQL Server 2008 database server
- Designing your first database
- Creating databases and tables in SQL Server 2008
- Imposing constraints on database tables and creating inter-table relationships
- Retrieving data from your database with simple and advanced Transact-SQL queries

✔ Creating basic reports with SQL Server Reporting Services

✔ Inserting data into your database via manual or bulk insertion

✔ Using stored procedures, functions and triggers to automate database tasks

✔ Keeping your database server running smoothly with indexes and partitions

✔ Limiting resource consumption with SQL Server 2008's new Resource Governor

✔ Automating database administration with SQL Server Agent and Maintenance Plans

✔ Troubleshooting and tuning SQL Server databases

✔ Protecting your database with security controls, backups, and transactions

✔ Creating high-availability database solutions for critical IT environments

✔ Using the Declarative Management Framework to create policies covering multiple SQL Server installations

SQL Server 2008 is the most powerful database product ever released by Microsoft. In this book, I scratch the surface of this product's powerful capabilities by providing you with the information you need to get up and running quickly.

Conventions Used in This Book

Throughout the book, I apply the following typography conventions to help guide you through some of the information I present:

✔ Text that appears in this `special font` is certain to be a URL (Web address), e-mail address, filename, folder name, or code.

✔ When I use a term that I think you might not be familiar with, I apply *italics* to that term to let you know that I go on to define it next.

✔ When I tell you to choose menu commands, I do it like this: Choose File⇨Save, which means choose the File command and then choose the Save command.

✔ When I want you to type a specific item, I put it in **bold** text.

What You Are Not to Read

There's quite a bit of material in this book. Some of it will be more important to you than others, depending on the way you use SQL Server and your role within your organization. If you're looking for a broad-based introduction to SQL Server, feel free to start reading at Chapter 1 and continue through the end of the book. Otherwise, I wrote each chapter with the intention that it stands on its own merit. Feel free to flip through the Table of Contents and skip directly to the chapters of most interest to you.

If you're not involved in designing or modifying database structures, you can skip Chapters 4, 5, and 6.

If you're not responsible for day-to-day administration of SQL Server, bypass Chapters 12, 13, 14, and 15.

Foolish Assumptions

I've made a few assumptions about you when writing this book. Here's what I guessed:

- ✔ You're already comfortable using a computer and with basic use of the Windows operating system. You should feel comfortable starting programs and opening files.

- ✔ You're familiar with the Internet and know how to locate specific information using a search engine.

- ✔ You're familiar with the use of a simple spreadsheet, such as Microsoft Excel, to organize information. You may not know all the advanced features of such software, but you're able to create a simple Excel spreadsheet.

If these assumptions don't describe you, you might be starting with the wrong book. I suggest going out and picking up a copy of *PCs For Dummies* or *Windows Vista For Dummies* to help you get started.

How This Book Is Organized

This book is made up of seven parts that introduce you to Microsoft SQL Server 2008:

- ✔ **Part I: Welcome to SQL Server 2008** provides you with an overview of SQL Server 2008. You find out about the differences between SQL Server's Express, Workgroup, Standard, and Enterprise editions so that you can select the one most appropriate for your needs. You also discover the decisions you need to make and actions you need to take to get your first SQL Server installation up and running.

✔ **Part II: Building Databases** walks you through the process of creating your first database in a SQL Server environment. I explain the planning process you should follow to build your database according to accepted design principles and walk you through the process of diagramming your database on paper before implementing it for real. I then describe the process to create your database, design tables, and enforce relationships between tables.

✔ **Part III: Retrieving Data from Databases** describes how to retrieve information from a SQL Server database. I introduce the Structured Query Language (SQL) and explain how you can use it to pull the exact information you need out of your database. I also describe some advanced database queries that allow you to combine information from multiple tables and take different actions based on the results of database queries.

✔ **Part IV: Inserting and Manipulating Your Data** takes you beyond simple retrieval of data and describes how you get new data into a database and modify information that exists within a database table. I describe the use of SQL statements and bulk import tools to add information to database tables. You also discover how stored procedures, functions, and triggers can help you automate tedious database tasks.

✔ **Part V: SQL Server Administration** is for those of you who have responsibility for administering SQL Server databases. You discover tips and tricks to help you keep your database operating in an optimal fashion by tuning performance parameters and governing resource utilization. I also provide you with advice on using SQL Server's administration tools to make the server do the routine work for you. I conclude this section with chapters dedicated to troubleshooting SQL Server problems and administering multiple servers in the same environment.

✔ **Part VI: Protecting Your Data** covers the basics you need to know to protect your SQL Server data from unwanted intruders and natural or technical disasters. You see how to implement access controls to limit the rights of database users and how to use encryption to protect your information from unauthorized access. I spend an entire chapter introducing the concept of transactions and explaining how they can protect the integrity of data stored within your database. Finally, you find out about techniques for backing up your database so that you can restore your data in the event of a disaster.

✔ **Part VI: The Part of Tens** is in every regular *For Dummies* book that you will ever pick up. In the first chapter in this part, I describe ten ways you can keep your database operating efficiently. In the second chapter, I provide you with ten tips for properly designing new SQL Server databases.

Icons Used in This Book

Icons are little pictures in the margins of the book that emphasize a point to remember, a warning to be aware of, or a tip that I think you might find helpful. Here are the ones I use in this book:

These are bits of information that I want to draw your attention to.

This icon means that I'm alerting you to something critical or I want you to think long and carefully about any action you might be about to take.

The information that shows up next to this icon might be more than you need (or want) to know, so you can skip it if you want, or come back to it when you have more time.

Here's a nugget of information that's worth storing in your memory because you'll need it from time to time.

Where to Go from Here

If you're looking for a broad introduction to SQL Server, just start reading at Chapter 1 and don't put the book down until you fall asleep or can't bear to read my writing any longer!

On the other hand, if you're looking for specific information about one aspect of SQL Server, feel free to pick and choose. Flip through the Table of Contents and select the chapters that interest you most. As I mentioned earlier, I wrote each chapter with the intention of making it a stand-alone chunk of information. Good luck in your SQL Server 2008 adventures!

Part I

Welcome to SQL Server 2008

The 5th Wave   By Rich Tennant

SNOW GLOBE DATA STORAGE

Okay, let's shake this thing and see what we come up with.

In this part . . .

In this first part, I give you an overview of SQL Server 2008. I point out the differences between SQL Server's various editions to help you figure out which one best suits your purposes. Here is where you also find out how to get your first SQL Server installation up and running.

Chapter 1

Introducing SQL Server 2008

SQL Server 2008 is Microsoft's enterprise-class database server, designed to compete with products such as Oracle and IBM's DB2. According to a Gartner study, SQL Server is rapidly gaining momentum, possessing more than 17 percent of the worldwide database market in 2006.

SQL Server allows you to store, retrieve, and manipulate data to meet your organization's business objectives. The platform provides a number of tools and technologies to assist you in managing and manipulating your data on your own terms. For example, using SQL Server 2008, you can

✔ Import and export data from a variety of file formats

✔ Link to other databases (both SQL Server and those of other manufacturers)

✔ Manipulate data from within Microsoft Excel and Microsoft Access

✔ Produce professional-quality dynamic reports based on SQL Server data

✔ Create automated tasks that trigger when data satisfies specified conditions

That's only scratching the surface of the functionality offered by SQL Server 2008! In this chapter, I focus on the basic knowledge you need to get started with SQL Server.

Starting Off on the Right Foot

There are a couple of decisions you need to make if you're building a new SQL Server installation. Before making an investment of time or money, take a few moments to think about the following questions:

- ✔ What SQL Server edition effectively balances your business needs against cost?
- ✔ What hardware and software platform are best suited for your SQL Server installation?

I help you answer these questions in this section.

Examining SQL Server editions

SQL Server is a complex product with a wide variety of services. Most organizations need only a subset of that functionality. Rather than charge a single high price for a one-size-fits-all software package, Microsoft offers SQL Server 2008 in a variety of editions, ranging from the low-end (but free!) Express Edition to the expensive, fully functional Enterprise Edition.

The right edition for your organization will depend upon your data processing needs. In fact, many organizations host a combination of several different SQL Server editions, used for different purposes.

Table 1-1 summarizes the differences between the various SQL Server 2008 editions.

Table 1-1	Comparing SQL Server Editions			
Feature	*Express*	*Workgroup*	*Standard*	*Enterprise*
Maximum Processors	1	2	4	Unlimited
Maximum RAM	1GB	3GB	Unlimited	Unlimited
Maximum Database Size	4GB	Unlimited	Unlimited	Unlimited
Database Mirroring	No	No	Yes	Yes
Log Shipping	No	Yes	Yes	Yes
Merge Subscriber	Yes	Yes	Yes	Yes
Merge Publisher	No	No	Yes	Yes

Feature	Express	Workgroup	Standard	Enterprise
Oracle Replication	No	No	No	Yes
SQL Agent	No	Yes	Yes	Yes
SQL Profiler	No	No	Yes	Yes
Analysis Services	No	No	Yes	Yes
Advanced Analytics	No	No	No	Yes
Partitioning	No	No	No	Yes
Data Compression	No	No	No	Yes
Resource Governor	No	No	No	Yes
Cost (per processor)	Free	$3,899	$6,000	$25,000

The prices listed in Table 1-1 are current as of the initial release date for SQL Server 2008 and are subject to change.

Table 1-1 presents only a high-level view of some common differences between the two platforms. For a complete feature comparison, see `http://msdn.microsoft.com/en-us/library/cc645993(SQL.100).aspx`.

One more SQL Server edition is available: Developer Edition. This edition is designed for application developers and offers functionality exactly the same as Enterprise Edition at an incredibly low price point of $50 per developer. What's the catch? You can use it only for development purposes. You may not use it in a production environment (even for disaster recovery purposes).

Microsoft plans to release two more editions of SQL Server 2008: Express Edition with Tools and Express Edition with Advanced Services. These two editions will include additional functionality.

Checking system requirements

Before you install SQL Server 2008, you need to verify that the hardware you intend to use meets Microsoft's minimum requirements for running SQL Server. In this section, I outline the requirements for each SQL Server edition.

Operating system

All editions of SQL Server 2008 will run on the following operating systems with at least the service pack (SP) level indicated:

- ✔ Windows Server 2003 Standard, Enterprise, or Data Center edition with SP2
- ✔ Windows Vista Ultimate, Home Premium, Home Basic, Enterprise, or Business
- ✔ Windows XP with SP2 (or later)
- ✔ Windows Small Business Server 2003 with SP2

Processor

SQL Server requires a minimum of a 1 GHz processor, but Microsoft recommends the use of 200 GHz or faster processors.

Microsoft charges per *physical processor* for SQL Server licenses. Current processor technology allows manufacturers to build multiple *cores* on the same physical processor. Each core is effectively an individual processor. So-called "dual core" processors include two discrete processors on the same chip, and "quad core" processors include four computing cores. Microsoft adopted a very generous licensing policy (unlike that of Oracle and IBM) that allows you to purchase licensing on a physical processor basis, regardless of the number of cores on those processors. Therefore, take this into account when choosing your hardware platform. You'll be much better off financially if you choose a single quad-core processor instead of four single-core processors!

Memory

The bare minimum amount of memory needed to run SQL Server 2008 is 512MB. Microsoft recommends a minimum of 2GB, but I suggest adding as much memory as your budget allows.

Hard drive

You need about 350MB of free hard drive space for SQL Server's software components. If you intend to install optional (but useful!) components such as SQL Server Books Online (described later in this chapter) or sample databases, plan on having about 1GB free. Don't forget that this is the requirement for SQL Server itself; you'll still need to save space to store your data!

Display

SQL Server 2008 requires at least a VGA (1024 x 768 pixels) video adapter and monitor.

Software

Before installing SQL Server, be sure you've installed the .NET Framework 3.5.

Understanding the Basic Components of SQL Server

You should begin your SQL Server 2008 adventure with a basic understanding of the components of SQL Server and their purposes. In this section, I explain how each of the major SQL Server components interact to help you manage your installation and manipulate data.

SQL and Transact-SQL

The Structured Query Language (SQL) is the language of databases. Any interaction between a user, program, or server and a database takes place through the use of SQL, even if the actual SQL code is buried deep within a graphical environment.

All major relational databases today (SQL Server, Oracle, Microsoft Access, IBM DB2, and so on) implement the same basic SQL commands. This common language allows database developers to easily migrate between platforms and create links between disparate database environments.

That said, every manufacturer of database software adds its own customizations to support functionality unique to its platform. Microsoft uses the name Transact-SQL (sometimes abbreviated as T-SQL) to refer to its extended version of SQL. Similarly, Oracle calls its enhanced version PL/SQL.

I provide an in-depth exploration of both SQL and Transact-SQL in Parts III and IV of this book.

SQL Server components

SQL Server provides a number of tools that facilitate your interactions with SQL Server. Each is designed for a specific set of tasks, although they do have some degree of overlap.

SQL Server Configuration Manager

SQL Server Configuration Manager (shown in Figure 1-1) allows you to perform basic administrative tasks that affect the configuration of your SQL Server installation. For example, this tool allows you to do the following:

✔ Start, stop, pause, and restart SQL Server services

✔ Configure the use of network protocols to access SQL Server

✔ Configure SQL Server Native Client connectivity

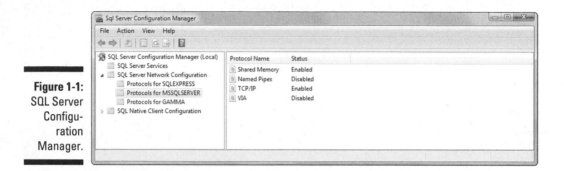

Figure 1-1:
SQL Server
Configu-
ration
Manager.

I discuss the use of SQL Server Configuration Manager in Chapter 3.

SQL Server Management Studio

SQL Server Management Studio (SSMS), shown in Figure 1-2, is the database administrator's primary interface to SQL Server 2008. It offers a fully functional management interface, allowing you to configure and interact with your databases from a single console.

I describe the use SSMS throughout this book, both to directly issue Transact-SQL commands to SQL Server databases and to build databases using SSMS's graphic user interface.

I provide an overview of SSMS in Chapter 3.

SQL Server Books Online

My intention in this book is to provide you with a practical, hands-on introduction to SQL Server's functionality in an easy-to-read fashion. I don't intend it to be a "deep dive" into the technology and syntax of SQL Server. Rather, it should provide you with a working knowledge of this powerful database platform's functionality.

Microsoft includes detailed online documentation with SQL Server 2008 in the form of SQL Server Books Online. This documentation contains the latest information on SQL Server functionality for administrators and developers alike. It's a great place to turn when you're seeking specific information about command syntax or advanced SQL Server features.

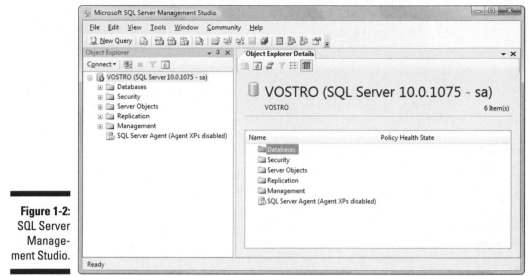

Figure 1-2:
SQL Server
Manage-
ment Studio.

Reporting Services

SQL Server Reporting Services underwent a significant overhaul before the
release of SQL Server 2008. This platform allows you to design and publish
dynamic reports based on SQL Server data. I show an example of a report
created with SQL Server Reporting Services in Figure 1-3.

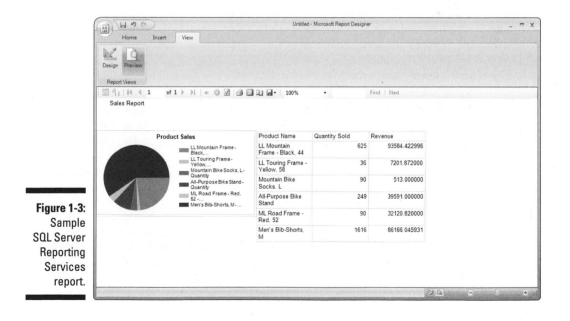

Figure 1-3:
Sample
SQL Server
Reporting
Services
report.

Analysis Services

SQL Server Analysis Services offers advanced analytical techniques, such as the use of online analytical processing (OLAP), data warehouses, and data mining. The use of this tool is beyond the scope of this book.

There are many other features of SQL Server — too many to list in this chapter. I discuss many of them later in this book. For example, I discuss SQL Profiler and the Database Engine Tuning Advisor in Chapter 14, and SQL Server Agent in Chapter 13.

Implementing Databases with SQL Server 2008

So how do you get started? SQL Server 2008 makes it simple to jump in feet first and begin working with databases.

Setting up your server

The first step is to create a SQL Server instance on an appropriate computing platform. Earlier in this chapter, I give you some advice for selecting the hardware, software, and SQL Server edition appropriate for your needs. In Chapters 2 and 3, I provide you with the information you need to set up a SQL Server instance.

Stocking it with databases

After you have SQL Server up and running, you need to create individual databases to house your data. In Chapter 4, I provide you with advice for planning and designing efficient databases. Chapters 5 and 6 describe the process for creating databases and tables and defining the relationships between different tables within the same database.

Accessing and updating your data

I dedicate a substantial portion of this book (Parts III and IV) to helping you put data in your database, update it, and retrieve it when necessary. My focus in this book is on the use of Transact-SQL and SQL Server Management Studio to manipulate your data.

Database developers use different techniques to manipulate databases. It still all boils down to Transact-SQL statements, but they use tools such as

Microsoft Visual Studio and the Microsoft Data Access Components (MDAC) to work with SQL Server 2008. Application development is beyond the scope of this book, but you can find more information in *Beginning Microsoft SQL Server 2008 Programming*.

Managing and protecting what you've built

Database administrators spend a large portion of their time keeping databases up and running daily. In Part V, I describe the tools and techniques you can use for ongoing administration of your SQL Server 2008 databases, including automation and troubleshooting tools. Part VI of this book discusses ways you can protect your data by applying SQL Server 2008's security and disaster recovery features.

What's New in SQL Server 2008

If you've used earlier versions of SQL Server, the first question in your mind is probably "What's new in SQL Server 2008?" The answer? Plenty! Microsoft promotes SQL Server 2008 as a major advance in its data platform vision and, as such, SQL Server 2008 offers a great deal of new functionality.

Rest easy, however, if you're already familiar with SQL Server 2005. Although SQL Server 2008 has a ton of new features, SSMS still has the same familiar look and feel. You should be able to get up and running quickly.

Declarative Management Framework

The Declarative Management Framework (DMF) is one of the most revolutionary features in SQL Server 2008. DMF allows database administrators to set high-level policies describing the allowed configuration status of DMF-managed SQL Server instances. DMF allows administrators to

- ✔ Create policies governing SQL Server configurations
- ✔ Evaluate an instance's current configuration against a policy and determine what deficiencies, if any, exist
- ✔ Apply a policy to a SQL Server instance
- ✔ Log or prevent any changes to a SQL Server instance that would bring it out of compliance with policy

I discuss the Declarative Management Framework in Chapter 20 of this book.

Encryption and Auditing

There are quite a few new security features in SQL Server 2008. Most notably:

- ✔ Transparent Data Encryption (TDE) allows the encryption of databases and backups with no user impact. I discuss TDE in Chapter 16.

- ✔ Enhanced auditing features allow the tracking of data access, in addition to data modification. I discuss SQL Server 2008's auditing features in Chapter 16.

Resource conservation

SQL Server 2008 includes two features designed to provide you with the ability to optimize server performance:

- ✔ Resource Governor allows you to set limits and priorities for different SQL Server workloads. This functionality offers you the ability to control the user experience by providing different users with a guaranteed level of performance. I discuss Resource Governor in Chapter 12.

- ✔ Backup compression shrinks the size of backup data before it is written to disk, reducing both the amount of time necessary to create a backup and the disk space used to store the backup. I discuss backup compression in Chapter 18.

Date/Time Data Types

I've been waiting for years for SQL Server to include date and time data types that match the way normal people think about dates and times! SQL Server 2008 provides four new data types that answer this formerly unmet demand:

- ✔ The DATE data type is a calendar date only, with no time information.

- ✔ The TIME data type is a time only, with no date information.

- ✔ The DATETIMEOFFSET data type is a date/time that allows for the inclusion of time zone information.

- ✔ The DATETIME2 data type allows the specification of a date anywhere within the range of the year 1 A.D. to the year 9999 A.D.

Chapter 2

Building Your SQL Server

*U*nless you're walking into an environment in which SQL Server 2008 is already in use, your first task will be installing a new SQL Server instance or upgrading an existing SQL Server 2005 (or earlier) instance to SQL Server 2008. In this chapter, I explore the process of installing SQL Server and performing the initial configuration tasks to get your database server up and running quickly.

Installing SQL Server 2008

Before you begin the installation of SQL Server 2008, you should ensure that the server you intend to use meets the minimum hardware and software requirements I discuss in Chapter 1. You also need a copy of the SQL Server 2008 installation package for the edition you want to install.

Before beginning the installation process, you should make several important configuration decisions. In the remainder of this section, I walk you through those decisions and then explain how to install SQL Server 2008 on your server.

Choosing between default and named instances

SQL Server allows you to install multiple instances on the same server. You can think of each instance as an individual "copy" of SQL Server running on the same server. Why might you want to run more than one copy of SQL Server on the same server?

✔ You may install different versions of SQL Server side by side on the same server using multiple instances. For example, if your organization is planning to upgrade to SQL Server 2008 but you want to approach the upgrade in a piecemeal fashion, you can run SQL Server 2005 and SQL Server 2008 instances on the same server and make the migration database by database.

✔ You can run separate instances for development and testing purposes. Doing so allows you to follow the best practice of separating production systems from development and test code, protecting your real data from the high likelihood of programming errors in a test environment.

✔ You can grant different users full administrative rights on different SQL Server instances running on the same server. This feature is most useful in a database hosting environment in which different customers might need to have databases on the same server.

SQL Server 2008 Setup provides you with two options for the instance name:

✔ **Default instance:** Takes the same name as the Windows name of your server. You can have only one default instance on each server.

✔ **Named instance:** Has a user-provided name and may coexist on a server with a default instance and other named instances.

If you want to run multiple instances of SQL Server on the same server, you must use named instances for all of the instances (although you may use the default instance for one of the instances, if you want).

In the remainder of this chapter, I assume that you're installing a server as the default instance because this is the most common SQL Server installation scenario.

Selecting an authentication mode

Authentication is the process that allows users to prove their identity to a server before gaining access to resources. In most cases, this is established through the use of a username and password. SQL Server supports two different authentication modes:

✔ **Windows authentication mode:** In this mode, SQL Server uses Windows account credentials to authenticate access to the database server. Users must have an operating system account in order to gain access to SQL Server.

✔ **Mixed authentication mode:** In this mode, SQL Server uses a mixture of Windows accounts and accounts created within SQL Server to manage user authentication.

Microsoft strongly recommends the use of Windows authentication mode as a security best practice. Using this approach, you maintain a single set of accounts for both server and database access, and errors are much less likely to occur. You should use mixed authentication mode only if you have a specific requirement for it in your organization, such as an application that doesn't support Windows authentication.

Choosing service accounts

During the installation process, you'll be asked to choose service accounts for several SQL Server services. Every program in Windows must run using the permissions of an account; when you make this decision, you're choosing the account(s) that will be used to run SQL Server and its components.

For security reasons, I strongly recommend that you ask your domain administrator to create dedicated domain accounts for the SQL Server Agent and SQL Server service accounts. These accounts should be configured with the minimum permissions necessary to run their respective services and should not be used for any other purpose.

Selecting the collation

Collations define how SQL Server stores and sorts data. They differ based upon the character set used in different parts of the world. Some common collations include:

- Latin1_General: collation for English and German
- Arabic collation for Arabic languages
- French: collation for French
- Modern_Spanish collation for Spanish

SQL Server Setup will choose a default collation for you based upon the settings of the underlying Windows operating system. In general, you should not change this default unless one of the following situations exists:

- The database collation must support a different language than that of the underlying operating system. For example, you might have a server hosted in one country supporting a database server used by individuals in another country.

- The database server participates in a replication relationship with another server that uses a different collation. A _replication relationship_ is when two servers are kept synchronized. (I discuss replication in more in Chapter 15.). In replication relationships, all servers must use the same collation.

Performing the installation

After making decisions about the instance, authentication mode, service accounts, and collation (covered in the preceding sections), you're ready to begin the SQL Server installation process. Here's how to install SQL Server:

1. **Insert the SQL Server DVD into your computer's DVD drive.**

2. **Click OK to install prerequisites, if necessary.**

   If your system doesn't have updated versions of the Microsoft .NET Framework and Windows Installer, the SQL Server installation program will pop up a warning message asking you to install them before beginning the SQL Server setup process. You may need to answer some additional questions regarding those installations before proceeding, and the system may require a reboot.

3. **When the SQL Server Installation Center appears, click the Installation link.**

4. **Click the New SQL Server Stand-Alone Installation or Add Features to an Existing Installation link.**

   SQL Server Setup performs a system configuration check to determine whether your system is ready for SQL Server 2008.

5. **Click the OK button to close the Setup Support Rules screen.**

6. **Select the appropriate licensing mode on the Product Key screen and click the Next button to continue.**

   If you have a license for SQL Server, you may enter your product key on this screen. If you don't have a license, you may select a 180-day trial of Enterprise Edition or the free installation of Express Edition.

7. **Select the I Accept the License Terms check box in the License Terms window and then click the Next button to continue.**

   SQL Server Setup displays a list of installation prerequisites, if any are necessary.

8. **If all checks pass, click the Next button to continue.**

   If some prerequisites are missing, you must click the Install button to install them before you can continue.

9. **In the Feature Selection window, select the check boxes next to the features you want to install.**

   At a minimum, you probably want to install the Database Engine Services, Client Tools, and Books Online, as shown in Figure 2-1.

10. **Click the Next button to continue.**

    The Instance Configuration window appears, as shown in Figure 2-2.

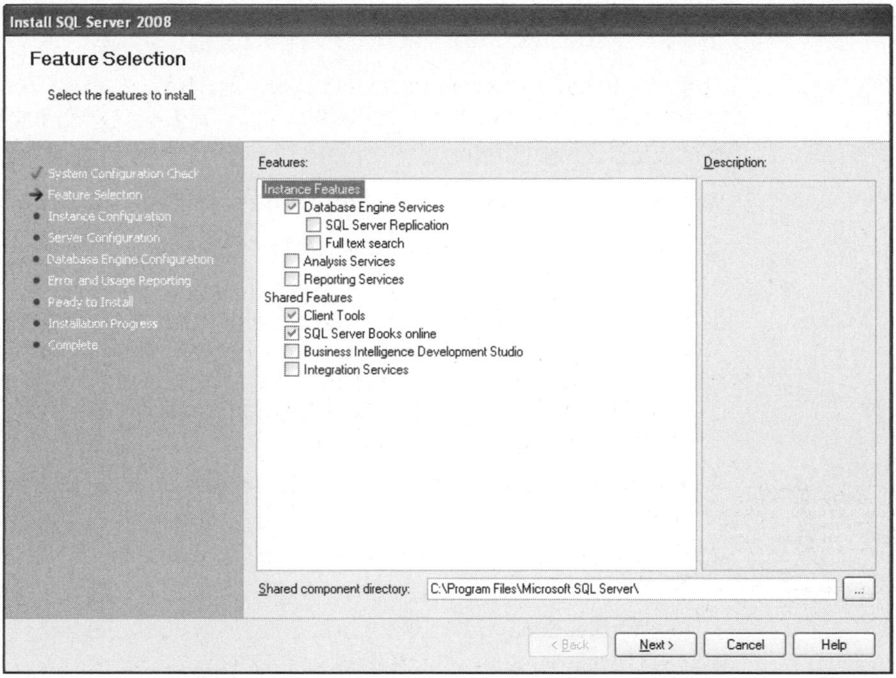

Install SQL Server 2008

Feature Selection

Select the features to install.

System Configuration Check
Feature Selection
Instance Configuration
Server Configuration
Database Engine Configuration
Error and Usage Reporting
Ready to Install
Installation Progress
Complete

Features:

Instance Features
☑ Database Engine Services
☐ SQL Server Replication
☐ Full text search
☐ Analysis Services
☐ Reporting Services
Shared Features
☑ Client Tools
☑ SQL Server Books online
☐ Business Intelligence Development Studio
☐ Integration Services

Description:

Shared component directory: C:\Program Files\Microsoft SQL Server\   [...]

< Back   Next >   Cancel   Help

Figure 2-1:
Selecting
your SQL
Server
features to
install.

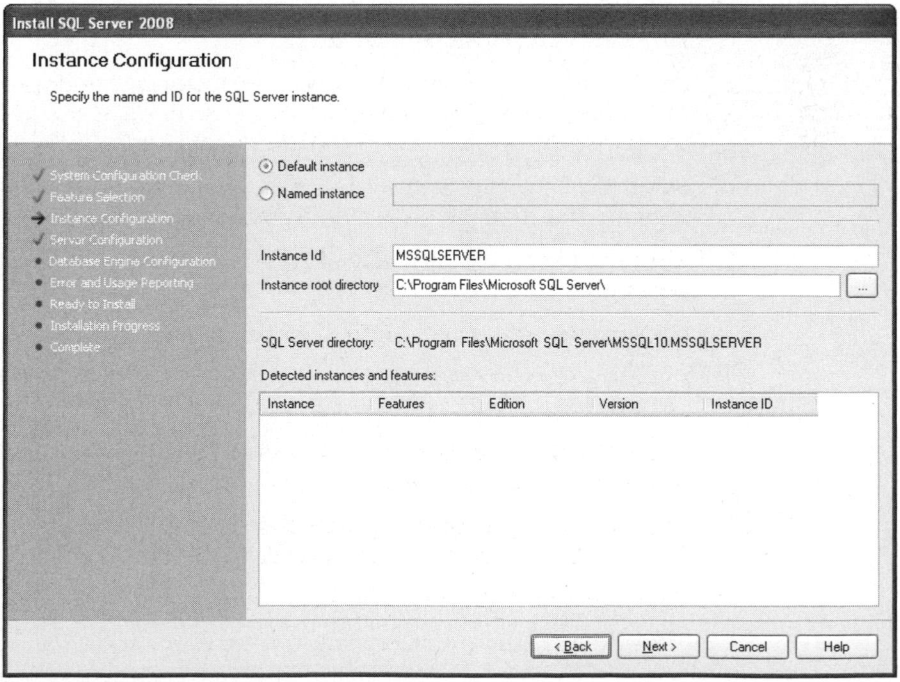

Install SQL Server 2008

Instance Configuration

Specify the name and ID for the SQL Server instance.

System Configuration Check
Feature Selection
Instance Configuration
Server Configuration
Database Engine Configuration
Error and Usage Reporting
Ready to Install
Installation Progress
Complete

⦿ Default instance
◯ Named instance   [   ]

Instance Id   MSSQLSERVER
Instance root directory   C:\Program Files\Microsoft SQL Server\   [...]

SQL Server directory: C:\Program Files\Microsoft SQL Server\MSSQL10.MSSQLSERVER

Detected instances and features:

Instance	Features	Edition	Version	Instance ID

< Back   Next >   Cancel   Help

Figure 2-2:
The
Instance
Configur-
ation
window.

11. **If you're installing a named instance, select the Named Instance radio button and provide a name for the instance in the adjacent text box.**

    If you are installing the server's default instance, you do not need to change any settings on this screen.

12. **Click the Next button to continue.**

13. **Review the Disk Usage Summary and click Next to continue.**

    SQL Server shows you the disk space requirements for the features you selected.

14. **In the appropriate text boxes, provide the username and password for the domain accounts that will be used to run each of the SQL Server services.**

    When providing account credentials, you must use an account that already exists on the system. SQL Server won't create an account for you. You may need to contact the system administrator for assistance.

    As noted earlier in the chapter, it is a best practice to use separate domain accounts for these services, as shown in Figure 2-3.

    Also, if you need to change the default collation, you may do so on this screen by clicking the Collation tab.

15. **Click the Next button to continue.**

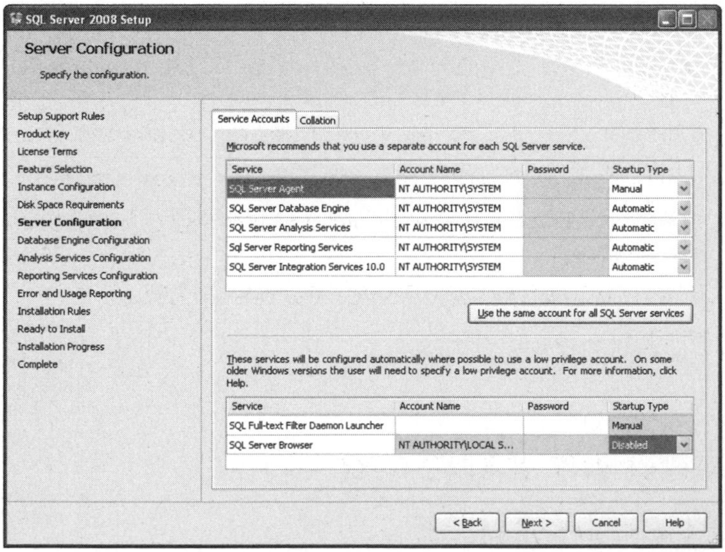

Figure 2-3: Setting SQL Server service accounts.

16. **Click the Next button in the Database Engine Configuration window to accept the default Windows authentication mode.**

You may also specify accounts that will serve as SQL Server administrators on this screen, as shown in Figure 2-4.

At this point in the process, you may need to provide additional configuration details for any optional components that you chose to install.

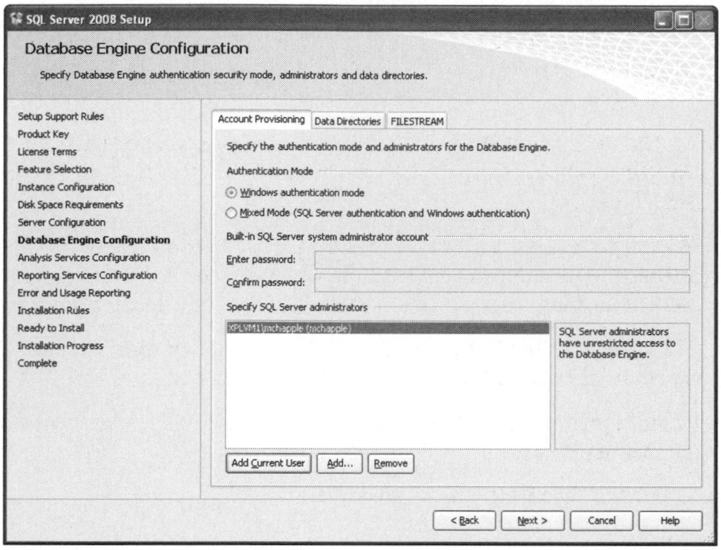

Figure 2-4:
Configuring
SQL server
authenti-
cation.

17. **Click the Next button to advance past the Error and Usage Reporting window.**

18. **Click the Next button to advance past the Installation Rules window.**

19. **Click the Install button to begin SQL Server installation.**

20. **Review the status screen to determine whether installation completed successfully.**

21. **Click the Next button to review the release notes.**

22. **Click the Close button.**

Upgrading an Existing SQL Server Installation

If you're already running SQL Server 2000 or SQL Server 2005 on your system and want to upgrade to SQL Server 2008, you have several options. In this section, I explain the preliminary steps you should perform to ensure that you're ready for the upgrade. Then I discuss your upgrade options.

Preparing for an upgrade with Upgrade Advisor

SQL Server Upgrade Advisor is included on the SQL Server 2008 installation DVD. It provides you with an automated means to determine whether your SQL Server 2000 and SQL Server 2005 databases are ready for an upgrade to SQL Server 2008. Here's how to install Upgrade Advisor:

1. **Insert the SQL Server 2008 DVD into the computer.**

2. **Select Install SQL Server Upgrade Advisor from the SQL Server Installation Center screen.**

3. **Click the Next button when the Installation Wizard appears.**

4. **Select the I Accept the Terms in the License Agreement radio button and then click Next.**

5. **Click Next to accept the default name and company; then click Next again to accept the default features.**

6. **Click the Install button to install SQL Server Upgrade Advisor.**

7. **Click the Finish button when the installation completes.**

When you've completed the installation process, run Upgrade Advisor as follows:

1. **From the Start menu, choose All Programs⇨Microsoft SQL Server 2008⇨SQL Server 2008 Upgrade Advisor.**

2. **When you see the Upgrade Advisor welcome screen, click the Launch Upgrade Advisor Analysis Wizard link.**

3. **Click the Next button to bypass the welcome screen.**

4. **Specify the server name in the appropriate text box and click the Detect button to automatically identify the service(s) for Upgrade Advisor to analyze (see Figure 2-5).**

   You may manually override the automatically detected services by using the check boxes.

5. **Click the Next button to continue.**

6. **On the Connection Parameters screen, select the instance you want Upgrade Advisor to analyze from the drop-down list.**

   If the server you want to analyze does not use Windows authentication, you also need to select SQL Server authentication from the authentication drop-down list and provide appropriate SQL Server credentials.

7. **Click the Next button to continue.**

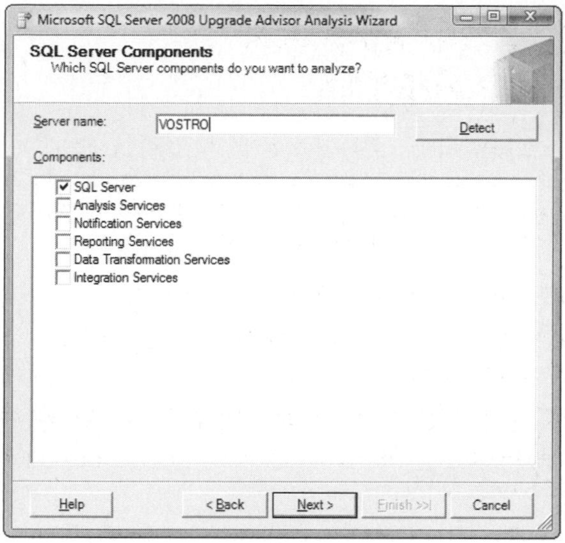

Figure 2-5:
Selecting
the services
to analyze.

8. **Click the Next button to accept the default setting of analyzing all databases on the instance.**

9. **Review the Upgrade Advisor Settings and click the Run button to begin the analysis.**

   This analysis may take several minutes or longer, depending upon the complexity of the database(s) analyzed.

10. **When the analysis completes, click the Launch Report button to view the results.**

    Review the report (a sample appears in Figure 2-6) and correct any issues before attempting an upgrade to SQL Server 2008.

Upgrading Your Installation

When you upgrade a SQL Server installation, you have two basic choices for a migration path: a side-by-side migration or a direct upgrade.

Side-by-side migration

In this approach, you build a SQL Server 2008 server and then transfer your databases to it one at a time. This approach is costly because it requires you to provision a second server, but it is the safest because it provides a fallback plan. If your migration fails for any reason, you can simply revert to the older database and try again later. I strongly recommend that you use this approach whenever possible.

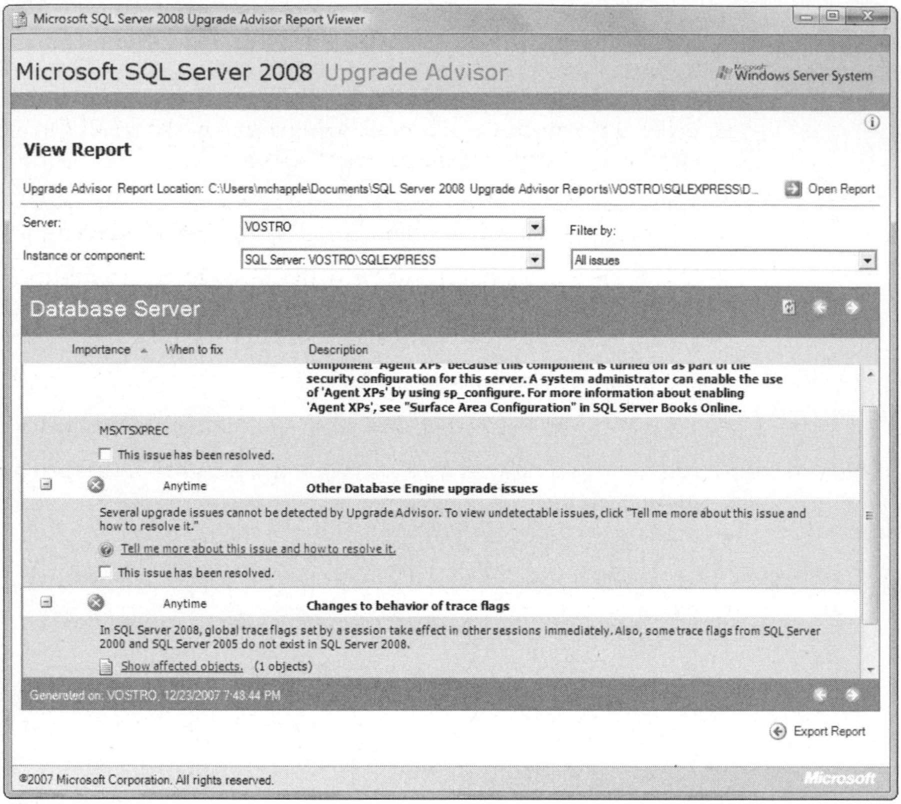

Figure 2-6:
SQL Server
Upgrade
Advisor
report.

Direct upgrade

If you do not have the resources available to perform a side-by-side migration, you can directly upgrade a SQL Server 2000 or SQL Server 2005 database instance to SQL Server 2008.

Performing a direct upgrade is dangerous and involves a significant risk of data loss. Be certain to back up your databases before attempting a direct upgrade.

The process of performing a direct upgrade is very similar to installing a new SQL Server 2008 instance. For more information on performing a direct upgrade, consult SQL Server Books Online (the reference material included with SQL Server.

Configuring Database Mail

SQL Server's Database Mail technology allows your applications to send e-mail messages. Most SQL Server instances require the use of Database Mail functionality. SQL Server does *not* enable Database Mail by default, so you must configure it using the Database Mail Configuration Wizard. Do so by following these steps:

1. **From the Start menu, choose All Programs⇨Microsoft SQL Server 2008⇨SQL Server Management Studio.**

2. **If you are connecting to a SQL Server instance other than the default instance, select it from the Server Name drop-down list.**

3. **If you are not using Windows Authentication, select SQL Server Authentication from the Authentication drop-down list and provide the login name and password in the appropriate text boxes.**

4. **Click the Connect button.**

5. **Click the plus sign (+)to the left of the Management folder.**

6. **Right-click Database Mail and select Configure Database Mail from the pop-up menu.**

7. **Click the Next button to advance past the welcome screen.**

   SQL Server displays the Select Configuration Task window, shown in Figure 2-7.

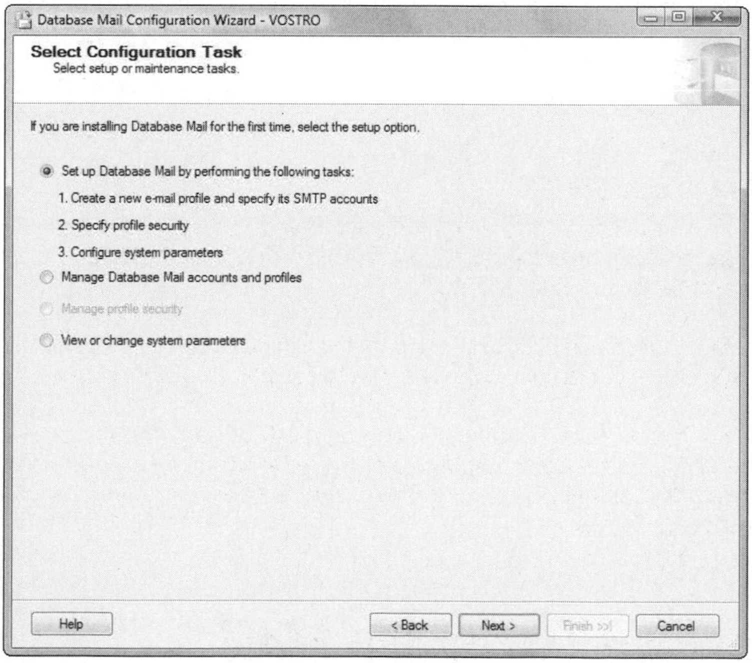

Figure 2-7: Selecting the Database Mail configuration task.

8. **Select Set up Database Mail by Performing the Following Tasks and click the Next button to continue.**

   SQL Server warns you that Database Mail is not currently enabled by displaying the message shown in Figure 2-8.

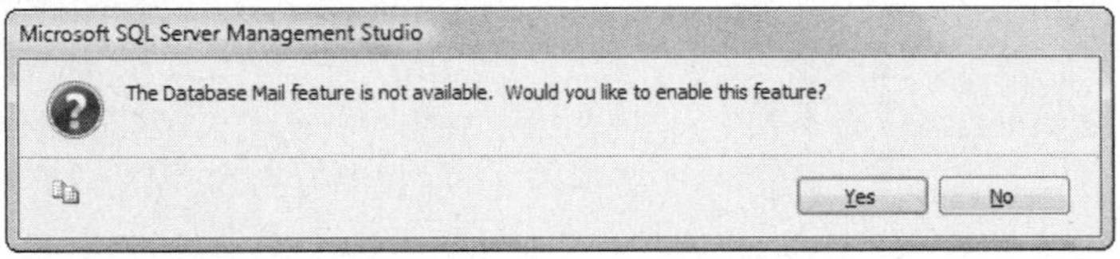

Figure 2-8: The Database Mail Not Enabled Message.

9. **Click the Yes button to confirm that you would like to install Database Mail.**

   The New Profile screen, shown in Figure 2-9, appears.

10. **Provide a name and description for your Database Mail profile by typing them in the appropriate text boxes.**

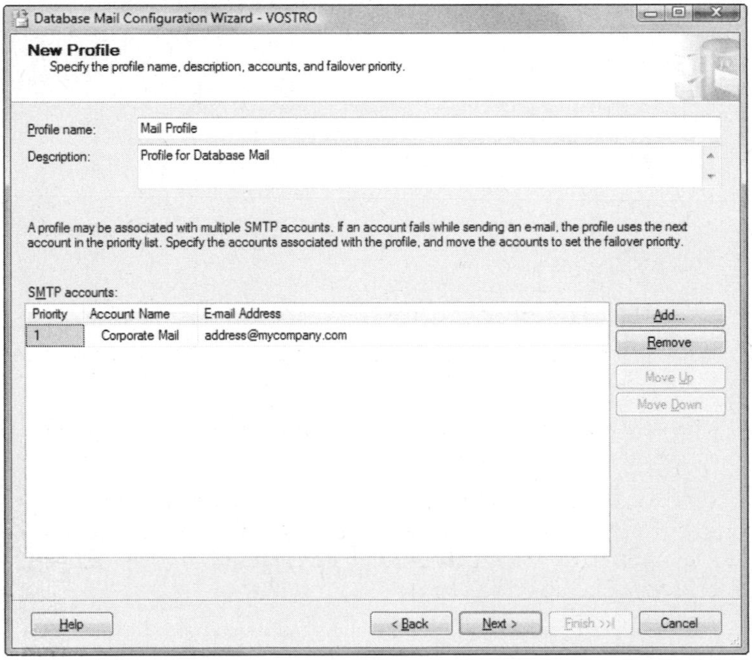

Figure 2-9: Creating a New Database Mail profile.

11. Click the Add button to add an SMTP account to the profile.

Database Mail uses the Simple Mail Transfer Protocol (SMTP) to communicate with mail servers. SMTP is the standard means for transmitting electronic mail. You may associate one or more SMTP accounts with each Database Mail profile.

When you click the Add button, SQL Server presents the New Database Mail Account window, shown in Figure 2-10.

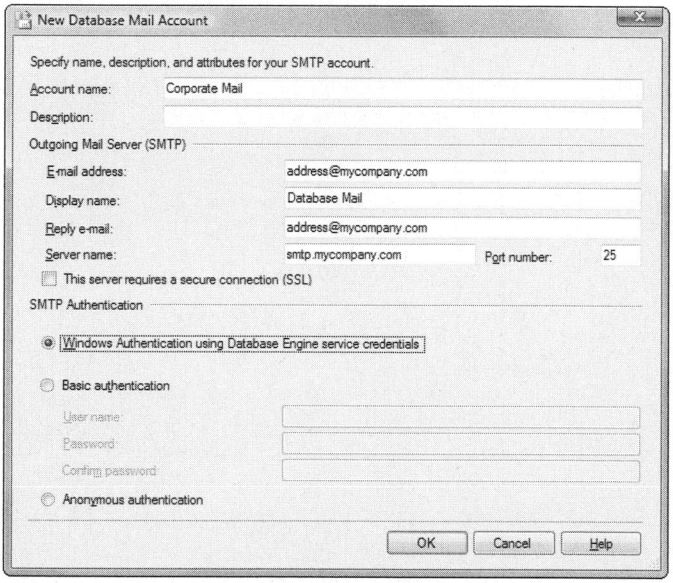

Figure 2-10:
Creating
a New
Database
Mail
account.

12. Fill in the SMTP account details provided by your mail server administrator and click OK.

13. Click the Next button to advance past the New Profile window.

SQL Server displays the Manage Profile Security window, shown in Figure 2-11.

14. Select the Public check box next to the name of the profile you just created.

Database Mail allows you to create a combination of public and private profiles. Any user authorized to use Database Mail may send messages using a public profile. Private profiles, on the other hand, may be restricted to specific users.

15. Choose Yes from the Default drop-down list next to the name of the profile.

If you select a default profile, any Database Mail messages sent without explicitly specifying a profile will use the default profile. You select the default profile by choosing Yes in the Default list for that item.

16. Click the Next button to continue.

17. Click the Next button to accept the default mail system parameters.

18. Click the Finish button to complete the configuration of Database Mail.

After you configure Database Mail, you must ensure that any users who might need to send mail are members of the msdb database's DatabaseMailUserRole role. (I discuss role membership in Chapter 16.)

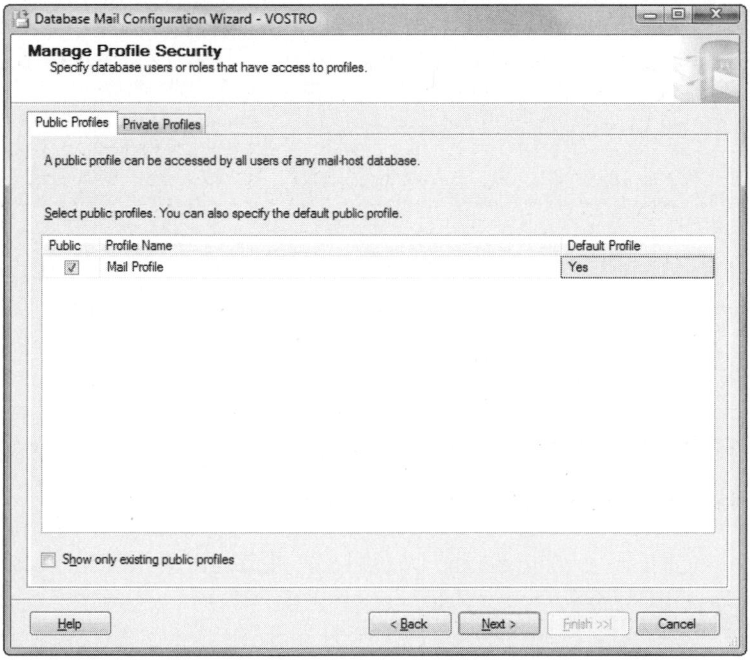

Figure 2-11:
Managing profile security.

Using SQL Server's Built-In Databases

SQL Server creates four databases when you install a new instance. These databases provide SQL Server with locations to store configuration information and temporary data and to use as a model for newly created databases.

Master database

SQL Server uses the master database to store configuration information that applies to the entire instance. For example, it includes:

- ✔ SQL Server configuration data
- ✔ Information on linked servers
- ✔ User logons
- ✔ High-level information about other databases on the instance

 The master database is the all-important glue that holds together all the individual databases stored on your server and is, therefore, extremely critical to the proper operation of your server. Therefore, you should back it up regularly. It's especially important to create a master database backup when you

- ✔ Create or delete a database
- ✔ Alter data or log files used by a database
- ✔ Add, remove, or change logins
- ✔ Add, remove, or change a linked server
- ✔ Modify the server configuration

I discuss more about backing up databases in Chapter 18.

The msdb database

QL Server and its components store scheduling and history information in a specialized database named msdb. Specifically, it contains information about any scheduled SQL Server Agent jobs (which I discuss in Chapter 13) and information about the backup and restore history of your SQL Server instance.

The model database

The model database serves as a template for all newly created databases on your server. Each time you create a new user database, SQL Server creates a copy of the model database to provide the initial configuration of the new database.

If you have default settings you'd like to apply to all your new databases, simply make the appropriate changes in the model database. For example, if you create a stored procedure in the model database, all new databases will automatically receive a copy of that stored procedure.

The tempdb database

SQL Server uses the tempdb database as a temporary storage location for working data, such as intermediate query results. Users may also explicitly create temporary tables, stored procedures, or other objects. SQL Server stores these temporary user objects in tempdb until they are no longer necessary.

Chapter 3

Working with SQL Server Tools

SQL Server 2008 provides a number of tools designed to make it easier for you to configure and manage your databases in a fashion comfortable to you. These tools include the graphical interfaces of SQL Server Configuration Manager and SQL Server Management Studio and the command-line utility SQLCMD.

In addition to these tools, SQL Server provides two important tools to help you tune and troubleshoot database server performance: Database Engine Tuning Advisor (DETA) and SQL Profiler. I discuss these latter two tools in Chapter 14.

In this chapter, you find out how to use SQL Server Configuration Manager, SQL Server Management Studio, and SQLCMD to take control of your SQL Server databases.

Using SQL Server Configuration Manager

SQL Server Configuration Manager is a lightweight tool that allows you to perform basic configuration of a SQL Server instance. You can use this tool to

✔ Start and stop services

✔ Change the service account used to start a service

✔ Change the start mode of a service

✔ Change the network protocols used by SQL Server

✔ Change the IP addresses and TCP ports used by SQL Server

Launching SQL Server Configuration Manager

You can start SQL Server Configuration Manager by selecting it from the Start menu, as follows:

1. **Click the Windows button (or the Start button in Windows XP) in the lower-left corner of your screen.**

2. **Click the All Programs item.**

3. **Click the SQL Server 2008 folder.**

4. **Click the Configuration Tools folder.**

5. **Click the SQL Server Configuration Manager item.**

   SQL Server Configuration Manager starts in a separate window and displays the interface shown in Figure 3-1.

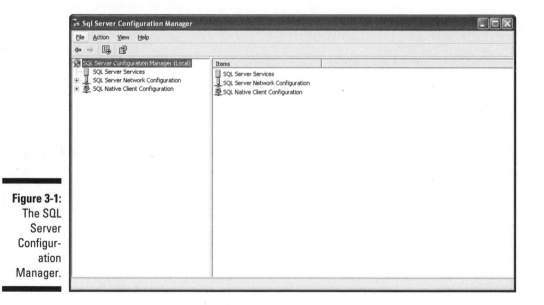

Figure 3-1:
The SQL
Server
Configur-
ation
Manager.

Starting and stopping services

You can use SQL Server Configuration Manager to start, stop, pause, resume, and restart Windows services running as part of SQL Server 2008. You may need to perform these actions for several reasons, as follows:

✔ You might want to start or stop a service that is infrequently used to enable it only when necessary. Doing so conserves system resources and improves the overall performance of your SQL Server.

✔ You may need to restart a service after making changes to its configuration, such as changing the service account.

✔ You may need to restart a service that is in a nonresponsive state to restore it to working order.

Here's how you can change the running state of a SQL Server service using SQL Server Configuration Manager:

1. **Open SQL Server Configuration Manager, as described in the previous section.**

2. **Click the SQL Server Services icon.**

   SQL Server Configuration Manager displays the status of all installed services in the main window pane, as shown in Figure 3-2. Notice that this window includes the following information:

   • Service name and type

   • Current state

   • Start mode

   • Service account ("Log On As")

   • Process ID

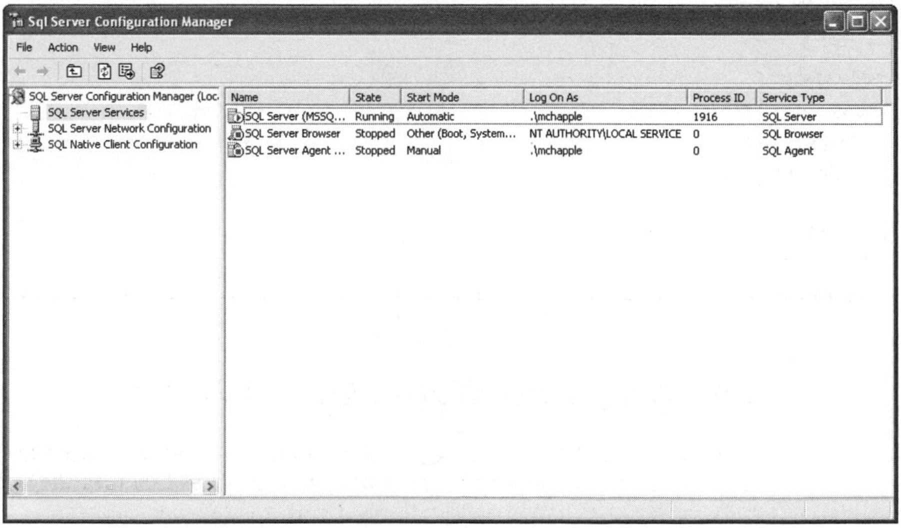

Figure 3-2:
SQL Server Services.

3. **Right-click the service you want to alter.**

4. **Select the action you want to perform (Start, Stop, Pause, Resume, or Restart) from the pop-up menu.**

5. **Wait while SQL Server Configuration Manager makes the requested change.**

   Figure 3-3 shows an example of the status screen displayed while starting a service.

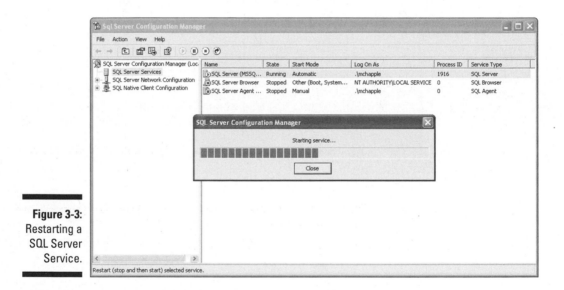

Figure 3-3:
Restarting a
SQL Server
Service.

Changing service accounts

During the installation process, you provided SQL Server with a set of accounts to use when starting each of its component services. If you later want to change those initial configuration decisions, you may do so using SQL Server Configuration Manager.

1. **With SQL Server Configuration Manager open, click the SQL Server Services folder.**

2. **Right-click the service you want to alter.**

3. **Choose Properties from the pop-up menu.**

   SQL Server displays the Properties window, shown in Figure 3-4.

4. **Type the account name in the appropriate textbox using the DOMAIN\ account format.**

   Alternatively, you may click the Browse button to search for an appropriate account.

Figure 3-4:
SQL Server
Service
properties.

5. **Provide the account password in both the Password and Confirm password textboxes.**

6. **Click the OK button.**

   SQL Server Configuration Manager warns you that it needs to restart the service to apply your change.

7. **Click the Yes button to restart the service.**

Changing service start modes

Each SQL Server service has a default start mode that you may configure. This start mode indicates the action that should occur for the service when the system restarts. Your start mode options include:

- **Automatic** mode configures services to start automatically when the operating system boots.

- **Disabled** mode prevents the service from starting (automatically or manually) unless you change the start model to automatic or manual.

- **Manual** mode does not start the service automatically, but allows users and other services with appropriate permissions to start the service manually.

You may verify the current start mode settings for each service by viewing them in the SQL Server Services section of SQL Server Configuration Manager, as I describe in the "Starting and stopping services" section, earlier in this chapter. If you want to change the start mode for a service, follow this process:

1. **With SQL Server Configuration Manager open, click the SQL Server Services folder.**
2. **Right-click the service you want to alter.**
3. **Choose Properties from the pop-up menu.**
4. **Click the Service tab.**

   The service properties appear, as shown in Figure 3-5.

5. **Choose the appropriate start mode from the drop-down menu.**
6. **Click the OK button.**

   After you click OK, the dialog box closes, and you return to SQL Server Configuration Manager.

Figure 3-5:
The Service
Properties
tab.

Modifying networking settings

SQL Server includes support for three major access protocols. These protocols dictate the way that users and other systems may connect to your SQL Server databases. Following are the most common protocols.

✔ **Shared Memory** allows connections on the local server to take place without using a network. You may use shared memory connections for access to a database instance on the local server only. There are no configuration options for this protocol.

✔ **Named Pipes** sets up a network connection using interprocess communication. It is most appropriate for use on a high-speed LAN, where it may offer enhanced performance.

✔ **TCP/IP** networking is the most common network protocol used with SQL Server. TCP/IP connections may easily and efficiently cross wide-area networks (such as the Internet) and are supported in almost any computing environment.

Enabling and disabling protocols

SQL Server Configuration Manager allows you to change the protocols used by SQL Server by either enabling or disabling them, which you can do by following these steps:

1. **With SQL Server Configuration Manager open, click the plus sign next to the SQL Server Network Configuration folder to expand the folder.**

2. **Click the Protocols folder corresponding to the instance you want to modify.**

   SQL Server Configuration Manager displays the status of that instance's networking protocols, as shown in Figure 3-6.

3. **Right-click the service you want to alter.**

4. **Choose the appropriate action (Enable or Disable) from the pop-up menu.**

   SQL Server Configuration Manager warns you that the changes will not take effect until you restart the service.

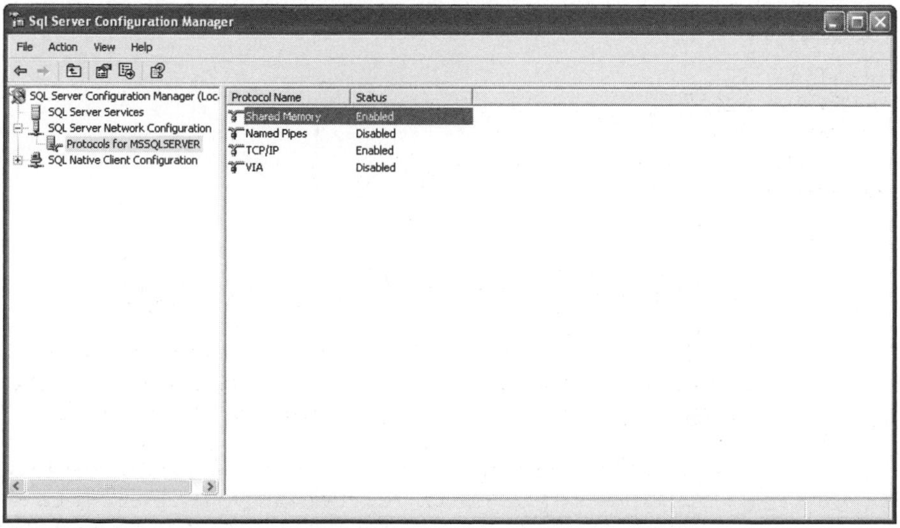

Figure 3-6:
SQL Server network configuration.

5. **Restart the SQL Server service.**

   Refer to the "Starting and stopping services" section, earlier in this chapter, where I describe how to restart a SQL Server service.

Changing protocol settings

You may also use SQL Server Configuration Manager to change networking settings, such as the IP address(es) and TCP ports used by SQL Server. To change network protocol settings, follow these steps:

1. **With SQL Server Configuration Manager open, expand the SQL Server Network Configuration folder.**

2. **Click the Protocols folder corresponding to the instance you want to modify.**

3. **Right-click the service you want to alter.**

4. **Choose Properties from the pop-up menu.**

   SQL Server displays the properties for the network protocol you selected. An example of the properties sheet for TCP/IP appears in Figure 3-7.

5. **Make any desired changes to the properties sheet and click OK to continue.**

   SQL Server Configuration Manager warns you that the changes will not take effect until you restart the service.

6. **Restart the SQL Server service.**

   Refer to the "Starting and stopping services" section, earlier in this chapter, where I describe how to restart a SQL Server service.

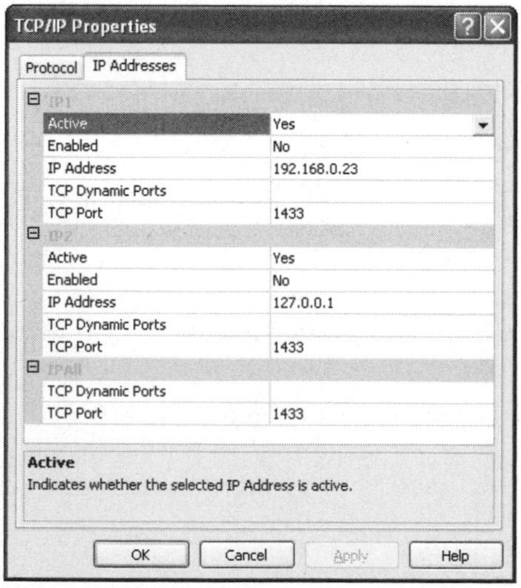

Figure 3-7: TCP/IP Properties.

Note that the TCP/IP properties are considerably more complex than those for other network protocols. If you need assistance configuring TCP/IP networking, you should consult your network administrator. Network configuration errors are one of the most common sources of server problems.

When configuring Named Pipes, the only option available to you is changing the name of the Named Pipe. The Shared Memory protocol offers no configuration options.

Managing Your Server with SQL Server Management Studio

You can perform most of the activities I describe in this book using SQL Server Management Studio (SSMS). Microsoft designed SSMS to be a one-stop replacement for piecemeal tools (such as Query Analyzer and Enterprise Manager) included in earlier versions of SQL Server. SSMS allows you to manage multiple SQL Server instances from a single platform.

Starting SSMS and connecting to an instance

As noted at the end of the preceding section, SSMS allows you to manage multiple SQL Server instances on both local and remote servers.

1. **Click the Windows button (or the Start button in Windows XP) in the lower-left corner of your screen.**

2. **Click the All Programs item.**

3. **Click the SQL Server 2008 folder.**

4. **Click the SQL Server Management Studio item.**

   SSMS opens and displays the Connect to Server dialog box, shown in Figure 3-8. If the authentication and server details are not correct, you may make any changes needed.

5. **After making any necessary changes to the connection data, click the Connect button.**

   SSMS displays the server options, as shown in Figure 3-9.

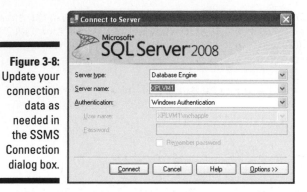

Figure 3-8:
Update your
connection
data as
needed in
the SSMS
Connection
dialog box.

Figure 3-9:
Server
options in
the SQL
Server
Manage-
ment Studio.

Exploring the SSMS Interface

The SSMS interface uses a folder-based navigation structure called Object Explorer. Notice that it uses five folders to organize SSMS options by the following categories:

- ✔ Databases
- ✔ Security
- ✔ Server Objects
- ✔ Replication
- ✔ Management

You can expand these folders to view the underlying detail by clicking the plus (+) sign that appears to the left of the folder. The folders each contain subfolders that you can expand the same way. When you click a root node, the main pane of the SSMS window displays detailed information about that item.

Throughout this book, I describe how you can use SSMS to manage your SQL Server instance.

Issuing Transact-SQL queries

One of the most important tasks you can perform using SSMS is executing Transact-SQL queries against your SQL Server databases.

Don't worry about the syntax of Transact-SQL commands just yet. I provide a detailed discussion of Transact-SQL in Parts III and IV of this book.

The following two Transact-SQL commands change the current database to the sales database and retrieve all information from the stock table in that database.

```
USE sales;

SELECT *
FROM stock;
```

Here's how you can execute that query using SSMS:

1. **With SSMS open, click the New Query button in the upper-left corner of SSMS.**

    The main SSMS pane changes to a blank window, where you may type in Transact-SQL statements.

2. **Type your Transact-SQL query into the main pane of SSMS.**

3. **Click the Execute button to run your Transact-SQL query.**

    After a moment, SSMS divides the main pane into two sections. The top half shows the query you executed, and the bottom half shows the results of that query. The resulting SSMS window appears in Figure 3-10.

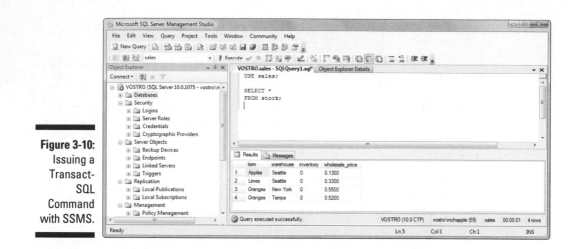

Figure 3-10:
Issuing a
Transact-
SQL
Command
with SSMS.

Working from the Command Line

If you prefer working at the command line to using the graphical interface of SSMS, SQL Server provides the SQLCMD utility that allows you to issue Transact-SQL statements from a command prompt. Here's a look at some of the important syntax options for this statement:

```
sqlcmd      [-S server_name [/instance_name]]
            [-U username [-P password]]
            [-d database_name]
            [-i input_filename]
            [-o output_filename]
```

In the following bullets, I discuss each one of these command line options. Next, I give you an example of SQLCMD in use.

✔ The –S option allows you to specify the name of the server and instance to which you wish to connect. For example, you could connect to the named instance MYDB on the server SQL2008 by specifying the command line option "–S SQL2008/MYDB". If you do not use this option, SQL Server will attempt to connect to a default instance on the local computer.

✔ The –U option allows you to specify the SQL Server login you wish to use, and the –P option allows you to provide the password. If you don't specify the login using this option, SQLCMD attempts to connect using Windows Authentication with the credentials of the user running SQLCMD.

✔ The –d option allows you to specify the database you want to use initially. If you don't specify this option, SQL Server defaults to the default database associated with the SQL Server login.

> ✔ The –i option allows you to specify the name of a file containing the Transact-SQL commands you want to execute.
>
> ✔ The –o option allows you to specify the name of a file in which SQLCMD will store your output.

Quite a few other command-line arguments that allow you to customize the use of SQLCMD are available. You won't need them to get up and running, but if you find yourself using SQLCMD for advanced applications, you may want to familiarize yourself with them.

Now that I've covered the basics of SQLCMD, I can give you an example to work with. Suppose that you want to execute the same Transact-SQL query used in the previous section against the sales database:

```
SELECT *
FROM stock;
```

To execute this query, follow these steps:

1. **Open a command prompt by choosing All Programs⇨Accessories⇨Command Prompt from the Start menu.**

2. **Type** SQLCMD –d sales **at the command prompt.**

3. **When the "1>" prompt appears, type** SELECT * FROM stock; **and press Enter.**

   You may type as many Transact-SQL statements as you want at this prompt and you may use as many lines as necessary to complete each statement. For example, you could have written **SELECT *** on the first line, pressed Enter, and typed **FROM stock;** on the second line. The key is to end each distinct Transact-SQL statement with a semicolon.

4. **When the** 2> **prompt appears, type GO and press Enter.**

   The GO command indicates to SQLCMD that you're finished entering Transact-SQL statements and want SQL Server to execute the commands.

5. **Review the results on the screen.**

   If you did not specify an output file, SQLCMD displays the results of your Transact-SQL command(s) on the screen. If you used the –o option to specify an output file, the query results are stored in that file.

6. **Type** EXIT **and press Enter.**

   SQLCMD closes, and you are returned to the Windows command prompt.

Figure 3-11 shows this entire sequence in a Windows command prompt session.

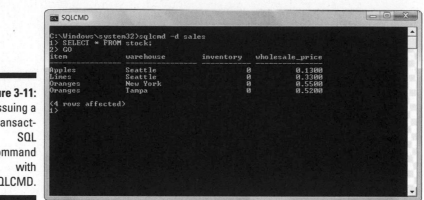

Figure 3-11:
Issuing a
Transact-
SQL
command
with
SQLCMD.

Part II
Building SQL Server 2008 Databases

The 5th Wave   By Rich Tennant

"Your database is beyond repair, but before I tell you our backup recommendation, let me ask you a question. How many index cards do you think will fit on the walls of your computer room?"

In this part . . .

This part shows you how to create your first database in a SQL Server environment. You need to know how to build your database according to accepted design principles, and a great way to plan your database is to first diagram it on paper before implementing it for real. After you've done all that, you're ready to really get rolling with SQL Server 2008: creating your database, designing tables, and enforcing relationships between tables.

Chapter 4

Planning Your Database

. . . .

. . . .

*T*here's an old saying in the military: "Prior planning prevents poor performance." This cliché proves true in the database world in several ways. If you take the time to map out your database on paper, the odds are on your side that you can build a scalable database that meets your business needs far into the future. You can enjoy a second benefit also: Well-designed databases simply perform better. They store and process data efficiently, helping you to minimize the demands on your computer systems and reduce the amount of time clients spend waiting for database transactions to complete.

In this chapter, I walk you through the process of properly designing a database. The techniques I discuss apply to any relational database system and work equally well in Microsoft SQL Server, Microsoft Access, Oracle, or any other database you encounter in the future. I also discuss diagramming techniques that can help you easily document your design decisions in a format understood by database professionals around the world.

Finally, database designers follow some basic principles intended to improve database efficiency and reduce redundant data. I conclude the chapter with a look at these techniques, showing you how to normalize your database design and how to choose appropriate data types for your database.

Introducing Database Design Concepts

Databases store data. You probably already knew that, but you should take a moment to reflect on that simple statement before you read on about database design. Everything I mention in this chapter is intended to help you store data efficiently and effectively in your SQL Server databases.

Databases store data efficiently when they minimize the amount of storage space they require to maintain your data. In addition to minimizing space requirements, efficient databases minimize the amount of time it takes the client to insert and retrieve data. These two requirements may sometimes conflict. For example, if you normally execute complex database queries that require quite a bit of computation, you can sometimes speed up those queries dramatically by storing precomputed results in your database. However, that storage requires additional space. No single answer exists for all such design decisions. You need to look at your storage and performance requirements and weigh them against each other to determine an appropriate balance for your organization.

Databases store data effectively when they provide you with the means to easily insert, retrieve, and modify data. Effective databases organize data in a fashion that's intuitive and allows users to interact with data in a natural way. For example, a user of a retail store database might find information about employees in one table, customers in another table, and products in yet another table.

 You can improve the effectiveness of your database by consulting with end users and other stakeholders early in the database design process. In my career, I've seen many cases in which database designers could have avoided expensive mistakes by simply sitting down and discussing the business goals of the project during the design phase. Don't fall victim to the temptation of diving right into the design, confident that you understand the business requirements. An assumption you make early in the design process may come back to haunt you down the road.

Understanding the Elements of a Database

You've already discovered that databases are computer systems that store data and facilitate the insertion, retrieval, and modification of that data. Now you need to understand a little more terminology before diving in to database design.

Database servers

Database software runs on specialized computer systems known as servers. These database servers have advanced hardware designed to optimize the system's performance for data storage, computation, and network communication. In contrast to user workstations, they're not designed for graphics work, word processing, or other applications. In fact, they usually don't even have a keyboard or mouse. Businesses often mount servers in racks and place them in data centers. Administrators normally interact with them using remote access techniques from their regular desktop systems.

Each database server runs a server operating system (such as Microsoft Windows Server 2003) and a database system (such as Microsoft SQL Server 2008). The database interacts with the operating system to gain access to server resources, such as hard drive storage, the processor(s), and network communications.

A database server may contain one or more separate databases. For example, you might use the same database server to store a database containing customer information and a completely separate database containing project management information. There's no need to build a separate server for each database. SQL Server ensures that the databases are isolated from each other. (In Chapter 16, I discuss how you can use database security controls to protect against users seeing data that they shouldn't be allowed to access.)

Relational databases

Most databases in use today are relational databases. What's that mean? They store data in a fashion that follows the relational model proposed by database pioneer Edgar F. Codd in 1969.

The relational model organizes data into a series of related tables. Each table contains rows and columns, as shown in Figure 4-1. Each column corresponds to an attribute: one type of information that you want to store. Each row corresponds to a record: one instance of each column. Each table may be related to one or more other tables.

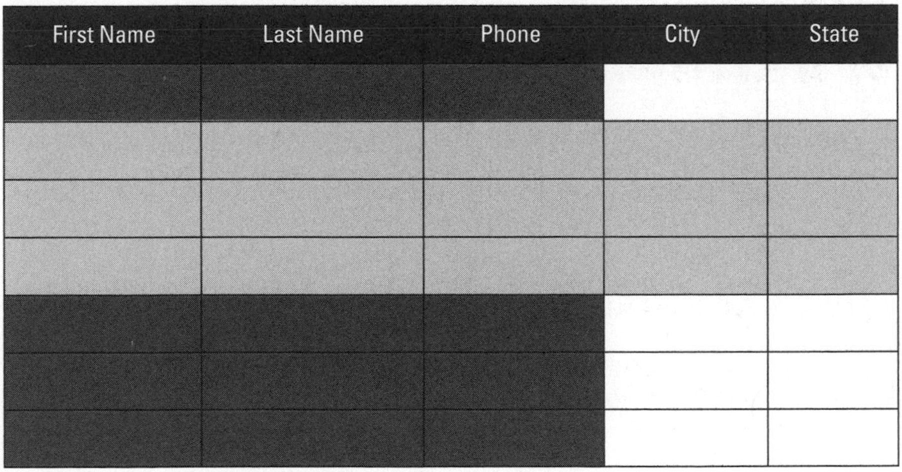

First Name	Last Name	Phone	City	State

Figure 4-1:
A basic database table.

You may find it easier to understand these principles in the context of an example. Suppose you wanted to create a database table containing address information for your relatives. You might create a table similar to that shown in Table 4-1. This table contains columns for each piece of information to store about each of your relatives: their first name, last name, address, city, state, and ZIP code. The table also contains rows for each relative. The row for each relative stores the information you know about that person.

Table 4-1		Relatives Table	
First Name	*Last Name*	*Address*	*ZIP*
Richard	Chapple	28 Cognac Street	46530
Matthew	Chapple	327 Scampi Avenue	33131
Christopher	Chapple	120 Hunter Terrace	21046
Renee	Chapple	116 Jasmine Street	08028
Mike	Chapple	223 Samantha Court	11579

The relatives table may also be related to other tables in the database. For example, your database might also contain a cities table (such as the one shown in Table 4-2) that contains information about each ZIP code in the country. The relatives table (which contains the ZIP code for each relative) is related to the cities table by the common key of the ZIP code. I discuss table relationships in further detail in Chapter 6.

Table 4-2	Cities Table	
City	*State*	*ZIP*
South Bend	IN	46530
Miami	FL	33131
Columbia	MD	21046
Glassboro	NJ	08028
Sea Cliff	NY	11579

Don't be confused by database terminology. When it comes to rows and columns, you find a few different terms that all mean the same thing. The terms *row* and *record* are interchangeable. Similarly, *columns* are sometimes called *fields, attributes,* or *variables.*

Databases vs. spreadsheets

At this point, you may be thinking, "A database table sounds a lot like a spreadsheet." You'd be correct! Database tables and spreadsheets have quite a bit in common. In fact, it may help you to think of a database as a collection of related spreadsheets.

Databases, however, offer a number of significant advantages over the use of simple spreadsheets. First, they allow you to create multiple tables and model the way they relate to each other. This grouping of data into tables reduces redundant storage of information, facilitates quick changes to information that affects large portions of the database, and allows you to pull together related information from multiple sources.

The similarity between databases and spreadsheets is a powerful one. In fact, you can use Microsoft Excel as an interface to a SQL Server database, but that's beyond the scope of this book.

Databases also provide powerful tools to help you interact with your data. For example, you can use a reporting facility called SQL Server Reporting Services (SSRS), which helps you provide business users with powerful, interactive reports in an automated fashion. Chapter 9 tells you more about SSRS.

Organizing a Database

Earlier sections in this chapter describe the relational database model and show you how databases organize related data into tables. In this section, you get started on designing databases that meet your business needs. You do that using a four-step process for organizing a database, as follows:

1. Define the objectives of your database.

2. Group related data into tables.

3. Identify primary keys that uniquely identify records.

4. Link related tables together.

I cover each of these four design steps in further detail in the following sections.

Defining your database objectives

If you were leaving town on a business trip, you wouldn't simply get in your car and start driving on the highway without knowing your destination. A trip without a clearly defined goal would be a terrible waste of time.

Things are no different in a database design project. Because of our technology and data focus, database designers often sit down and ask themselves the question "What data do I have and how can I organize it?" That's equivalent to our business traveler asking "How much gas do I have and how far can it take me?"

Instead, begin your journey with the end in mind. Ask yourself these questions:

- ✔ What's prompting your database design project?
- ✔ Who will benefit from the proper implementation of this database?
- ✔ Who are the end users of the database?
- ✔ Is this database project intended to support a new business process or improve an existing one?
- ✔ What are the business requirements for the database?
- ✔ What capabilities must the database provide to support those requirements?
- ✔ What data elements are necessary to provide those capabilities?
- ✔ How do users prefer to interact with the database?

Notice that the question "What data do I have?" doesn't appear anywhere in that list. Instead, I encourage you to think about database design differently. Walk through the preceding questions to determine what data your business processes require, and only then look at methods you can use to obtain that data and organize it effectively.

This type of thinking will help you overcome the tendency to act like a data packrat, squirreling away all the data you can find. It forces you to focus on business requirements and put in your database only data that is likely to result in business value down the road.

Grouping data into tables

After you've collected all the data elements that you wish to store in your database, you should organize them into tables for your relational database.

When you design tables, keep in mind that your goal is to group related data and reduce redundancy. If you create too many tables, queries against your database will take a long time to complete. If you create too few tables, you'll probably wind up storing redundant data in those tables that will consume unnecessary space on your server's hard drive.

Here's an example of how you can organize data into tables. Suppose you are tasked with creating a database for a newspaper delivery service. After completing your business requirement analysis, you determine that you need to store the following data:

- ✔ Customer name (first and last)
- ✔ Customer street address
- ✔ Customer ZIP code
- ✔ Customer phone number
- ✔ Day(s) of the week the customer receives the paper
- ✔ Carrier name for each customer (first and last)
- ✔ Phone number for each carrier
- ✔ Carrier's driver's license number
- ✔ Carrier's hire date

If you followed the spreadsheet mentality, you might simply create a single table with all this information. However, having just one table would create two significant problems for you:

- ✔ **Large quantities of redundant data.** Assume that each carrier has 1,000 customers. If you used a single table design, you'd wind up storing that carrier's name, telephone number, driver's license number and hire date in each of those 1,000 rows. That's a lot of wasted space!
- ✔ **Difficulty updating data after a change.** What if a carrier quits and you need to reassign customers to a new hire? You'd need to edit all 1,000 records for that carrier!

Instead, you can improve your design by grouping related data into tables. First, look at the data and see what discrete entities already exist in your data. This example already has the notion of a customer and the separate notion of a carrier. Each of those entities already has some data associated with it. There are two of your tables! The Customers table and Carriers table are shown in Tables 4-3 and 4-4.

TIP

If you don't understand some of the fields in these tables, don't worry. I introduce you to routes and subscription types later in this section.

Next, analyze the data and determine whether you can find any abstract concepts that you can use to extract other groups of related data. You might notice that I'm storing the days of the week each customer receives the paper in the database. Perhaps your business process analysis revealed that your newspaper offers only three subscription types: weekday delivery, weekend delivery, and full-week delivery. You can create a table containing information about each of these subscription types and reduce the amount of information stored in the customer table, as shown in Table 4-5.

Table 4-3 Customers Table

Customer ID	First Name	Last Name	Subscription Type	Address	ZIP	Route ID	Phone Number	Hold Status
1	John	Abrams	2	123 Main Street	49242	1	(502) 555-2352	No
2	Bob	Allen	1	482 Main Street	49242	1	(502) 555-1252	No
3	Mary	Smith	1	912 First Street	49243	2	(502) 555-1942	No
4	Beth	McDeer	3	922 First Street	49243	2	(502) 555-9120	Yes

Table 4-4 Carriers Table

Carrier ID	First Name	Last Name	Phone Number	DL Number	Hire Date
1	Jeremy	Hinton	(502) 555-9221	129522902	7/19/2007
2	Kate	Jones	(502) 555-5125	092481982	6/10/2000

Table 4-5 Subscription Types Table

Subscription Type	Sunday	Monday	Tuesday	Wednesday	Thursday	Friday	Saturday
1	Y	N	N	N	N	N	Y
2	N	Y	Y	Y	Y	Y	N
3	Y	Y	Y	Y	Y	Y	Y

Your business process analysis might also reveal that you organize your customers into routes and assign carriers to those routes. Some carriers may have multiple routes, and carriers frequently switch from one route to another. You should also include this concept by introducing a route table and assigning each customer to a route rather than a carrier. A customer's carrier may change often, but the carrier's route will change rarely, if at all. An example routes table appears in Table 4-6.

Table 4-6	Routes Table
Route ID	*Carrier ID*
1	2
2	1
3	1

Notice that the routes table is quite simple. The sole purpose of this table is to link route and carrier information. I discuss linking of related tables later, in the "Linking related tables" section of this chapter.

Selecting primary keys

Each table in a well-designed database should have a primary key that uniquely identifies each row in the table. The primary key is usually a single attribute that the database guarantees will be unique for each row. You can, if you wish, use the combination of two or more columns as a table's primary key, but you'll find it easier to use a single column when possible.

When you look for a primary key, first examine the attributes that already exist in the table. Are any of the attributes guaranteed to be unique for every row? If so, those attributes may be a good choice for a primary key.

Make sure that your choice of a primary key is *guaranteed* to be unique. Some bad choices are people's names (very likely to repeat; how many John Smiths are in the phone book?) and telephone numbers (often reassigned to different people).

Social Security Numbers (SSNs) also make poor primary keys for a number of reasons:

✔ People are often understandably reluctant to provide their SSN because of privacy and identity theft concerns.

> ✔ Businesses don't like to store SSNs unless absolutely necessary because of the potential liability if they are lost.
>
> ✔ Not everyone has an SSN. Generally speaking, only U.S. citizens and others authorized to work in the United States receive SSNs.

Good examples of primary keys include unique identifiers issued by an organization. Many businesses issue employee identification numbers to each employee. If these numbers are never reused, they make excellent primary key candidates. Similarly, colleges and universities issue student identification numbers as an alternative to using SSNs. These also make great primary keys.

Any attribute or combination of attributes that uniquely identifies records in a table is known as a candidate key. The candidate key that you select to uniquely identify those records in the database is known as the primary key. Therefore, a table may contain several candidate keys but only one primary key.

If you can't find an appropriate primary key in your table, you may need to create one. One common approach is to create an "ID" column in your table that contains a unique integer. An example of this approach appears earlier in this chapter in Table 4-3 (which used "Customer ID" as the primary key), and Table 4-4 (which used "Carrier ID"), and Table 4-6 (which used "Route ID").

Linking related tables

After you've identified the primary key for each table in your database, you can harness the true power of relational databases by linking related tables. You accomplish this task by selecting foreign keys. *Foreign keys* identify records in other tables that are related to records in the primary table. Typically, the foreign key in the primary table contains the value of the primary key from the related table.

For example, consider Table 4-3, the customers table, which appears in the "Grouping data into tables" section, earlier in this chapter. For that table, I introduce the notion of a subscription type and create a business rule requiring a subscription type for each customer. I don't include details of each subscription type in the customer records because doing so would introduce redundant data into the database. Instead, I created a foreign key in Table 4-3 called "Subscription Type." This foreign key corresponds to the "Subscription Type" primary key in the subscription types table (Table 4-5, also shown earlier). If you want to determine the days of the week a given customer receives the newspaper, you must first retrieve that customer's subscription type from the customers table and then use that code to retrieve the days of the week from the subscription types table.

I discuss relationships between tables in further detail in Chapter 6.

Diagramming Your Database

The adage "A picture is worth a thousand words" holds true in the world of database design. The previous section of this chapter presents you with a few tables and describes the relationships between them in words. Figure 4-2 shows the same concept using a diagram.

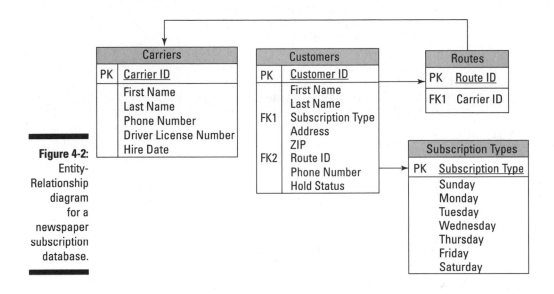

Figure 4-2: Entity-Relationship diagram for a newspaper subscription database.

Isn't that easier to understand than the written descriptions in the previous section? The diagram in Figure 4-2 is an Entity-Relationship (ER) diagram. An ER diagram is a common tool that database designers use to document their designs and share them in a commonly understood format.

When you see an ER diagram, there are a few elements you should examine to identify various features of the relational database:

- ✔ **Each box in the diagram represents a table.** The name of the table appears centered in the shaded area of the box.

- ✔ **Attributes appear in the unshaded portion of each table's box.** Each attribute appears in a separate row.

- ✔ **Attribute(s) that compose a table's primary key appear in the top portion of the unshaded area, above the horizontal line.** They also have the designation "PK" to their left.

- ✔ **Foreign key attributes have the designation "FK" to their left.** In addition, an arrow points from the table containing the foreign key to the referenced table.

> ✔ **Required fields appear in boldface font.** Attributes that may contain
> NULL values (discussed later in this chapter) appear in a regular typeface.

I used Microsoft Visio to create the ER diagram shown in Figure 4-2. Visio is a
great tool that allows you to quickly and easily build many kinds of technical
diagrams.

The form of ER diagrams presented in this book is a simplified approach to
the diagramming process. Advanced approaches allow you to include additional information in your diagram, such as the type of relationship that exists
between tables.

Staying Fit and Trim with Normalization

In addition to creating the concept of relational databases, Eugene F. Codd
(see the "Relational databases" section, earlier in this chapter) also set forth
principles of good database design. He called these principles *normalization
techniques* and created several sets of requirements known as *normal forms*.

In this section, I discuss the three most common normal forms: first normal
form (abbreviated 1NF), second normal form (2NF), and third normal form
(3NF). A database that meets the requirements of a normal form is said to be
"in" that form. The normal forms are cumulative. That is, a database that is in
2NF must also be in 1NF, and a database in 3NF must also be in 2NF.

Normalization techniques provide you with guidelines for sound database
design. Keep in mind that they are *only* guidelines, not inviolable rules.
Sometimes business necessity or expediency may dictate deviating from these
best practices.

First normal form

There are two requirements for a table to be in first normal form:

> ✔ **The table must have no duplicate records.** This criteria is automatically
> met if you define a primary key for the table.

> ✔ The table must have no multi-valued attributes. This one's a little more
> complicated. Basically, it says that you can't combine multiple values
> that are valid for a column in a single column. I provide an example
> to help you understand this concept. Look back at the carriers table
> in Table 4-4. If I didn't care about 1NF, I could have simply created a
> "Routes" column in the carriers table, as shown in Table 4-7.

Table 4-7		Carriers Table Not in 1NF				
Carrier ID	First Name	Last Name	Phone Number	DL Number	Hire Date	Routes
1	Jeremy	Hinton	(502) 555-9221	129522902	7/19/2007	2,3
2	Kate	Jones	(502) 555-5125	092481982	6/10/2000	1

However, this table contains a multi-valued attribute. The "Routes" column contains two values ("2" and "3") for Jeremy Hinton.

An alternative approach would be to create the table shown in Table 4-8.

Table 4-8			Carriers Table in 1NF				
Carrier ID	First Name	Last Name	Phone Number	DL Number	Hire Date	Route1	Route2
1	Jeremy	Hinton	(502) 555-9221	129522902	7/19/ 2007	2	3
2	Kate	Jones	(502) 555-5125	092481982	6/10/ 2000	1	

This table does meet the requirements of 1NF, but it's still not great database design. What happens if Jeremy wants to add a third route? With the approach shown in Table 4-8, you'd need to add another column to the table. The original approach (Table 4-4) creates a separate table to link routes and carriers and allows for an unlimited number of routes per carrier.

Second and third normal forms

The second normal form (2NF) introduces one additional requirement: all attributes that are not part of a candidate key must be functionally dependent upon the entire primary key.

The third normal form (3NF) also requires that all attributes that are not part of a candidate key must be nontransitively dependent upon each candidate key in the table. This means that the attributes may not be dependent only upon the primary key, because they are dependent upon another attribute that is dependent upon the primary key.

What does all of this boil down to? You shouldn't include data in a table that's not directly related to the table's primary key. Imagine if you tried to combine the routes table in Table 4-6 with the carriers table in Table 4-4 to get the result shown in Table 4-9.

Table 4-9		Routes Table Not in 2NF or 3NF			
Route ID	First Name	Last Name	Phone Number	DL Number	Hire Date
1	Kate	Jones	(502) 555-5125	092481982	6/10/2000
2	Jeremy	Hinton	(502) 555-9221	129522902	7/19/2007
3	Jeremy	Hinton	(502) 555-9221	129522902	7/19/2007

The primary key of this table is "Route ID", but there's quite a bit of information in the table that's not dependent upon that primary key. For example, the driver's license number in the third row is not determined by the route ID. It's linked to Jeremy Hinton, so it appears in each row representing a route served by Jeremy.

Normalization requires that you separate this table into a carriers table and a routes table, as I do earlier in the chapter.

The three normal forms described previously are the ones most commonly implemented in databases. There are other, more advanced, normal forms that impose more burdensome requirements that are difficult to implement and often result in significant inefficiencies. They include fourth normal form (4NF), fifth normal form (5NF), sixth normal form (6NF), Boyce-Codd normal form (BCNF) and domain/key normal form (DKNF).

Choosing Data Types for Your Tables

After you have a normalized design, you need to transform your ER diagram into a SQL Server database design. The primary task to perform is the selection of appropriate data types for each of the attributes in your database. The data type tells SQL Server how to interpret the data stored in each column.

I discuss the process of creating SQL Server databases and tables in Chapter 5. Here, you can focus on discovering the various data types and mapping them to your design.

Numeric data types

Numeric data types store any type of information that you'd like SQL Server to use in mathematical computations. They include data types capable of storing both integers and decimal numbers.

The numeric data types supported by SQL Server 2008 appear in Table 4-10.

Table 4-10	Numeric Data Types	
Data Type	*Description*	*Length*
int	Stores integer values ranging from −2,147,483,648 to 2,147,483,647	4 bytes
tinyint	Stores integer values ranging from 0 to 255	1 byte
smallint	Stores integer values ranging from −32,768 to 32,767	2 bytes
bigint	Stores integer values ranging from −263 to 263−1	8 bytes
money	Stores monetary values ranging from −922,337,203,685,477.5808 to 922,337,203,685,477.5807	8 bytes
smallmoney	Stores monetary values ranging from −214,748.3648 to 214,748.3647	4 bytes
decimal(p,s)	Stores decimal values of precision *p* and scale *s*. The maximum precision is 38 digits.	5-17 bytes
numeric(p,s)	Functionally equivalent to decimal	
float(n)	Stores floating point values with precision of 7 digits (when n=24) or 15 digits (when n=53)	4 bytes (when n=24) or 8 bytes (when n=53)
real	Functionally equivalent to float(24)	

You need to be familiar with a few mathematical terms and concepts to understand the differences between the numeric data types, so here's a brief refresher:

- ✔ Integers are numbers with no decimal point. The following numbers are all integer values:

  - 2

  - 32,420

  - 1,000,000,000,000,000

  - 0

  - –15

- ✔ The precision of a decimal number is the number of digits that may be stored on both sides of the decimal points. Here are a few examples:

  - The value 32 has a precision of 2.

  - The value 3.14159 has a precision of 6.

  - The value 19402.4391024 has a precision of 12.

- ✔ The scale of a decimal number is the number of digits that may be stored on the right side of the decimal point. Here are a few examples:

  - The value 32 has a scale of 0.

  - The value 3.14159 has a scale of 5.

  - The value 19402.4391024 has a scale of 7.

- ✔ Floating-point numbers (both the float and real data types) are less accurate than other decimal types because of the way they are stored in binary form.

Always use the smallest-length variable that will accommodate all anticipated values stored in a column. Consider the case of an integer value that stores values between 1 and 50. If you use a standard int data type, each row will require 4 bytes for that column. On the other hand, if you use a tinyint, that column will require only 1 byte per row. That might not sound like much, but the use of a tinyint reduces the column's space consumption by 75 percent. That's a significant difference in a large database!

Date and time data types

SQL Server provides several data types specifically designed for the storage of date and time data. SQL Server 2008 includes the new date and time data types, features long requested by SQL Server users.

Table 4-11	Date and Time Data Types		
Data Type	*Description*	*Length*	*Example*
date	Stores dates between January 1, 0001, and December 31, 9999	3 bytes	2008-01-15
datetime	Stores dates and times between January 1, 1753, and December 31, 9999, with an accuracy of 3.33 milliseconds	8 bytes	2008-01-15 09:42:16.142
datetime2	Stores date and times between January 1, 0001, and December 31, 9999, with an accuracy of 100 nanoseconds	6–8 bytes	2008-01-15 09:42:16.1420221
datetimeoffset	Stores date and times with the same precision as datetime2 and also includes an offset from Universal Time Coordinated (UTC) (also known as Greenwich Mean Time)	8–10 bytes	2008-01-15 09:42:16.1420221 +05:00
smalldatetime	Stores dates and times between January 1, 1900, and June 6, 2079, with an accuracy of 1 minute (the seconds are always listed as ":00")	4 bytes	2008-01-15 09:42:00
time	Stores times with an accuracy of 100 nanoseconds	3–5 bytes	09:42:16.1420221

Character string data types

Character string data types allow you to store text in a Microsoft SQL Server database. Table 4-12 shows the character string data types.

Table 4-12	Character String Data Types	
Data Type	**Description**	**Length**
char(n)	Stores *n* characters	*n* bytes (where *n* is in the range of 1–8,000)
nchar(n)	Stores *n* Unicode characters	2*n* bytes (where n is in the range of 1–4,000)
varchar(n)	Stores approximately *n* characters	actual string length + 2 bytes (where *n* is in the range of 1–8,000)
varchar(max)	Stores up to $2^{31}-1$ characters	actual string length + 2 bytes
nvarchar(n)	Stores approximately *n* characters	2*(actual string length) + 2 bytes (where *n* is in the range of 1–4,000)
nvarchar(max)	Stores up to $((2^{31}-1)/2)-2$ characters	2*(actual string length)+2 bytes

Here are a few facts you should know about character string data types:

- ✔ If the number of characters in a string is fairly constant, you should use the char or nchar data type. Doing so avoids the 2-byte overhead of the varchar and nvarchar data types.

- ✔ If the number of characters in a string varies significantly, use the varchar or nvarchar data types. Doing so avoids wasting space storing short strings in large spaces.

- ✔ If your database supports only English attributes, use the char or varchar data types. These use half the space that the nchar and nvarchar data types use.

- ✔ SQL Server supports the text and ntext data types for the storage of large strings, but these are scheduled for removal in a future version of SQL Server. You should avoid them to ensure the compatibility of your database with future versions. Use varchar(max) or nvarchar(max) instead.

Binary data types

SQL Server's binary data types allow you to store basically any type of data represented in binary form. The binary data types are shown in Table 4-13.

Table 4-13	Binary Data Types	
Data Type	**Description**	**Length**
bit	Stores a single bit of data	1 byte per 8 bit columns in a table
binary(n)	Stores *n* bytes of binary data	*n* bytes (where n is in the range of 1-8,000)
varbinary(n)	Stores approximately *n* bytes of binary data	actual length+2 bytes (where *n* is in the range of 1–8,000)
varbinary(max)	Stores up to $2^{31}-1$ bytes of binary data	actual length+2 bytes

Examples of binary data include documents, images, encrypted text, and any other data that can be represented in binary form.

 SQL Server also supports the image data type but, as is true of text and ntext, image will not be supported in future releases of SQL Server. You should use another binary data type in its place to ensure the compatibility of your database with future versions of SQL Server.

Other data types

SQL Server also provides six additional built-in data types that don't neatly fit into any of the classifications described in previous sections of this chapter. These types appear in Table 4-14.

Table 4-14	Other Built-In Data Types	
Data Type	**Description**	**Length**
cursor	Stores a reference to a cursor	N/A (cannot be used in a table)

(continued)

Table 4-14 *(continued)*

`sql_variant`	May store any data type other than `sql_variant`, `text`, `ntext`, `image`, and `timestamp`	Up to 8,000 bytes
`table`	Stores a temporary table (such as a query result)	N/A (cannot be used in a table)
`rowversion`	Stores a value of the data-base time (a relative number that increments each time you insert or update data in a database. It is not related to calendar/clock time)	8 bytes
`uniqueidentifier`	Stores a globally unique identifier	2 bytes
`xml`	Stores formatted XML documents	Up to 2GB

The timestamp data type is one of the least understood aspects of SQL Server. It does *not* contain an actual date and time but contains a value from the data-base's internal counter. You can use it for comparing the relative sequence of events, but honestly, it's not a very useful data type.

In case all these data types aren't enough for you, SQL Server lets you create your own data types to meet your specific needs. You can create user-defined types (UDTs) to develop your own, nonstandard data types. For example, you might make a UDT for telephone numbers that enforces consistent number formatting throughout your organization's databases.

Working with NULL Values

The value NULL holds special meaning for database developers. It means "nothing," and you use it to indicate either missing information or a value of "not applicable." NULL does *not* mean "empty" or "zero."

For example, suppose you have a customer management database that contains a variable storing the number of times each customer visits your stores.
If you did not know the number of times a customer visited your store, you
would use the NULL value. If a customer has never visited your store, you would
use a value of 0.

When you create a database table, you may specify whether each column
may contain NULL values. If you do not allow a column to contain NULLs,
users may not create a row without entering an appropriate value for that
column. I cover the creation of tables that permit and deny NULL values in
Chapter 5.

When you compare database values, you need to consider the possibility
that a column might contain a NULL value and remember that it may affect
the results of your comparison. Here are a few pointers:

- If you want to test whether a value is NULL, use the IS NULL condition
  in a query's WHERE clause. I discuss doing so in Chapter 7.

- If you test two conditions joined with an AND (such as "X AND Y") and
  one of the values is NULL, the result will be NULL. The only exception to
  this result is if one of the values is known to be false. In that case, the
  clause will be false no matter what.

- Similarly, if you test two conditions joined with an OR (such as "X OR Y")
  and one of the values is true, that clause will always be true. However, if
  there are no true values and there is at least one NULL value, the result
  will be NULL.

Chapter 5

Creating Databases and Tables

In This Chapter

▶ Creating a new SQL Server database

▶ Working with files and filegroups

▶ Creating, modifying, and deleting database tables

After you install SQL Server 2008, you can get down to the nuts and bolts of SQL Server databases. And as with any database, you want to apply the basics of good database design, which I cover in Chapter 4. In this chapter, I take you through the process of creating a database on a SQL Server. You find out how easily you can configure a new database, populate it with the tables that hold your data, and modify existing tables.

Remember that a *database* is a collection of related tables that store your data. Each time you install SQL Server on a system, you have the ability to create one or more databases to store different kinds of data. When you install SQL Server, you don't actually create a database. Rather, you create a server that has the capability to store databases. In this chapter, I show you how to create a single database on your new SQL Server.

If you just opened the book and skipped to this chapter, you probably want to take a few minutes to look over Chapter 4, where I discuss the proper way to design a database. If you try to create your database and tables without under-standing that information, you might make design decisions that will make your life difficult down the road. For example, if you don't design your tables efficiently at first, you may need to redesign them later. Redesigning existing database tables requires modifying all the queries and reports that use those tables — a time-consuming task.

Creating a Database

SQL Server 2008 makes the creation of a new database simple and pain free. Although this powerful platform certainly enables you to customize your database, it also includes a great set of default options that can have you up and running in a matter of minutes. Follow these steps to create a new SQL Server database:

1. **Choose Start➪All Programs➪Microsoft SQL Server➪SQL Server Management Studio to start SQL Server Management Studio (SSMS).**

   SSMS opens and prompts you to connect to an installation of Microsoft SQL Server, as shown in Figure 5-1.

2. **Click the Connect button to connect to your server.**

   Simply clicking Connect works if you're running SSMS on the same computer you used to install SQL Server and you configured it to use Windows Authentication mode (see Chapter 2 for more about Windows Authentication mode).

   If you're connecting to the server from a remote system, you need to specify the server name in the Connect to Server dialog box. If your server uses SQL Server Authentication, you also need to provide your username and password in the same window.

3. **Right-click the Databases folder, which you find in the Object Explorer pane of the resulting SSMS window, and select New Database from the pop-up menu.**

   You see the first screen of the New Database wizard, shown in Figure 5-2, which assists you in configuring your database.

4. **Type a name that describes your database into the Database Name textbox.**

   Every database on a SQL Server system must have a unique name. For this example in this chapter, I use the name Cookies.

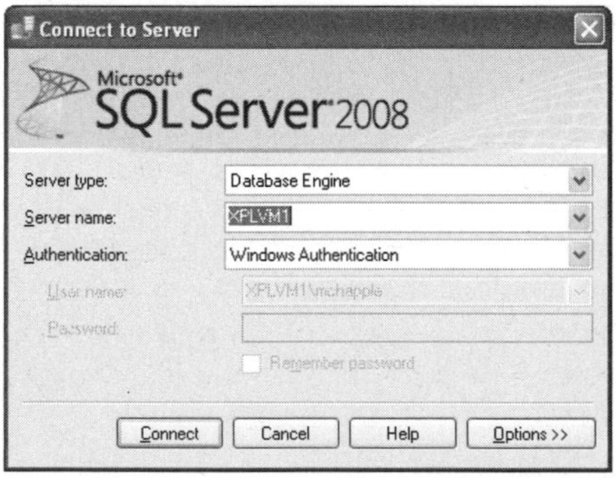

Figure 5-1:
Connecting to a SQL Server 2008 server.

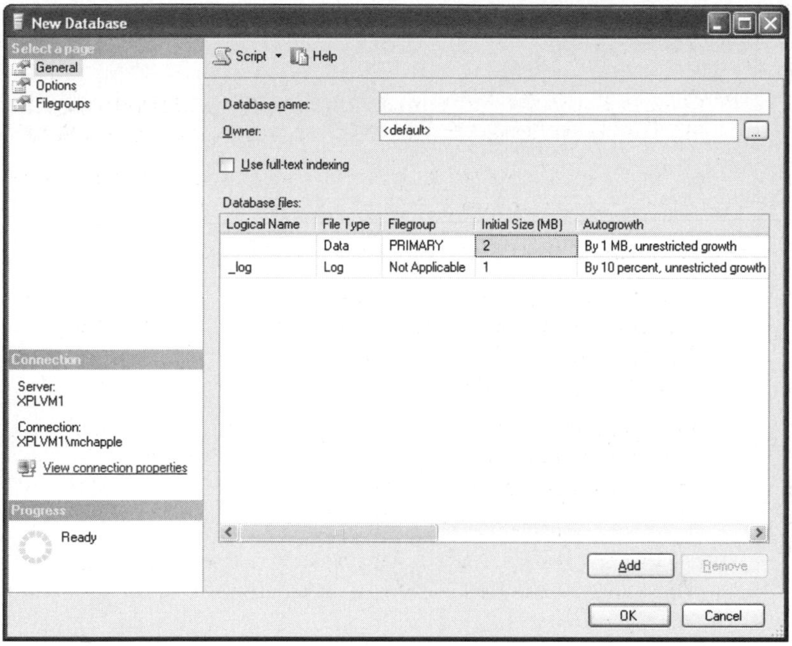

Figure 5-2:
You can
configure
your data-
base using
the New
Database
Wizard.

5. Click through the various pages by using the Select a Page pane in the upper-left corner of the New Database Wizard window.

The New Database Wizard allows you to set a number of different options when you create a new database, including

- Using files and filegroups to specify how SQL Server should store your data. (You can find more details on this in the section "Specifying Files and Filegroups," later in this chapter.)

- Setting the database owner.

- Configuring a recovery model. (I discuss recovery models in Chapter 17.)

- Making your database backwards compatible with earlier versions of SQL Server.

Figure 5-3 shows the Options page with default options. In the interest of keeping your first database simple, I recommend accepting all the default options for now.

5. Click OK to create your database.

The computer will probably take a while to build your database. While SQL Server is working, the Progress pane in the lower-left corner of the New Database Wizard says "Executing," as shown in Figure 5-4.

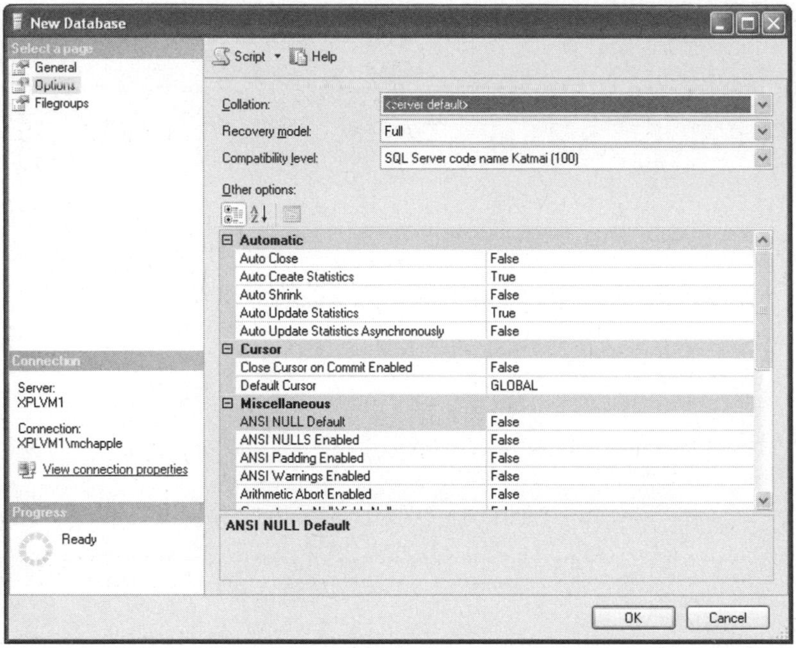

Figure 5-3:
The Options
page of
the New
Database
Wizard.

6. **View your database in SSMS after the New Database window disappears.**

If you don't see any entries underneath the Databases folder, expand it by clicking the + sign to the left of the Databases folder icon. Doing so expands the list of databases, and you should now see your new database underneath the System Databases and Database Snapshots entries. Figure 5-5 shows a SQL Server 2008 installation with the new database that I named Cookies.

Figure 5-4:
The
Progress
pane
displays
while your
database is
being built.

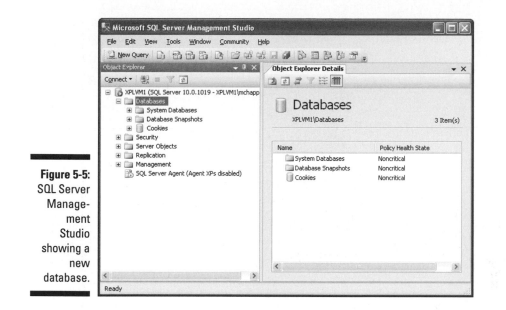

Figure 5-5:
SQL Server
Manage-
ment
Studio
showing a
new
database.

That's all there is to it. Congratulations, you've now built your own SQL Server database!

Altering database properties

You might want to change some of your initial design decisions after you've finished creating your database. For example, suppose that you rarely use a database and decide that you'd like SQL Server to close it automatically when not in use. Now you want to change options so that the database automatically closes. No problem! SQL Server Management Studio makes doing so easy.

1. **With SQL Server Management Studio open, use Object Explorer to navigate to the database you'd like to modify by expanding the Databases folder (click the plus sign next to the folder icon) and clicking the desired database.**

2. **Right-click the database and choose Properties from the pop-up menu.**

   The database Properties window appears and shows the currently selected options.

3. **Browse the property pages by clicking their titles in the Select a Page pane of the Properties window; then, modify any option(s) you want.**

   Some common changes to make to database properties include the following:

   - Configuring a database to automatically close when not in use. To do so, you set go to the Options page and set the Auto Close property to True.

   - Adding files to a database on the Files page.

   - Altering database mirroring settings on the Mirroring page. (I discuss mirroring in Chapter 19.)

4. **Click OK to confirm your changes.**

Deleting or renaming a database

Occasionally, you may need to delete an entire database when you no longer need it. Also, you might want to change the name you initially assigned to a database based upon changes you make after the initial design. The modification process is slightly different if you'd like to delete or rename a database. To delete a database, follow these steps:

1. **With SQL Server Management Studio open, navigate to the database you'd like to delete by expanding the Databases folder in Object Explorer and clicking the desired database.**

Doing things the hard way

In Chapter 1, I mention that the only language that databases understand is the Structured Query Language (SQL). At this point in Chapter 5, you might be asking yourself "Where's the SQL?" Rest assured that it's there in the background. SSMS conveniently translates your mouse clicks and data entry into SQL code that's sent to the database. You can actually write a SQL statement to create a database rather than use the New Database Wizard. If you were to choose the SQL way, your statement would read like this:

```
CREATE DATABASE Cookies;
```

Similarly, you can rename the database with this statement:

```
ALTER DATABASE Cookies
MODIFY NAME = Brownies;
```

2. **Right-click the object and choose Delete from the pop-up menu.**

   SSMS presents a Confirmation window similar to the one shown in
   Figure 5-6. This window gives you one last chance to confirm that you'd
   like to delete the database.

3. **Verify the information in the Confirmation window and, if you're pre-
   pared to delete the database, click OK to continue.**

Backing up your database before you delete it is a good idea. After you delete
it, your structure and data are gone, and restoring from backup is the only
way to bring the database back online.

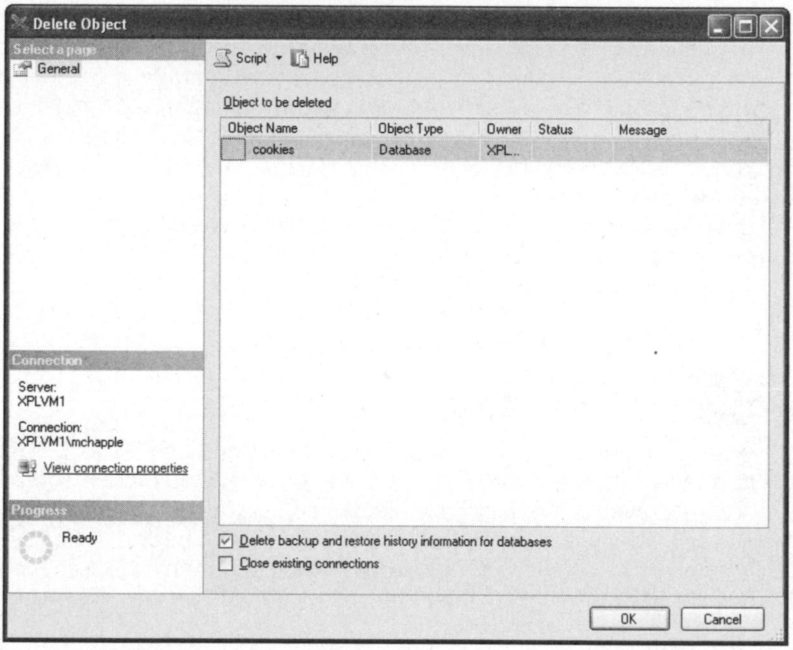

Figure 5-6:
Confirming
the deletion
of a data-
base.

If your use of a database changes over time, you can rename the database
to match the revised use. If you explored the database property sheets, you
probably noticed that the database name appears as a property, but you
can't change it in the property sheet. To change the name of a database,
follow these steps:

1. **With SQL Server Management Studio open, navigate to the database
   you'd like to rename by expanding the Databases folder in Object
   Explorer.**

2. **Right-click the object and select Rename from the pop-up menu.**

3. **Type the new name over the old name and press Enter.**

Specifying Files and Filegroups

If you're familiar with desktop database products (such as Microsoft Access), you might be wondering where SQL Server actually stores your data. After all, to open an Access database, you simply browse your computer and double-click the database file.

SQL Server also uses files to store your data, but they're kept behind the scenes. Database users don't even need to know that these files exist, because the users interact with databases and database applications through other interfaces, such as Web applications, instead. Administrators, however, should be aware of these files, because their location and configuration can affect database performance.

In this section, I offer you a look at the files that make up a SQL Server database and then turn your attention to the use of *filegroups,* which help you group related files for convenient file management.

SQL Server files

When you create a database using the New Database Wizard, SQL Server automatically creates the necessary files for you on disk. By default, SQL Server creates a primary data file named *database*.mdf and a log file named *database*_log.mdf, where *database* is the name of your database. These files are stored in SQL Server's data directory. Unless you've changed it, this directory is C:\Program Files\Microsoft SQL Server\MSSQL.1\MSSQL\DATA.

If you can't find a particular file, you can look up the location on the database's Files property sheet. I explain how to view database properties in the "Altering database properties" section, earlier in this chapter.

SQL Server 2008 uses three file types to store database information and logs:

✔ **Primary data files** serve as the "hub" of the database. Each database has one and only one primary data file. By default, this file contains all the data stored in your database. It also contains important configuration information and the location of other database files. Most administrators use the .mdf file extension to indicate a primary data file.

✔ **Secondary data files** are an optional way to spread your database content over multiple files. It's common practice to use the .ndf file extension on secondary data files.

✔ **Log files** store your database's transaction logs. They're critical if you ever need to restore your database from backup. I discuss transaction logs in Chapter 18. Most administrators use the .ldf file extension when naming log files.

Separating your data files and log files onto separate physical disks helps optimize database performance. For example, if you have four physical disks, you can have a primary data file, two secondary data files, and a log file all on separate disks, improving data access times.

Adding a file

If you'd like to spread your data across multiple files to take advantage of multiple disks, you can add secondary data files to your database. It's a simple process, as follows:

1. **With SQL Server Management Studio open, navigate to the database where you'd like to add a file by expanding the Databases folder in Object Explorer.**

2. **Right-click the database name and select Properties from the pop-up menu.**

   The Properties dialog box appears.

3. **Click the Files page in the Select a Page pane.**

   SSMS displays the files associated with the current database.

4. **Click the Add button to add a new data file.**

   You see the new data file appear as a new, unnamed row in the Database files table located in the center of the window.

5. **Click in the Logical Name cell and type the name of your file (Figure 5-7).**

6. **Use the scroll bar to view the right side of the Database files table and click the ellipsis (. . .) icon next to the file path field if you'd like to change the storage location of your new file.**

7. **Click OK to confirm the addition.**

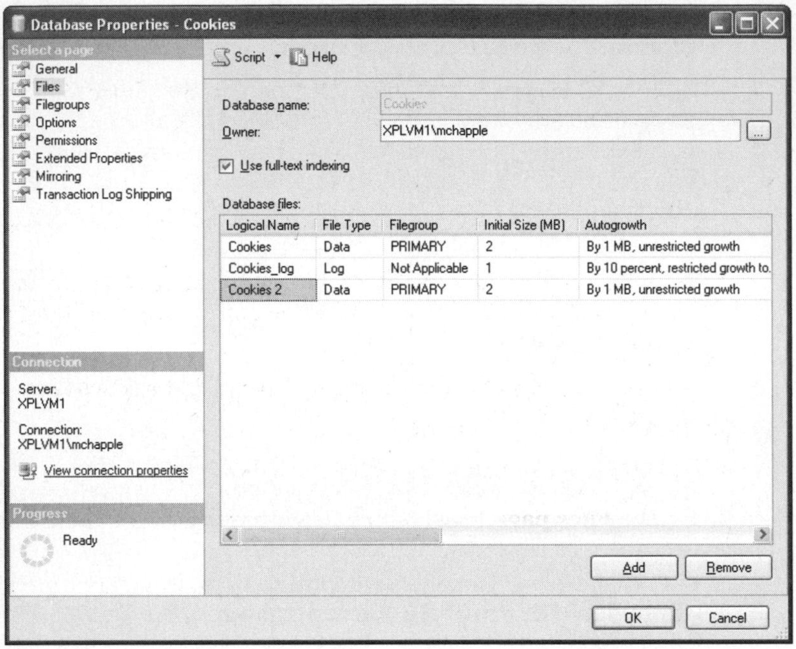

Figure 5-7:
Adding a
secondary
data file to a
database.

Adding log files follows the same process. Just choose the Log file type from the drop-down menu in the Database files table to add a new log file to your database.

Removing a file

You may want to rearrange the way you stored your database files on disk. For example, you might plan to remove a drive from a system for maintenance purposes. Before doing so, you need to remove the database files stored on that disk. Removing a file from a database is a two-step process: You first need to ensure that the file is empty and then you can remove it from the database.

Ensure that the file is empty by following these steps:

1. **With SQL Server Management Studio open, navigate to the database where you'd like to remove a file by expanding the Databases folder (click the plus sign next to it) in Object Explorer.**

2. **Right-click the database name and choose Tasks⇨Shrink⇨Files.**

   SSMS displays the Shrink File window, which allows you to specify the shrinking options you'd like to use.

3. **Use the File Type, Filegroup, and File Name drop-down boxes to identify the file you plan to remove.**

4. **Select the Empty File by Migrating the Data to Other Files in the Same Filegroup radio button.**

5. **Click OK to empty the file.**

After you've emptied the file, you can delete it by following these steps:

1. **With SQL Server Management Studio open, navigate to the database where you'd like to remove a file by expanding the Databases folder in Object Explorer.**

2. **Right-click the database object and select Properties from the pop-up menu.**

3. **Click the Files page in the Select a Page pane.**

4. **On the Files page, single-click the file you'd like to delete.**

   The filename is now highlighted.

5. **Click the Remove button.**

   The file disappears from the list.

6. **Click OK to confirm the deletion.**

Using filegroups

If you have a large, complex SQL Server environment, managing individual files may be cumbersome. SQL Server provides the ability to group related files into filegroups to help ease your administrative burden.

Each primary and secondary data file may be a member of one and only one filegroup. A filegroup may contain one or more data files. Log files may not belong to a filegroup.

Creating a new filegroup

To add a new filegroup to a SQL Server 2008 database, follow these steps:

1. **With SQL Server Management Studio open, navigate to the database where you'd like to add a filegroup.**

2. **Right-click the database object and select Properties from the pop-up menu.**

   SSMS displays the Database Properties window.

3. **Click the Filegroups page in the Select a Page pane.**

4. **Click the Add button to add a new filegroup.**

   The new filegroup appears as a new, unnamed entry.

5. **Click in the Name cell and type the name of your filegroup.**

   Figure 5-8 illustrates this process.

6. **Click OK to confirm the addition.**

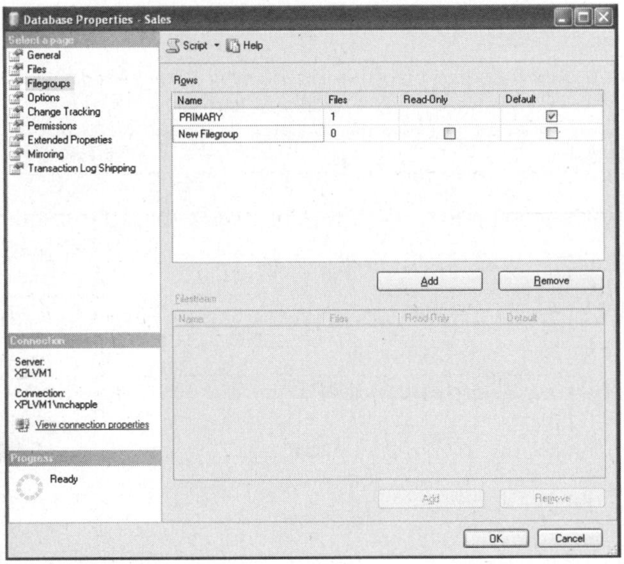

Figure 5-8:
Creating a
new file-
group.

You've now created a new filegroup. The next time you add a data file to your database, you'll notice the new filegroup's name in the Filegroup drop-down box.

Understanding the PRIMARY filegroup

SQL Server 2008 creates a filegroup called the PRIMARY filegroup in each new database at the time of creation. The PRIMARY filegroup contains a variety of system information and, unless you specify otherwise, serves as the default filegroup for all new data files.

You may change the default filegroup using SSMS by checking the Default box in the desired entry on the filegroups page of the database properties sheet.

Creating a Table

Tables serve as the basic structure for storing data in a relational database. In this section, you find out how to create a new table, assign it a name, add data columns, and select a primary key.

Imagine that you're the database administrator for a chain of cookie stores and you want to create a database to manage store information. You might create a shops table that holds essential information about each one of the stores in your cookie empire. Your table might contain the columns shown in Table 5-1:

Table 5-1	Shops Table	
Column Name	*Data Type*	*Allow Nulls*
Unit Number	`tinyint`	No
Address	`varchar(50)`	No
City	`varchar(20)`	No
State	`Char(2)`	No
ZIP	`Char(5)`	No
Phone	`Char(12)`	No
Fax	`Char(12)`	Yes

Getting started

The first thing you need to do is create the basic structure of your table in SQL Server. You can build your table using SQL Server Management Studio's graphical table interface. Here's the process you can follow:

1. **With SSMS open, navigate to the database where you'd like to build a new table by expanding the Databases folder (click the plus sign next to it) in Object Explorer.**

2. **Expand the database's folder.**

3. **Expand the Tables folder.**

   If your database already has tables, you see a listing of them here. If you're working with a new database, the only object in this folder is the System Tables folder.

4. **Right-click the Tables folder and select New Table from the pop-up menu.**

   You now see SSMS' table creation interface (Table Designer), set up and ready to go with a new table, as shown in Figure 5-9.

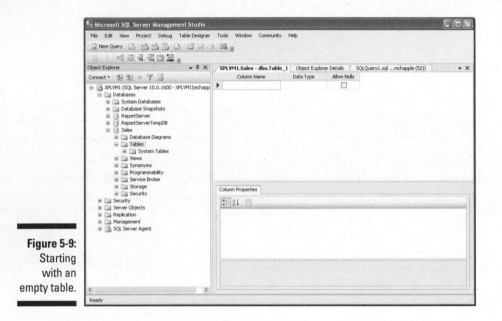

Figure 5-9:
Starting
with an
empty table.

Adding columns

After you create the basic table structure, you need to add columns to your table that correspond to the data elements in your design. I outlined the columns of a Shops table in Table 5-1, shown previously, and now you can use them to duplicate the table by following these steps:

1. **Click in the empty cell in the Column Name column (in the middle pane of the Table Designer window) and enter the name of your column (for example,** Unit Number**).**

2. **Select the appropriate data type using the Data Type drop-down box.**

   If you're working with data types that allow you to specify the length (such as `char`, `varchar`, and `binary`), you may edit the value in parentheses to indicate the appropriate length. For example, if you want a column of type `char` with length 2, you first select `char(10)` from the drop-down box and then edit the length, changing it from 10 to 12.

3. **Select the Allow Nulls check box if you'd like to allow users to store NULL values in the column.**

   You may repeat this process as many times as necessary to create all the columns for your database table.

Selecting a primary key

In Chapter 4, I discuss the importance of selecting an appropriate primary key for your table. You may select either a single column or a combination of columns to serve as your table's primary key.

The primary key *must* be unique. SQL Server will not allow you to insert a new row in a table that contains a primary key value duplicating another table entry. For similar reasons, SQL Server will not allow you to select the Allow Nulls attribute on a column used in the primary key.

If you're not certain that a key value will always remain unique, you can use an identity column to automatically generate a unique key. You may set the Identity Column property in the Table Designer category of the Property pane.

Here's how to set a table's primary key:

1. **In the Table Designer window, select the column(s) involved in your primary key.**

   If your key uses more than one column, hold down the Ctrl key and click each one.

2. **Click the primary key icon (shown here in the margin).**

   This icon appears in the Table Designer toolbar that is, by default, right above the Object Explorer pane in the table window.

3. **Verify that the row(s) involved in the key now have the primary key icon next to their entries in the table window.**

Save your table often! If you close SSMS without saving your work, you'll lose it! You can save your table by choosing Save from the File menu, clicking the disk icon in the Standard toolbar, or pressing Ctrl+S. SQL Server lets you know when your table design contains unsaved changes by putting an asterisk (*) next to the table name in the tab above the column definitions.

Figure 5-10 shows the completed Shops table. Notice that this table is in need of a save!

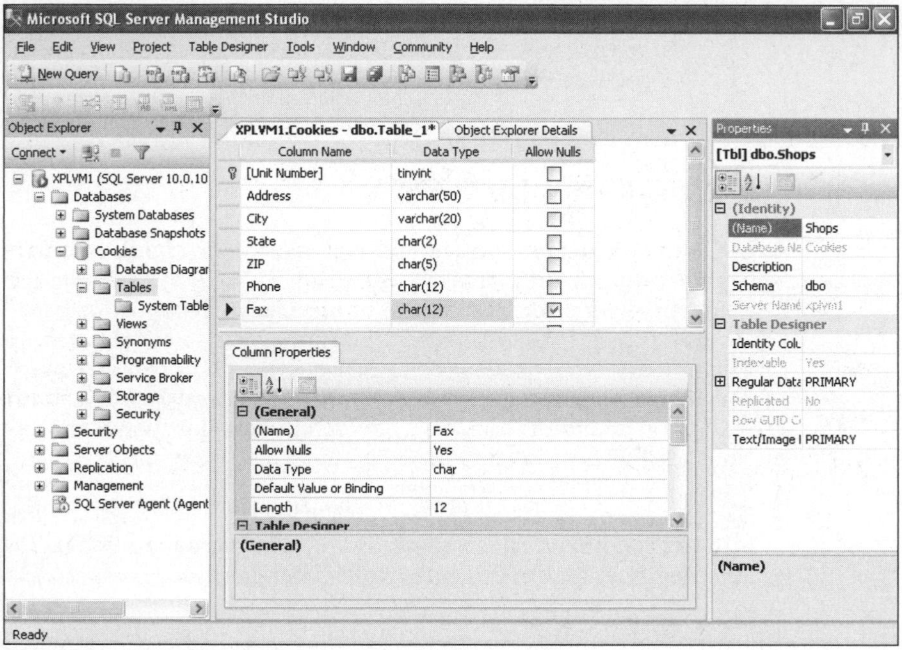

Figure 5-10:
The completed Shops table.

Doing it the Transact-SQL way

As with all other database activities, you may create a table using nothing other than Transact-SQL statements. The Transact-SQL required to create the same Shops table used in this chapter is as follows:

```
USE [Cookies];
CREATE TABLE [dbo].[Shops](
    [Unit Number] [tinyint]
NOT NULL,
    [Address] [varchar](50)
NOT NULL,
    [City] [varchar](20) NOT
NULL,
    [State] [char](2) NOT
NULL,
    [ZIP] [char](5) NOT
NULL,
    [Phone] [char](12) NOT
NULL,
    [Fax] [char](12) NULL,
) ON [PRIMARY]
```

You may view the Transact-SQL statement for an existing table by right-clicking a table's name in the Object Explorer and choosing Edit from the pop-up menu.

If you return to the Object Explorer, you'll now notice that the name of your table appears in the Tables folder for your database. The "dbo." string before your table name indicates that the dbo (database owner) account maintains ownership of the table.

If you'd like to discover more about the CREATE TABLE Transact-SQL statement and its options, consult SQL Server Books Online.

Modifying tables

You'll often need to modify the design of an existing table to meet the changing business requirements of your organization. For example, if your cookie stores go online, you might need to modify the Shops table from the previous section to add an e-mail address column. SSMS makes this a simple process:

1. **With SSMS open, navigate to the database object that contains the table you'd like to modify by expanding the Databases folder (click the plus sign next to it).**

2. **Expand the Tables subfolder for the appropriate database.**

3. **Right-click the name of the table you plan to modify and select the Design option from the pop-up menu.**

   The table opens in Design view.

4. **Use Table Designer to modify your table.**

   The Table Designer interface is exactly the same as the one you used to create a new table in the Creating a Table section of this chapter. You may modify table properties or add, edit, or remove table columns.

5. **Save the table when you're finished by clicking the Save icon.**

If you're a Transact-SQL junkie, the ALTER TABLE statement allows you to modify table characteristics without using the graphic interface of Table Designer.

Deleting tables

Occasionally, you may need to delete a table that's no longer needed in your database. For example, suppose your database contains a table of Social Security numbers, and new privacy regulations require that you no longer store sensitive personal data. Here's how you can easily delete the table:

1. **With SSMS open, navigate to the database object that contains the table you'd like to delete.**

2. **Expand the Tables folder for the appropriate database by clicking the plus sign next to it.**

3. **Right-click the name of the table you plan to delete and select the Delete option from the pop-up menu.**

4. **Confirm the deletion by clicking OK.**

   SQL Server displays the confirmation screen shown in Figure 5-11 and asks you to confirm the deletion prior to finalizing it.

You may also delete tables using the DROP TABLE Transact-SQL statement. For example, to delete a table named Test, you use the following code:

```
DROP TABLE Test;
```

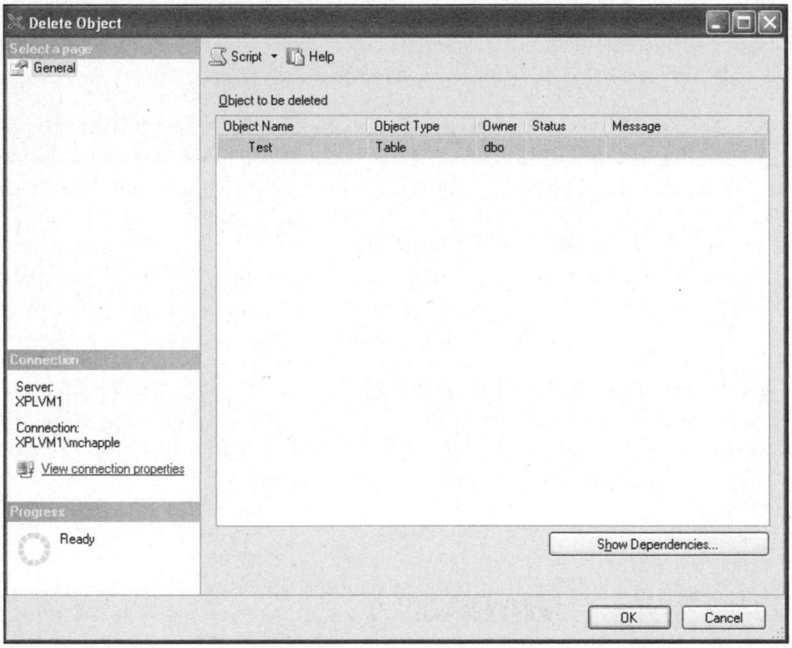

Figure 5-11:
Confirming a table deletion.

Chapter 6

Imposing Constraints and Relationships

As you work with SQL Server, you'll often want to control the contents of your database to ensure the quality of the data it contains. For example, you might want to ensure that your customers database doesn't contain two duplicate records for the same customer. Similarly, you wouldn't want an orders table in that database to contain an order for an item that doesn't exist in your catalog. Both of these situations could cause embarrassing situations for your business and possibly have a negative impact on your organization's profitability.

Database administrators refer to this type of quality assurance as ensuring the integrity of the database. Microsoft SQL Server provides a number of mechanisms for enforcing database integrity. Collectively, these mechanisms are known as constraints, and this chapter shows you how to effectively use them to control the contents of your databases.

Introducing Constraints

SQL Server 2008 supports five different types of database integrity constraints. Two of them primarily enforce business rules imposed upon the database, whereas the other three ensure the integrity of database row uniqueness and relationships.

The two types of constraints that primarily serve to enforce business logic in your databases are the following:

- ✔ **DEFAULT constraints** supply values to fill fields when the user doesn't provide a value.
- ✔ **CHECK constraints** limit the values that users may insert into a particular database field.

The three rules designed to support database relationships and enforce uniqueness are as follows:

- ✔ **PRIMARY KEY constraints** ensure that specified column(s) always contain a unique value so that the column(s) may serve as a table's primary key.
- ✔ **UNQIUE constraints** provide functionality similar to primary key constraints, but do not specify that the column(s) subject to the constraint are a table's primary key.
- ✔ **FOREIGN KEY constraints** link two tables in a database by requiring that the data in the column(s) governed by the constraint contain values stored in the primary key column(s) of the linked table.

Each of these constraints serves a unique purpose in a SQL Server 2008 database. In the rest of this chapter, you discover how each one can help you enforce business logic and ensure the integrity of your SQL Server databases.

Controlling Database Contents Using Constraints

Databases allow you to do much more than simply store and retrieve data. They also allow you to enforce business rules that ensure that your data meets the business requirements of your organization. DEFAULT constraints and CHECK constraints are two powerful mechanisms that SQL Server 2008 provides to help you enforce business logic. Read on to find out how to put these mechanisms to best use.

Filling in empty values with DEFAULT constraints

In an ideal world, users providing data for your database will always provide a set of complete rows, containing a value for every field in the relevant table. Unfortunately, this isn't usually the case. You'll often receive data with missing or unknown values, and your database should provide mechanisms to handle these situations.

Chapter 4 explains the concept of NULL, which is the value used by a database to indicate an unknown or missing value. Sometimes, however, you may not wish to use a NULL value for every case in which the user does not supply data.

Deciding how to handle missing data

Consider the case of an inventory table containing information about the products stocked in a retail store along with a current count of the on-hand inventory of each product. If the store manager wishes to add a new product to the catalog, but does not yet have any of the product on hand, he or she might go ahead and insert a new record into the products table but leave the inventory field blank.

You have several possible ways to deal with this situation:

- ✔ You could interpret the blank value literally and have the database store a NULL value to indicate the missing data. However, this approach doesn't take advantage of all the information at your disposal. You know that the store manager is entering the product into the catalog for the first time and that there is no current inventory in stock. The database, on the other hand, will contain a NULL value, indicating that you do not know the current inventory status of the product. This solution is not ideal because you're losing information that could be valuable to the organization for inventory planning purposes.

- ✔ You could mark the column as not allowing NULL values. This approach would require that the store manager provide a value for the column by refusing to accept a new record containing a NULL value. This solution might be the most technically correct, but it's annoying to the store manager. Your primary goal should be to design usable systems that meet your business and technical requirements while imposing as little burden upon the organization as possible. This solution fails to meet that objective.

- ✔ You could set a value of zero by default, acknowledging the fact that when a product is first ordered, you know there is no inventory on hand. This solution is the ideal one because it ensures the integrity of your database and stores all the available information for future use. It also reduces the burden upon the store manager, providing a workable solution.

You may implement the third scenario by using SQL Server's DEFAULT constraint. DEFAULT constraints provide a value that SQL Server will automatically insert in a column when the data source does not explicitly provide a value.

Creating a DEFAULT constraint

Here's how to create a DEFAULT constraint in SQL Server 2008:

1. **With SQL Server Management Studio open, navigate to the database containing the table where you'd like to implement a DEFAULT constraint by expanding the Databases folder in Object Explorer.**

2. **Click the plus (+) icon next to the database name to expand the relevant database.**

3. **Click the plus (+) icon next to the Tables folder icon to expand the Tables folder for the relevant database.**

4. **Right-click the name of the desired table and select Design from the pop-up menu.**

   The table opens in Design view, and you see a screen similar to the one shown in Figure 6-1.

5. **Select the name of the column for which you want to provide a default value.**

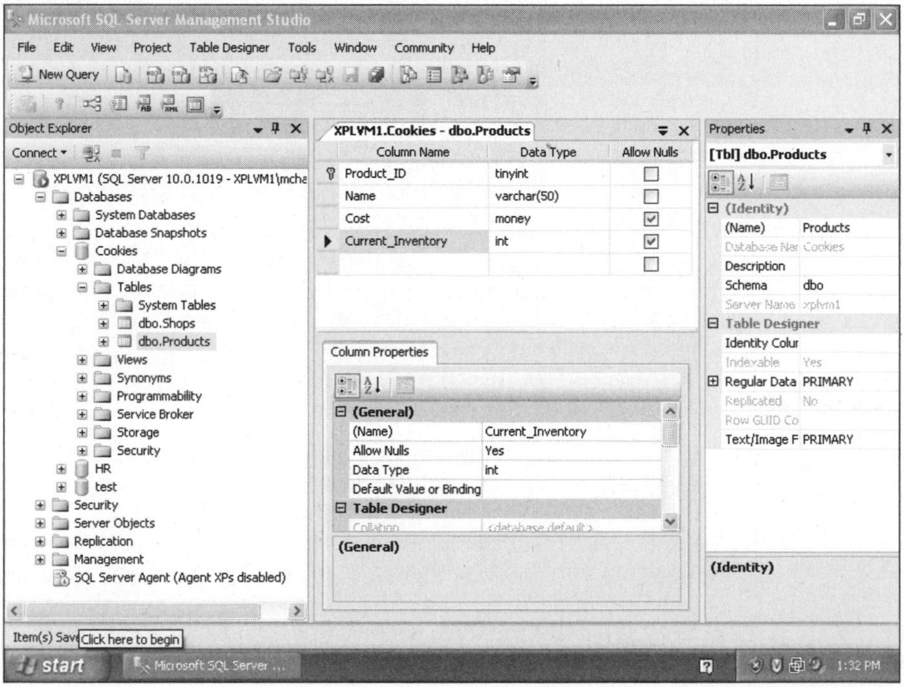

Figure 6-1:
Design view of a database table.

6. In the Column Properties pane, click in the Default Value or Binding cell and type in the default value.

If you're entering a numeric default, simply type in the numeric value. If you're providing a character string default value for a text field, enclose it within single quotation marks. Figure 6-2 shows an example in which I've provided a default value of 0 for the `Current_Inventory` column within the Products table of a database.

7. Click the Save icon to save your modified table.

That's all there is to creating a `DEFAULT` constraint in a SQL Server 2008 database. You can remove a `DEFAULT` constraint from a column by simply deleting the value in that column's Default Value or Binding property.

As you may have already noticed, the Design view used to add a `DEFAULT` constraint is the same one used to create a new database table. You may, in fact, add `DEFAULT` constraints for columns when you create a new table by providing a value for the Default Value or Binding property of those columns.

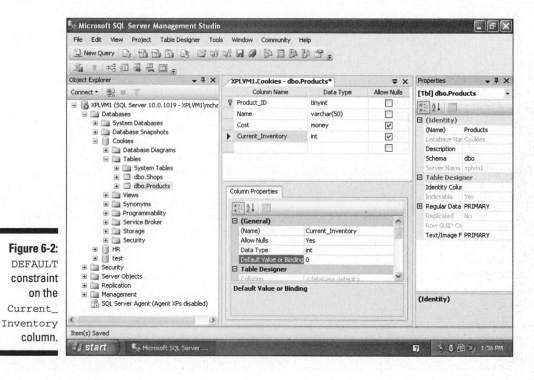

Figure 6-2:
`DEFAULT`
constraint
on the
`Current_`
`Inventory`
column.

Coordinating NULL values and DEFAULT constraints

As mentioned earlier, a definite relationship exists between NULL values and DEFAULT constraints: Both provide different ways to handle the scenario where a user doesn't provide data. However, these two concepts aren't mutually exclusive. You can have NULL values in a column that also contains a DEFAULT constraint.

Consider the example I provide earlier in this section about a store's product inventory. In that example, I suggest that a DEFAULT constraint on the inventory column is appropriate in that situation for times when the store manager enters a new product into the database but doesn't provide an inventory value.

You might also want to store NULL values in that same column. For example, suppose the same store conducts a quarterly audit of inventory, and that audit returns inconsistent results for a particular product. At that time, you're not sure about the current number of products in your inventory, so a NULL value is appropriate.

A NULL value for any column that allows that value will always trump any DEFAULT constraint on that column. So, if a user explicitly provides a NULL value for a column, and the column allows it, that column will take on a value of NULL — no matter what DEFAULT constraint the column might contain.

Limiting column values with CHECK constraints

SQL Server 2008 allows you to limit the values that may be entered in a database table with the use of CHECK constraints. CHECK constraints are simply statements of business rules that apply to the data stored within your database.

For example, suppose you're managing the database for a retail store and have a table that contains information about all your products, including the current selling price of each item in your inventory. Your store might have a policy of not selling any items valued at greater than $100 and never giving away items for free. This is a perfect example of a scenario in which you might want to use a CHECK constraint to limit the sales price of products to values greater than $0 and less than $100.

Another common use of CHECK constraints is to ensure that values match an appropriate format. For example, suppose your store database has a table containing information about each store location, including the store's nine-digit ZIP Code (in the form 12345-6789). You can use a CHECK constraint to ensure that all values entered in the ZIP Code field match the nine-digit ZIP Code format.

Writing CHECK constraints

You write CHECK constraints as SQL expressions, similar to those used to create the WHERE clause in a SQL query. To do so, you use the Transact-SQL syntax, which I discuss in more detail in Chapter 7 but provide a few examples of here.

If you want to create a CHECK constraint that limits the maximum cost of an item to $100, you use the following SQL expression:

```
Cost <= 100
```

Similarly, if you want to ensure that there is a non-negative, nonzero cost, you use a CHECK constraint with this expression:

```
Cost > 0
```

Things get a little more complicated when you use CHECK constraints to enforce pattern matching. You need to use wildcards to specify the various patterns you wish to allow. Here are a few common expressions you might use to create patterns:

✔ The underscore character (_) matches any single character.

✔ The percent sign (%) matches any sequence of zero or more characters.

✔ Enclosing a list or range of characters in square brackets ([ ]) matches any single character in the list or range. For example:

- [aeiou] matches any vowel

- [a-z] matches any letter

- [0-9] matches any digit

- [a-d] matches the letters a, b, c or d

✔ Putting a carat symbol (^) as the first character within square brackets makes the expression match any character that is *not* within the list or range that follows. For example:

- [^aeiou] matches any character other than a vowel

- [^a-z] matches any character other than a letter

- [^0-9] matches any character other than a digit

- [^a-d] matches any character other than the letters a, b, c, or d

If you wanted to write a CHECK constraint that matched nine-digit ZIP Codes, you would use the following syntax:

```
ZIP_Code LIKE '[0-9][0-9][0-9][0-9][0-9]-[0-9][0-9][0-9]
          [0-9]'
```

Using this syntax would ensure that you have a sequence of five digits, followed by a hyphen, followed by four digits.

Similarly, if your company had a bizarre business rule that said it won't open stores in cities that start with the letter *A*, you could enforce that with a CHECK constraint using the following expression:

```
City LIKE '[^a]%'
```

You could also accomplish the same goal by using the following expression in your CHECK constraint:

```
City NOT LIKE 'a%'
```

Note that in the two preceding examples, I used square brackets in one case but not the other. The first example requires square brackets because you're telling SQL Server to match anything other than the character *a*. In that case, the square brackets delimit the portion of the statement that includes the list of characters that may not be matched. For example, if you wanted to match all cities that started with letters other than *A* and *B*, you would write:

```
City LIKE '[^ab]%'
```

On the other hand, if you wanted to match cities that had a starting letter other than *A* and a second letter that is *b*, you would write:

```
City LIKE '[^a]b%'
```

CHECK constraints are quite versatile, and you can use them to enforce a variety of business rules. If you can express a business rule in SQL, you can enforce it with a CHECK constraint.

Determining when to enforce CHECK constraints

When you create a CHECK constraint, SQL Server offers you three options for enforcing the constraint:

- ✔ You may enforce the constraint on data that already exists in the table when you create (or reenable) the constraint by using the Check Existing Data on Creation or Enabling option.
- ✔ You may enforce the constraint for new data added to the table by using the Enforce for INSERTs and UPDATEs option.
- ✔ You may enforce the constraint for data added by replication agents by using the Enforce for Replication option. I discuss database replication in Chapter 15.

These options are most relevant when you're adding a CHECK constraint to an existing database. If you select Check Existing Data on Creation or Enabling, you won't be able to create the CHECK constraint until you go through the table and correct any entries that don't meet the requirements of the constraint.

Creating a CHECK constraint

You can create a CHECK constraint using SQL Server Management Studio's Table Designer. I walk you through the process of creating the constraint that limits the city field to values that start with a letter.

Before you begin, you need to determine the correct expression for your CHECK constraint. In this case, I want to ensure that values in the City field start with a letter. The business rule doesn't specify what follows the letter, so you can check for a single letter followed by any sequence of zero or more characters using this expression:

```
City LIKE '[a-z]%'
```

Now you can create the CHECK constraint in SQL Server, as follows:

1. **With SQL Server Management Studio open, navigate to the database containing the table where you'd like to implement a CHECK constraint and expand the Databases folder in Object Explorer by clicking the plus (+) icon to its left.**

2. **Click the plus (+) icon next to the relevant database name to expand that database.**

3. **Click the plus (+) icon next to the Tables folder icon to expand the Tables folder for the relevant database.**

4. **Right-click the name of the desired table and select Design from the pop-up menu.**

   The table opens in Design view, and you see a screen similar to the one shown in Figure 6-1.

5. **Click the Table Designer menu at the top of the screen and choose Check Constraints from the drop-down list.**

   If the table contains no CHECK constraints, you see the empty window shown in Figure 6-3.

6. **Click Add to create a new CHECK constraint.**

7. **Type your expression into the Expression field under the "(General)" heading.**

   If you've already written the expression elsewhere, you can simply cut and paste it into this field.

8. **Review the remaining information in the window.**

   The other properties of the new constraint appear below the expression. They include the name of the constraint and the three enforcement options discussed in the previous section. You may choose to accept the default values for these properties or modify them to suit your business requirements. Figure 6-4 provides an example of the completed CHECK constraint.

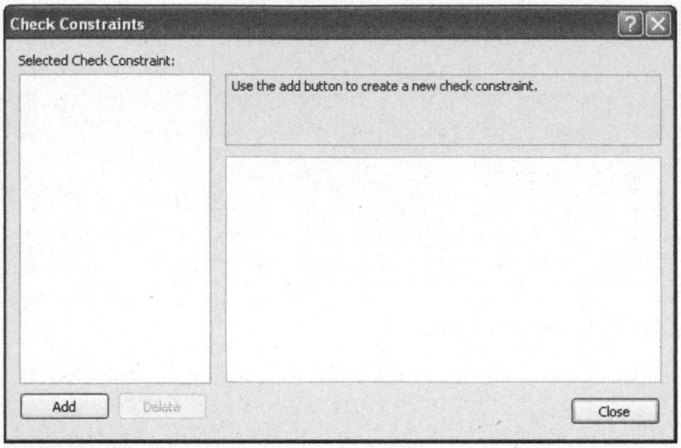

Figure 6-3:
Check
Constraints
window.

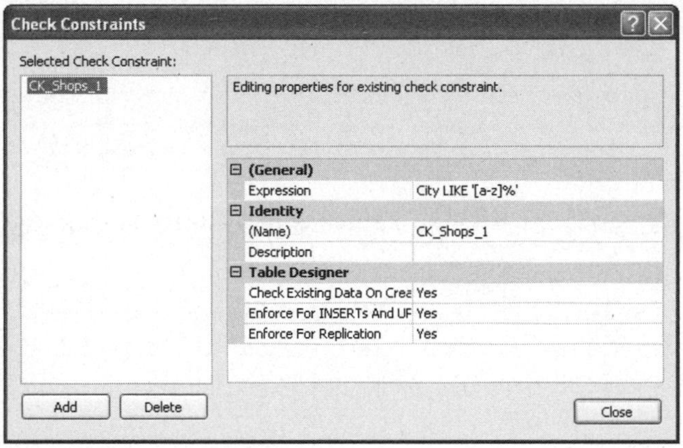

Figure 6-4:
CHECK
constraint
on the
Shops table.

9. **Click the Close button to close the Check Constraints window.**

10. **From the File menu, choose Save to commit your new constraint to the database.**

It's important to realize that the database will not enforce the constraint until after you complete this last step.

Disabling CHECK constraints

After you add a CHECK constraint to your database, it won't be possible to add new rows to a table that violate the constraint (provided, of course, that you chose the Enforce for INSERTs and UPDATEs option). If you try to insert a row that violates the constraint, you'll see an error message similar to the one shown in Figure 6-5.

Microsoft SQL Server Management Studio [?][X]

ⓘ No row was updated.

The data in row 1 was not committed.
Error Source: .Net SqlClient Data Provider.
Error Message: The INSERT statement conflicted with the CHECK constraint
"CK_Shops". The conflict occurred in database "Cookies", table "dbo.Shops", column
'City'.
The statement has been terminated.

Correct the errors and retry or press ESC to cancel the change(s).

[OK]

Figure 6-5:
Constraint
violation
error
message.

However, in some cases, you may wish to temporarily disable a constraint to allow the insertion of data that violates the business logic enforced by the constraint. Here's how you can disable a constraint in SQL Server Management Studio:

1. **With the Check Constraints window open, select the constraint you'd like to disable in the Selected Check Constraint list.**

2. **In the Table Designer section of the constraint properties, change the value for Enforce For INSERTs and UPDATEs from Yes to No.**

3. **Click the Close button.**

4. **Choose File⇨Save to commit your changed constraint to the database.**

If you inserted rows that violate the CHECK constraint while the constraint is disabled, you won't be able to enable the constraint again if you have the Check Existing Data on Creation or Enabling option selected. If you try to do so, you'll see an error message similar to the following:

```
'Shops' table
- Unable to add constraint 'CK_Shops_1'.
The ALTER TABLE statement conflicted with the CHECK
constraint "CK_Shops_1". The conflict occurred in
database "Cookies", table "dbo.Shops", column 'City'.
```

CHECK constraints and rules

If you used earlier versions of SQL Server, you might be familiar with the concept of database rules that offer similar functionality to the CHECK constraint but can be reused across different database tables and columns. Rules also have a significant limitation: You can apply only one rule to a database column, whereas you can apply multiple CHECK constraints to the same column.

SQL Server 2008 still supports database rules, but Microsoft no longer encourages their use. Microsoft announced that it will remove rule functionality from future versions of SQL Server and recommends that you "avoid using this feature in new development work, and plan to modify applications that currently use this feature. Use CHECK constraints instead."

Enforcing Database Integrity

As I mention at the beginning of the chapter, SQL Server offers three types of constraints that you may use to enforce the integrity of your database: PRIMARY KEY constraints, UNIQUE constraints, and FOREIGN KEY constraints. I cover the selection and creation of primary keys in Chapter 5, so I discuss the remaining two types in this section.

Enforcing uniqueness

UNIQUE constraints allow you to enforce the uniqueness property of columns other than the primary key in a table. They act in a similar manner to PRIMARY KEY constraints, but with two important differences:

✔ Columns subject to a PRIMARY KEY constraint may not contain NULL values. Columns subject to a UNIQUE constraint may contain one row with a NULL value. (If you had two rows with a NULL value in the same option, that would be a duplicate value, which violates the UNIQUE constraint.)

✔ A table may have only one PRIMARY KEY constraint but may have multiple UNIQUE constraints.

Here's how to create a UNIQUE constraint on a column in an existing SQL Server table:

1. **Open the table in Design View using SQL Server Management Studio by right-clicking the table and selecting Design from the pop-up menu.**

2. **From the Table Designer pull-down menu, select Indexes/Keys.**

   The Indexes/Keys window, shown in Figure 6-6, opens. Notice that in this example, the table already has a PRIMARY KEY constraint.

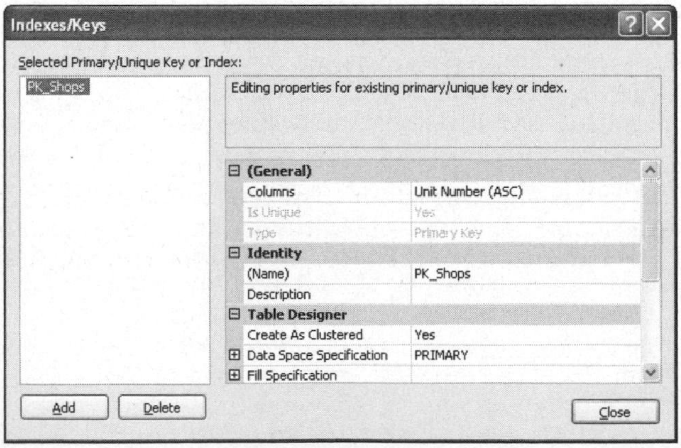

Figure 6-6: The Indexes/ Keys window showing a table with a PRIMARY KEY constraint.

3. **Click the Add button to create a new key.**

4. **Click the Type property and change the value from Index to Unique Key.**

5. **Click the ellipsis (. . .) next to the Columns property and select the columns you want to include in your UNIQUE constraint.**

   You may also change the name of the key, if you want. I like to use the naming convention UK_name (for Unique Key) to help identify my constraints. Figure 6-7 shows the completed window.

6. **Click the Close button.**

7. **Choose Save from the File menu to save your new constraint.**

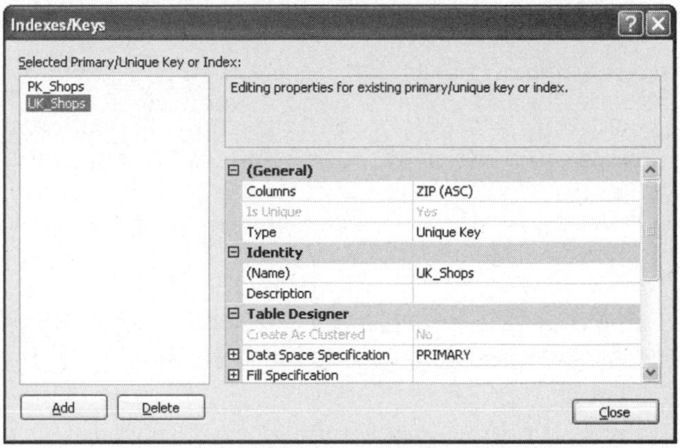

Figure 6-7:
Creating a
Unique Key.

Enforcing referential integrity with FOREIGN KEY constraints

Your database tables will often contain related information. For example, the retail store database I discuss in this chapter contains a table with information about each store owned by the company. I might also wish to have an Employees table containing information about each of the company's employees. It would be logical to include the store that hired each employee in that employee's record.

The easiest way to include this information is to create a Unit_Number field in the Employees table. This field would contain the Unit_Number (the primary key of the Shops table) of the employee's store, creating a link between the two tables.

However, including the field creates a potential issue down the road. What happens if a store closes? All the employees associated with that store would then be "orphaned" because they would be associated with a Unit_Number that didn't exist. Similarly, if no business logic is used in creating the table, a data entry clerk might accidentally create an orphaned employee by mistyping an employee's Unit_Number and entering a number that's not assigned to any store.

These issues are known as *referential integrity* issues, and SQL Server provides the FOREIGN KEY constraint to prevent their occurrence. A foreign key creates a relationship between two tables by linking the foreign key in one table to the primary key (or any other unique key) in the referenced table. In the stores example, the Unit_Number field in the Employees table would be a foreign key to the Unit_Number primary key in the Shops table.

When you create a foreign key relationship between two columns, the columns must have the same data type. Additionally, if you create a foreign key relationship that involves multiple-column keys, the two keys must contain the same number of columns.

Here's how to create a FOREIGN KEY constraint in SQL Server Management Studio:

1. **Open the table that will contain the foreign key in Design View using SQL Server Management Studio by right-clicking the table and selecting Design from the pop-up menu.**

   In my example, the Shops table contains the foreign key.

2. **From the Table Designer drop-down list, select Indexes/Keys.**

   The Foreign Key Relationships window, shown in Figure 6-8, opens.

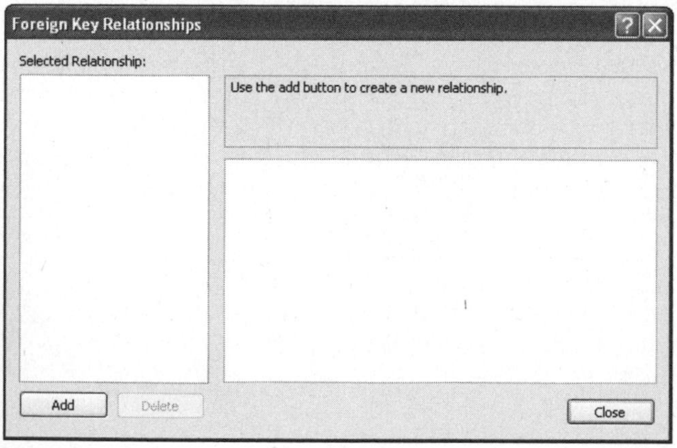

Figure 6-8: The Foreign Key Relationships window.

Foreign Key Relationships

Selected Relationship:

Use the add button to create a new relationship.

Add   Delete   Close

3. Click the Add button to create a new FOREIGN KEY constraint.

4. Click the ellipsis (. . .) next to the Tables and Columns Specification property.

   The Tables and Columns window opens.

5. Select the table that your foreign key refers to in the Primary Key Table drop-down list.

6. Select the names of the column(s) involved in your primary key from the drop-down lists in the grids below the primary key table name and the foreign key table name.

   When you're finished, the window should look like the example in Figure 6-9.

7. Click OK to close the Tables and Columns window.

8. Click Close to close the Foreign Key Relationships window.

9. Choose Save from the File menu to save your new constraint.

After you've created a foreign key relationship between the two tables, SQL Server will require that all values associated with the constraint in the foreign key table have corresponding values in the primary key table. The constraint does not, however, require that all values in the primary key table have corresponding values in the foreign key table. Additionally, there may be multiple values in the foreign key table that reference the same record in the primary key table.

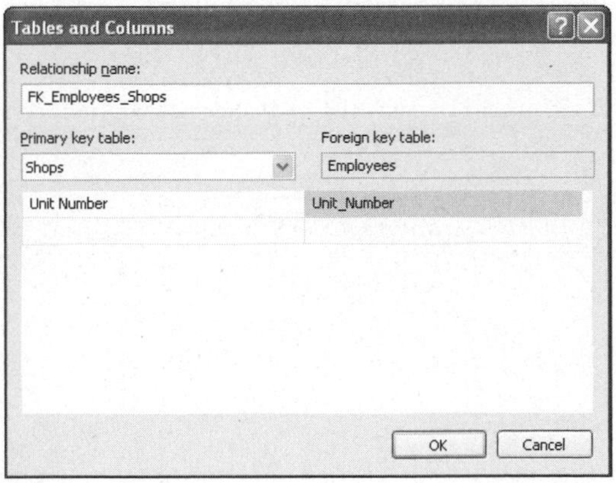

Figure 6-9: The Tables and Columns window with a FOREIGN KEY constraint.

Part III
Retrieving Data from Databases

The 5th Wave   By Rich Tennant

AUTO SHOW FOR COMPUTER STORAGE EXECUTIVES

GLOVE COMPAR

In this part . . .

In this part, you find out how to retrieve information from a SQL Server database. I introduce the Structured Query Language (SQL) and show you how to use it to pull the exact information you need out of your database. You also find out about some advanced database queries that let you combine information from multiple tables and take various actions based on the results of your database queries.

Chapter 7

Constructing Simple Database Queries

. . . .

In This Chapter

▶ Using SELECT statements to retrieve data from a SQL Server database

▶ Summarizing data with aggregate functions

▶ Grouping results by attributes

▶ Formatting SQL Server output

. . . .

*I*n most databases, the vast majority of SQL statements issued are designed to retrieve information from a database. You can use the SQL SELECT statement to retrieve information from database tables. The beauty of this statement is that it's quite simple to use in its basic form, but it also contains quite a bit of flexible power, allowing you to precisely specify the exact information you'd like to retrieve.

In this chapter, I dissect the SELECT statement, clause-by-clause, and show you how to put together simple database queries. I recommend that you master this material before you check out the more powerful uses of the SELECT statement that I present in Chapter 8.

Retrieving Data with SELECT Statements

The SQL command used to retrieve data from a database is the SELECT statement. As do other SQL statements, the SELECT statement reads almost like an English statement. If you can fill in the blanks in the following sentence, you can compose a SELECT statement:

```
Select ____columns____ from ___table___ where ____
           conditions____ .
```

That's really all there is to it. You simply need to identify three things to compose a proper SELECT query:

- ✔ The columns you want to retrieve
- ✔ The table you want to retrieve them from
- ✔ The conditions (if any) that the data must satisfy

You then take this information and plug it into the proper SQL syntax. For example, suppose you wanted to retrieve a list of students from a school database to determine which students might qualify for a boys' hockey team. It's a boy's team, so you're interested in only male students. Also, you're planning to give this list to the team's coach, so you want to include only names and telephone numbers, omitting any other personal information stored in the database. Here's how that would look in SQL:

```
SELECT first_name, last_name, phone
FROM students
WHERE gender = 'male'
```

That query would produce the following results:

```
first_name        last_name         phone
---------------   ---------------   ---------------
Richard           Jones             574-555-0125
Matthew           Jones             574-555-0125
Christopher       Murphy            574-555-8224
Mike              Abrams            574-555-1925
Edward            Sorin             574-555-1902

(5 row(s) affected)
```

I discuss using SQL Server Management Studio to execute SQL statements in Chapter 3.

As you can probably imagine, there are more advanced SELECT statements as well. This basic format allows you to retrieve data from a single table using simple conditions. In Chapter 8, I discuss advanced concepts, including combining data from multiple tables and writing complex SELECT queries.

The SELECT. . .FROM clause

The first two components of the SELECT statement (the columns you want to retrieve and the table that contains them) appear in the SELECT. . .FROM clause.

What does the number of rows affected mean?

Notice at the end of the query that SQL Server reports the number of rows "affected" by the query. In the case of a SELECT statement, this report includes the number of rows that your query returned. If you don't want SQL Server to produce this summary reporting, issue the following SQL command:

SET NOCOUNT ON

This command causes SQL Server to suppress reporting the number of rows affected by future queries. You can restore the default behavior with the following command:

SET NOCOUNT OFF

If you'd like to select a single column, simply type the name of the column between the SELECT and FROM keywords. If you'd like to include multiple columns, include a comma-separated list, as I demonstrate in the previous section's query.

You may also choose to retrieve all the columns from a database table by substituting an asterisk (*) for the column listing.

After you've listed the names of the column(s) you want to retrieve, simply type the name of the table containing those columns after the FROM keyword.

The SELECT...FROM clause is the only required component of a SQL SELECT query. For example, if you wanted to retrieve all columns from the students table, you could use this simple query:

```
SELECT *
FROM students
```

which would produce the following results:

```
first_name    last_name    student_id   phone          gender
-----------   -----------  -----------  -------------  ------
Richard       Jones        1            574-555-0125   male
Matthew       Jones        2            574-555-0125   male
Christopher   Murphy       3            574-555-8224   male
Renee         Smith        4            574-555-9201   female
Mike          Abrams       5            574-555-1925   male
Edward        Sorin        6            574-555-1902   male
Mary          Keenan       7            574-555-9889   female
Susan         Davis        8            574-555-9124   female

(8 row(s) affected)
```

The WHERE clause

The WHERE clause allows you to be specific about the types of data you'd like to retrieve from the tables identified in the SELECT...FROM clause. You may include condition(s) that each row in the result set must satisfy.

For example, if you wanted to identify all the members of the Jones family enrolled in your school, you might use the following SQL statement:

```
SELECT first_name, last_name
FROM students
WHERE last_name = 'Jones'
```

which would produce the following results:

```
first_name        last_name
---------------   ----------------
Richard           Jones
Matthew           Jones

(2 row(s) affected)
```

Combining several conditions

You're not limited to including a single condition in your WHERE clause. For example, suppose you wanted to identify all the students in your school who are male and are among the first five students to enroll (meaning their student_id is less than or equal to 5). You could retrieve the names of the students who meet both of these two conditions by joining those conditions with the AND keyword, as shown in the following SQL statement:

```
SELECT *
FROM students
WHERE gender = 'male' AND student_id <= 5
```

which would produce the following results:

```
first_name    last_name    student_id   phone           gender
-----------   ----------   ----------   -------------   ------
Richard       Jones        1            574-555-0125    male
Matthew       Jones        2            574-555-0125    male
Christopher   Murphy       3            574-555-8224    male
Mike          Abrams       5            574-555-1925    male

(4 row(s) affected)
```

Similarly, you can use the OR conjunction to retrieve all rows that meet either one of the conditions. If you modified the previous query to use the OR conjunction, as follows:

```
SELECT *
FROM students
WHERE gender = 'male' OR student_id <= 5
```

you would retrieve the following rows from the database:

```
first_name    last_name    student_id   phone          gender
------------  -----------  -----------  -------------  ------
Richard       Jones        1            574-555-0125   male
Matthew       Jones        2            574-555-0125   male
Christopher   Murphy       3            574-555-8224   male
Renee         Smith        4            574-555-9201   female
Mike          Abrams       5            574-555-1925   male
Edward        Sorin        6            574-555-1902   male

(6 row(s) affected)
```

Note that the results include the same four rows as the previous query (those that met both criteria), but also includes two additional rows. Renee Smith is included in the results because she meets one condition (she's student #4) but not the other (she's female). Similarly, Edward Sorin wasn't included in the first query results because he wasn't among the first five students, but he is included in this set because he meets the gender condition.

Using the BETWEEN condition

Sometimes you need to retrieve records that satisfy a range condition. That is, they contain a value that's within a specified range of values. For example, you might want to retrieve a list of all students born between 1997 and 2004. One way to accomplish this task is by using two conditions joined by an AND conjunction, as follows:

```
SELECT first_name, last_name, birthdate
FROM students
WHERE birthdate >= '1-Jan-1997' AND birthdate <=
        '31-Dec-2004'
```

As you'd expect, the result of this query is a list of all students born between the two dates:

```
first_name      last_name        birthdate
--------------  ---------------  ------------------------
Richard         Jones            2001-02-23 00:00:00
Matthew         Jones            1999-03-27 00:00:00
Renee           Smith            2004-11-06 00:00:00
Susan           Davis            2000-06-10 00:00:00

(4 row(s) affected)
```

You'd probably agree that this looks a little clumsy and makes it difficult to tell what the query is actually doing. SQL provides an alternative that's a little more readable: the BETWEEN clause, which allows you to specify a range of values in "BETWEEN x AND y" format. For example, you could rewrite the previous query as:

```
SELECT first_name, last_name, birthdate
FROM students
WHERE birthdate BETWEEN '1-Jan-1997' AND '31-Dec-2004'
```

This query produces the same results as the previous query.

Negating conditions with NOT

Sometimes it is easier to express your query in terms of the data that you *don't* want to retrieve. SQL provides the NOT keyword for such cases. For example, if you wanted to pull a list of students who *aren't* in the Jones family, you could use the following SQL statement:

```
SELECT first_name, last_name
FROM students
WHERE NOT last_name = 'Jones'
```

As you've probably noticed already, there are often several ways to accomplish the same thing in SQL. Some people prefer to write the preceding query using the <> (greater than or less than) operator. Using that notation, you would issue the following SQL command:

```
SELECT first_name, last_name
FROM students
WHERE last_name <> 'Jones'
```

Using list conditions

If you have a list of values you'd like to search for, you can use the SQL IN keyword to provide that list in your SQL statement. For example, you can retrieve a list of all students from the Jones, Smith, and Keenan families with the following SQL command:

```
SELECT first_name, last_name
FROM students
WHERE last_name IN ('Jones', 'Smith', 'Keenan')
```

When executed, that statement produces the following results:

```
first_name       last_name
---------------  ---------------
Richard          Jones
Matthew          Jones
Renee            Smith
Mary             Keenan

(4 row(s) affected)
```

Similarly, you can combine the IN and NOT keywords to obtain a list of students who are *not* in those families with this SQL statement:

```
SELECT first_name, last_name
FROM students
WHERE last_name NOT IN ('Jones', 'Smith', 'Keenan')
```

As you'd expect, that command lists the other four students in the school database:

```
first_name       last_name
---------------  ---------------
Christopher      Murphy
Mike             Abrams
Edward           Sorin
Susan            Davis

(4 row(s) affected)
```

Matching text patterns with LIKE

In some cases, you won't be able to describe the condition you wish to place on a text variable in the simple form:

```
WHERE variable = 'value'
```

For example, you might want to retrieve a list of students who have first names beginning with the letter *M.* You can do this by using a LIKE clause with wildcard values that can represent more than one possible character. Here's an example:

```
SELECT first_name, last_name
FROM students
WHERE first_name LIKE 'M%'
```

This query produces the following results:

```
first_name       last_name
---------------  ---------------
Matthew          Jones
Mike             Abrams
Mary             Keenan

(3 row(s) affected)
```

The LIKE clause allows you to match patterns in text variables using several different wildcard types, as listed in Table 7-1.

Table 7-1	Wildcard Types
Wildcard	*Description*
_	Any single character
%	Any series of zero or more characters
[a-f]	Any single character in the range a–f
[^a-f]	Any single character *not* in the range a–f
[abc]	Any single character contained in the list (a, b, or c)
[^abc]	Any single character *not* contained in the list (a, b, or c)

These are the same wildcard values used in CHECK constraints, as I discuss in Chapter 6.

You can use combinations of these wildcards to construct complicated patterns. For example, the following query will select any students who have last names starting with J, K, or S but that do not end with an S:

```
SELECT first_name, last_name
FROM students
WHERE last_name LIKE '[j,k,s]%[^s]'
```

This statement produces the following results:

```
first_name       last_name
---------------  ---------------
Renee            Smith
Edward           Sorin
Mary             Keenan

(3 row(s) affected)
```

In addition to pattern matching with LIKE conditions, SQL Server 2008 supports Full Text Search (FTS) capabilities that allow you to perform advanced text searches. FTS is beyond the scope of this book.

Selecting rows with NULL values

In Chapter 4, I explain how databases use the special value NULL to represent unknown or missing values. If you want to use the value NULL in a WHERE condition, you should use the special keywords IS NULL and IS NOT NULL to do so. The following example shows you how.

Say that you wanted to retrieve a birthday list for students in your school and you used the following query to do so:

```
SELECT first_name, last_name, birthdate
FROM students
```

which produces the results:

```
first_name        last_name         birthdate
---------------   ---------------   -----------------------
Richard           Jones             2001-02-23 00:00:00
Matthew           Jones             1999-03-27 00:00:00
Christopher       Murphy            NULL
Renee             Smith             2004-11-06 00:00:00
Mike              Abrams            2007-01-21 00:00:00
Edward            Sorin             NULL
Mary              Keenan            1995-02-08 00:00:00
Susan             Davis             2000-06-10 00:00:00

(8 row(s) affected)
```

Note that the database doesn't contain birthdates for two students: Christopher Murphy and Edward Sorin. If you want to omit those names from the query results, you can use the IS NOT NULL clause, as shown in this query:

```
SELECT first_name, last_name, birthdate
FROM students
WHERE birthdate IS NOT NULL
```

Executing this query produces the following list:

```
first_name        last_name         birthdate
---------------   ---------------   -----------------------
Richard           Jones             2001-02-23 00:00:00
Matthew           Jones             1999-03-27 00:00:00
Renee             Smith             2004-11-06 00:00:00
Mike              Abrams            2007-01-21 00:00:00
Mary              Keenan            1995-02-08 00:00:00
Susan             Davis             2000-06-10 00:00:00

(6 row(s) affected)
```

If you want to produce a list of students who have missing birthdates, perhaps to follow up and obtain that information, you can use the following SQL query:

```
SELECT first_name, last_name, birthdate
FROM students
WHERE birthdate IS NULL
```

The query would produce the following results:

```
first_name       last_name        birthdate
---------------  ---------------  -------------------------
Christopher      Murphy           NULL
Edward           Sorin            NULL

(2 row(s) affected)
```

Organizing Query Results

Retrieving the correct data from SQL Server is only half the battle. When you've successfully retrieved data using a SELECT statement, you can use the power of SQL to help you organize your results. In this section, I cover techniques you can use to sort, summarize, group, and format the data you retrieve from your database.

Sorting output

One of the simplest ways you can manipulate your data is to sort it, alphabetically or numerically. SQL Server allows you to sort by any attribute or combination of attributes using the ORDER BY clause in your SELECT statement. For example, to retrieve an alphabetical list of students, you might use the following SQL statement:

```
SELECT first_name, last_name
FROM students
ORDER BY last_name
```

This statement produces a list of students, sorted alphabetically by last name, as follows:

```
first_name       last_name
---------------  ---------------
Mike             Abrams
Susan            Davis
Richard          Jones
Matthew          Jones
Mary             Keenan
Christopher      Murphy
Renee            Smith
Edward           Sorin

(8 row(s) affected)
```

Note that the output is sorted by last name, but there are two students named Jones. You may wish to specify a secondary sort attribute to further sort rows for which the primary sort attribute has the same value. The following SQL statement sorts primarily by last name but then further sorts by first name for cases in which students have the same last name:

```
SELECT first_name, last_name
FROM students
ORDER BY last_name, first_name
```

Matthew and Richard Jones are now sorted by first name within the results sorted by last name:

```
first_name       last_name
---------------  ---------------
Mike             Abrams
Susan            Davis
Matthew          Jones
Richard          Jones
Mary             Keenan
Christopher      Murphy
Renee            Smith
Edward           Sorin

(8 row(s) affected)
```

You can sort by any attribute in your table. SQL Server determines the appropriate way to sort based upon the data type. For example, you could sort the list by birth date using this SQL command:

```
SELECT first_name, last_name, birthdate
FROM students
WHERE birthdate IS NOT NULL
ORDER BY birthdate
```

This produces a list of students sorted by birth date, in ascending order:

```
first_name       last_name        birthdate
---------------  ---------------  ------------------------
Mary             Keenan           1995-02-08 00:00:00
Matthew          Jones            1999-03-27 00:00:00
Susan            Davis            2000-06-10 00:00:00
Richard          Jones            2001-02-23 00:00:00
Renee            Smith            2004-11-06 00:00:00
Mike             Abrams           2007-01-21 00:00:00

(6 row(s) affected)
```

SQL Server always assumes that you want to sort your results in ascending order (A–Z for text and smallest to largest for numeric values). You may override this behavior by specifying the sort order with the keywords ASC (for ascending order) or DESC (for descending order) after each attribute in your ORDER BY clause. For example, to re-sort your birthday list so that the youngest student appears first (descending order), you can use the following SQL statement:

```
SELECT first_name, last_name, birthdate
FROM students
WHERE birthdate IS NOT NULL
ORDER BY birthdate DESC
```

This statement produces the desired sorting as follows:

```
first_name          last_name          birthdate
--------------      --------------     ------------------------
Mike                Abrams             2007-01-21 00:00:00
Renee               Smith              2004-11-06 00:00:00
Richard             Jones              2001-02-23 00:00:00
Susan               Davis              2000-06-10 00:00:00
Matthew             Jones              1999-03-27 00:00:00
Mary                Keenan             1995-02-08 00:00:00

(6 row(s) affected)
```

I instructed the database to omit records with NULL birth date values from the results. If your result set does include NULL values, SQL Server will treat them as the smallest value in your result set. This means that they will appear at the top of results in ascending order and at the bottom in descending order.

Summarizing data with aggregate functions

SQL Server also allows you to answer more complicated questions about datasets. For example, you might want to know the number of records that meet a certain condition or the average value in a recordset. For this purpose, SQL provides a class of functions called *aggregate functions*. These functions work on groups (or aggregations) of data.

Table 7-2 lists the common aggregate functions used in Transact-SQL programming.

Table 7-2	Transact-SQL Aggregate Functions
Function	*Description*
AVG	Returns the average of the values in the group
COUNT	Returns a count of the number of items in the group
MAX	Returns the largest value in the group
MIN	Returns the smallest value in the group
SUM	Returns the sum of all values in the group
STDEV	Returns the statistical standard deviation of all values in the group
VAR	Returns the statistical variance of all values in the group

To help illustrate these functions, I've added a new column to the students table that appears earlier in this chapter. It now includes the number of absences for each student in the current school year. Here are the values now inserted in the table:

```
first_name        last_name          absences
--------------    --------------     --------
Richard           Jones              3
Matthew           Jones              NULL
Christopher       Murphy             5
Renee             Smith              2
Mike              Abrams             8
Edward            Sorin              14
Mary              Keenan             0
Susan             Davis              6
```

Read on for some examples of using aggregate functions.

Counting records

Suppose you want to count all the students in your school. You can use the COUNT aggregate function, as follows:

```
SELECT COUNT(*)
FROM students
```

This returns the following output:

```
-----------
8

(1 row(s) affected)
```

You should notice a few interesting things about this output:

- ✔ The value 8 is the answer to the question. How many rows are in the students table?

- ✔ The output value has no variable name; nothing is listed above the header. I show you how to correct this problem in the Formatting Output section later in this chapter.

- ✔ The statement 1 row(s) affected refers to the number of rows of output, not the number of rows counted by the query. I asked a question that takes only a single line (8) to be answered, so only one row is "affected" by the query.

Working with unique records

SQL Server also allows you to count unique instances of a variable using the DISTINCT keyword. For example, suppose you wanted to know how many different last names exist in your student body. You could use COUNT DISTINCT as follows:

```
SELECT COUNT(DISTINCT(last_name))
FROM students
```

This produces the following output:

```
-----------
7

(1 row(s) affected)
```

You can also use the DISTINCT keyword with a regular SELECT statement. For example, the following statement retrieves a list of all student last names without duplicates:

```
SELECT DISTINCT(last_name)
FROM students
```

Finding minimum, maximum, and average values

Aggregate functions can also help you identify the smallest or largest value in a dataset using the MIN and MAX functions. Similarly, the AVG function determines the mathematical average of the specified variable.

The following SQL statement demonstrates these three functions on the absences attribute:

```
SELECT min(absences), max(absences), avg(absences)
FROM students
```

It produces the following results:

```
---- ---- -----------
0    14   5
Warning: Null value is eliminated by an aggregate or other
         SET operation.

(1 row(s) affected)
```

From these results, the smallest number of absences in your database is 0, the largest is 14, and the average is 5. The Warning statement in the output indicates that SQL Server ignores NULL values when calculating aggregate functions. This means that the two NULL absence values were not used when calculating the average number of absences.

Totaling values

The SUM function allows you to determine the total of a variable in a record-set. For example, the following statement allows you to determine the total number of days missed by all of your students:

```
SELECT sum(absences)
FROM students
```

Once again, SQL Server reminds you that the result (38 total days) does not include NULL values:

```
-----------
38
Warning: Null value is eliminated by an aggregate or other
         SET operation.

(1 row(s) affected)
```

You can also add WHERE clauses to your aggregate functions to limit the records considered by the SQL statement. For example, if you wanted to know the total number of absences recorded by male students, you could use the following SQL statement:

```
SELECT sum(absences)
FROM students
WHERE gender = 'male'
```

Grouping results

In the example in the preceding section, I show you how you can limit the use of aggregate functions to results that meet condition(s) specified in a WHERE clause. SQL also allows you to group results into categories and use aggregate functions to summarize data across those categories instead of across the entire dataset.

For example, suppose you want to investigate whether boys or girls are more likely to skip school. You can determine the average number of absences for each gender using the following SQL statement:

```
SELECT gender, avg(absences)
FROM students
GROUP BY gender
```

SQL Server then groups the results by gender, showing you the average for each gender:

```
gender
------ -----------
female 2
male   7


(2 row(s) affected)
```

Renaming columns in your output

The examples that appear so far in this chapter are missing some headers, as you may have noticed if you've read straight through this chapter. By default, SQL Server provides header names for regular variable columns but does not do so for computed columns, such as those generated by aggregate functions.

For example, the query

```
SELECT gender, min(absences), max(absences), avg(absences)
FROM students
GROUP BY gender
```

produces the following results:

```
gender
------ ---- ---- -----------
female 0    6    2
male   3    14   7

(2 row(s) affected)
```

You can provide reader-friendly column headings for those results by using the AS clause in your SQL statement. You simply include the phrase AS column-name after each expression listed in your SELECT...FROM clause. For example, you can rewrite the previous query as:

```
SELECT gender AS 'Gender', min(absences) AS 'Lowest
         Absences', max(absences) AS 'Highest Absences',
         avg(absences) AS 'Average Absences'
FROM students
GROUP BY gender
```

which produces the nicely formatted results that follow:

```
Gender Lowest Absences Highest Absences Average Absences
------ --------------- ---------------- ----------------
female 0               6                2
male   3               14               7

(2 row(s) affected)
```

Note that I also renamed the gender column to capitalize the first letter, making it consistent with the other columns in the results.

Chapter 8

Joins and Other Advanced Queries

Transact-SQL provides SQL Server users with a variety of advanced functionality that allows you to harness the power of a relational database. In this chapter, I describe a number of these technologies and explain how you can use them to issue powerful, compact database commands.

I begin by exploring Transact-SQL's JOIN functionality that allows you to easily combine related data from multiple tables. I then describe several twists on the standard SQL queries: computed values, subqueries, and CASE statements. I wrap up this chapter by taking a brief look at SQL views.

Joining Data from Multiple Tables

In the previous chapter, I describe simple queries that you can use to extract data from a single table. However, in many cases, you'll need to combine data from multiple tables to meet business requirements. Transact-SQL allows you to do this through the use of JOIN statements.

In this section, I explain three types of JOIN statements:

✔ INNER JOINs allow you to match related records from different tables.

✔ OUTER JOINs also include records from one or both tables that do not have corresponding record(s) in the other table.

✔ Self-joins are a special case in which you join a table with itself to compare records in the same table.

Matching records with INNER JOINs

The most common type of JOIN statement is the INNER JOIN. This statement, also known as an equi-join, combines records from two tables that have one or more specified attributes in common. For example, suppose you have a school database containing the students table shown in Table 8-1.

first_name	last_name	student_id	Gender	teacher
Richard	Jones	1	Male	1
Matthew	Jones	2	Male	2
Christopher	Murphy	3	Male	2
Renee	Smith	4	Female	1
Mike	Abrams	5	Male	NULL
Edward	Sorin	6	Male	2
Mary	Keenan	7	Female	2
Susan	Davis	8	Female	1

Table 8-1 — **Students Table**

If you've been following along, you may be noticing that this is a simplified version of the students table used in Chapter 7. I added the teacher column to the table as a foreign key to the teachers table shown in Table 8-2.

teacher_id	first_name	last_name
1	Richard	Allen
2	Mary	Brady
3	Ann	Edwards

Table 8-2 — **Teachers Table**

The school principal might ask you to generate a class list showing each student's name and the name of his or her teacher. This is a reasonable, straightforward request, but you can't fulfill it with a basic SELECT statement. The best you'd be able to do is retrieve a list of students with the ID number of their teacher and provide the principal with two separate lists: students with teacher IDs and teacher IDs and teacher names. That's certainly not a business-friendly answer!

This is where the INNER JOIN simplifies your life. You can use this statement to retrieve data from both the student and teacher tables!

Writing an INNER JOIN statement

You create an INNER JOIN by including the two tables in the FROM clause with the INNER JOIN keyword and specifying the join condition using the ON keyword. For example, if you want to fulfill the principal's request, you may do so with the following SQL statement:

```
SELECT students.first_name, students.last_name, teachers.
          first_name, teachers.last_name
FROM students INNER JOIN teachers
ON students.teacher = teachers.teacher_id
```

Note that I use a different form for attribute names in this query than those I use in earlier chapters. Instead of simply writing the attribute name, I specified the table name as well, using the form table_name.attribute_name. This is necessary when two tables share common attribute names. For example, both the students and teachers tables contain an attribute named "first_name." If I hadn't specified the table name, SQL Server would have refused to process the query, returning the following error:

```
Msg 209, Level 16, State 1, Line 1
Ambiguous column name 'first_name'.
```

NULL is a special value that corresponds to missing or unknown data. Therefore, records that have NULL values for the join condition do *not* match each other and will not appear in the output of an INNER JOIN statement.

Technically, it's necessary to use the table_name.attribute_name format when only working with attributes that appear in both tables. However, most SQL Server users consider it good practice to use this format any time you write queries involving multiple tables.

Analyzing the results

Here are the results of the INNER JOIN statement:

```
first_name        last_name          first_name         last_name
---------------   ---------------    ----------------   ----------------
Richard           Jones              Richard            Allen
Matthew           Jones              Mary               Brady
Christopher       Murphy             Mary               Brady
Renee             Smith              Richard            Allen
Edward            Sorin              Mary               Brady
Mary              Keenan             Mary               Brady
Susan             Davis              Richard            Allen

(7 row(s) affected)
```

You should notice two important things about the results of this INNER JOIN:

✔ There is no record for the student Mike Abrams. Refer back to Table 8-1 and you'll notice that his teacher is NULL. INNER JOINs don't print records where the join attribute has a NULL value in either table.

✔ There are no records for the teacher Ann Edwards. Again, refer back to Table 8-1 and notice that there are no students assigned to Ann (her teacher ID is 3). INNER JOINs do not print records that don't have corresponding matches in the other table.

Cleaning things up with aliases

One thing you probably noticed is that both the SELECT statement and the results in the previous example are quite ugly! The SELECT statement repeats the table names ("students" and "teachers") multiple times, while the output doesn't specify table names at all, leaving us with ambiguous attribute names.

Fortunately, you can clean up these situations by using aliases. I describe one use of aliases, renaming columns, in Chapter 7 when I discuss using the AS clause to rename output columns. You can also use the AS clause to rename table names within a query. For example, you can rename the students table as "s" and the teachers table as "t" to simplify your SQL.

The following SQL statement uses aliases to both rename tables for brevity and rename columns to disambiguate the output:

```
SELECT s.first_name AS 'Student FN', s.last_name AS
         'Student LN', t.first_name AS 'Teacher FN',
         t.last_name AS 'Teacher LN'
FROM students AS s INNER JOIN teachers AS t
ON s.teacher = t.teacher_id
```

Using this SQL statement, you get the following results:

```
Student FN        Student LN        Teacher FN        Teacher LN
---------------   ---------------   ---------------   ---------------
Richard           Jones             Richard           Allen
Matthew           Jones             Mary              Brady
Christopher       Murphy            Mary              Brady
Renee             Smith             Richard           Allen
Edward            Sorin             Mary              Brady
Mary              Keenan            Mary              Brady
Susan             Davis             Richard           Allen

(7 row(s) affected)
```

That's certainly easier to understand than the previous example!

In this chapter, I discuss using INNER JOIN statements where the join condition contains an equality statement (for example, attribute X = attribute Y). This covers the vast majority of INNER JOINs used in the real world. However, you can also use other operators to write the join condition. That's beyond the scope of this book, but you can find more information in *SQL For Dummies*.

Including nonmatching records with OUTER JOINs

In some cases, you'll need to include records in your results that don't have any matching records in the second table. The various OUTER JOIN statements, LEFT OUTER JOIN, RIGHT OUTER JOIN, and FULL OUTER JOIN, help you accomplish this.

All three OUTER JOINs begin with the results of the INNER JOIN. They include all records in the left table along with their matching records in the right table. However, they go one step further: Each type of OUTER JOIN includes additional information on nonmatching records.

LEFT OUTER JOINs

The LEFT OUTER JOIN includes rows that appear in the left table (the Students table in my example) but don't have a matching record in the right table (the teachers table). It includes both records that have a nonmatching value for the join attribute(s) and records that have NULL values for the join attribute(s).

The SQL code that follows shows the format of a LEFT OUTER JOIN for the students and teachers table:

```
SELECT s.first_name AS 'Student FN', s.last_name AS
        'Student LN', t.first_name AS 'Teacher FN',
        t.last_name AS 'Teacher LN'
FROM students AS s LEFT OUTER JOIN teachers AS t
ON s.teacher = t.teacher_id
```

The results of this query appear below:

```
Student FN        Student LN       Teacher FN        Teacher LN
--------------    --------------   ---------------   ---------------
Richard           Jones            Richard           Allen
Matthew           Jones            Mary              Brady
Christopher       Murphy           Mary              Brady
Renee             Smith            Richard           Allen
Mike              Abrams           NULL              NULL
Edward            Sorin            Mary              Brady
Mary              Keenan           Mary              Brady
Susan             Davis            Richard           Allen

(8 row(s) affected)
```

Notice that Mike Abrams appears in the results of this query. This is the only difference between these results and the results of the INNER JOIN I discuss earlier in this chapter. Also, notice that the values of all attributes from the right table are NULL for records that appeared in the left table but did not have matching values in the right table.

RIGHT OUTER JOINs

The RIGHT OUTER JOIN is very similar to the LEFT OUTER JOIN; it simply reverses the direction of the query. In this case, the results include records that appear in the right table but don't have a matching record in the left table.

Here's the familiar student/teacher query written as a RIGHT OUTER JOIN:

```
SELECT s.first_name AS 'Student FN', s.last_name AS
        'Student LN', t.first_name AS 'Teacher FN',
        t.last_name AS 'Teacher LN'
FROM students AS s RIGHT OUTER JOIN teachers AS t
ON s.teacher = t.teacher_id
```

The results of this query are as follows:

Student FN	Student LN	Teacher FN	Teacher LN
Richard	Jones	Richard	Allen
Renee	Smith	Richard	Allen
Susan	Davis	Richard	Allen
Matthew	Jones	Mary	Brady
Christopher	Murphy	Mary	Brady
Edward	Sorin	Mary	Brady
Mary	Keenan	Mary	Brady
NULL	NULL	Ann	Edwards

(8 row(s) affected)

In this case, Mike Abrams no longer appears in the results because he has no match in the right table. However, there is now a new row corresponding to the teacher Ann Edwards. She has no students assigned to her in the students table, so she didn't appear in the INNER JOIN or LEFT OUTER JOIN version of this query.

FULL OUTER JOINs

The FULL OUTER JOIN is essentially a combination of the LEFT OUTER JOIN and the RIGHT OUTER JOIN. The output includes records that appear in either the left or right table. The FULL OUTER JOIN version of the query is as follows:

```
SELECT s.first_name AS 'Student FN', s.last_name AS
        'Student LN', t.first_name AS 'Teacher FN',
        t.last_name AS 'Teacher LN'
FROM students AS s FULL OUTER JOIN teachers AS t
ON s.teacher = t.teacher_id
```

Here are the results of that query:

```
Student FN        Student LN        Teacher FN        Teacher LN
---------------   ---------------   ---------------   ---------------
Richard           Jones             Richard           Allen
Matthew           Jones             Mary              Brady
Christopher       Murphy            Mary              Brady
Renee             Smith             Richard           Allen
Mike              Abrams            NULL              NULL
Edward            Sorin             Mary              Brady
Mary              Keenan            Mary              Brady
Susan             Davis             Richard           Allen
NULL              NULL              Ann               Edwards

(9 row(s) affected)
```

In this case, the output set has nine rows: the seven rows from the INNER JOIN results along with the Mike Abrams result from the LEFT OUTER JOIN and the Ann Edwards result from the RIGHT OUTER JOIN.

Joining a table with itself

In some cases, you'll want to join a table with itself. This situation is known as a self-join, and it occurs when you want to compare records in a table to each other. The classic example of a self-join is a "flattened" employees table that contains information on an organizational hierarchy, as shown in Table 8-3.

Table 8-3		Employees Table		
employee_id	*first_name*	*last_name*	*title*	*manager_id*
1	Mike	Kristov	President	NULL
2	Betsy	Simon	Executive Vice President	1
3	Mark	Edmond	Senior Vice President	2

(continued)

Table 8-3 *(continued)*

employee_id	first_name	last_name	title	manager_id
4	Ellen	Jacobs	Senior Vice President	2
5	Bob	Quinn	District 1 Manager	3
6	Ben	Reilly	District 2 Manager	3
7	Kelly	Smith	District 3 Manager	4
8	Anita	Jober	District 4 Manager	4

This is known as a self-referential table: Each record contains a reference to another record in the same table. In this case, the manager ID for each employee is simply the employee ID of the individual's manager. The data in this table can be expressed visually in the organizational chart shown in Figure 8-1.

If you wanted to retrieve a listing of all employees and their managers, you could use a self-join SQL statement. There's nothing special about the syntax — you simply use the same table name on both sides of the join clause. You must use table renaming to eliminate ambiguity, because both tables have the same attribute names. Here's the Transact-SQL statement you could use to retrieve the desired list:

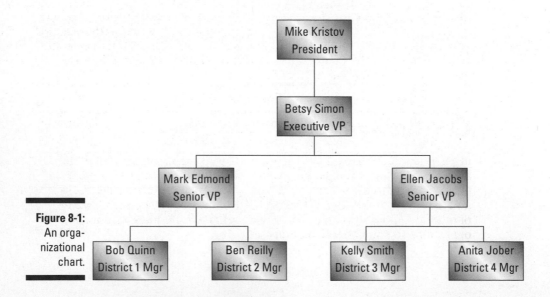

Figure 8-1:
An orga-
nizational
chart.

```
SELECT e.first_name AS 'Employee FN', e.last_name AS
         'Employee LN', e.title AS 'Employee Title',
         m.first_name AS 'Manager FN', m.last_name AS
         'Manager LN'
FROM employees AS e LEFT OUTER JOIN employees AS m
ON e.manager_id = m.employee_id
```

This statement produces the following output:

```
Employee FN Employee LN Employee Title            Manager FN Manager LN
----------- ----------- ------------------------- ---------- ----------
Mike        Kristov     President                 NULL       NULL
Betsy       Simon       Executive Vice President   Mike       Kristov
Mark        Edmond      Senior Vice President      Betsy      Simon
Ellen       Jacobs      Senior Vice President      Betsy      Simon
Bob         Quinn       District 1 Manager         Mark       Edmond
Ben         Rilley      District 2 Manager         Mark       Edmond
Kelly       Smith       District 3 Manager         Ellen      Jacobs
Anita       Jober       District 4 Manager         Ellen      Jacobs

(8 row(s) affected)
```

It's still very important to select the right type of join statement when writing a self-join. In this case, if I used an INNER JOIN instead of a LEFT OUTER JOIN, my employee list would have omitted the company's president, who has no manager!

Taking SELECT to the Next Level

The SELECT statement offers a number of other bells and whistles designed to help you squeeze more efficiency out of your SQL queries. In this section, I describe how you can compute values within your SELECT statement, nest SQL statements with subqueries, and handle different cases in different manners within the same SQL statement.

Computing values

In Chapter 7, I describe how you can use aggregate functions to find the average, minimum, or maximum value for a column, count the number of rows that match certain criteria, and perform other computations. In addition to these functions, Transact-SQL allows you to perform a variety of other computations on query results, ranging from basic arithmetic operations to complex calculations.

Returning to the school database example from earlier in the chapter, suppose you wanted to provide the principal with a report detailing the number of absences for each student. You could accomplish this with a simple SQL query:

```
SELECT first_name, last_name, absences
FROM students
WHERE absences IS NOT NULL
```

This query would provide the results:

```
first_name          last_name          absences
---------------     ---------------     --------
Richard             Jones              3
Christopher         Murphy             5
Renee               Smith              2
Mike                Abrams             8
Edward              Sorin              14
Mary                Keenan             0
Susan               Davis              6

(7 row(s) affected)
```

Many schools allow students a number of "free" absences before triggering parental notification. If your school has a policy of allowing two "free" absences, you may want to provide the principal with a report that takes that into account. You can do this by creating an "Absence Score" column that subtracts two from the number of absences using this query:

```
SELECT first_name, last_name, absences-2 as 'Absence
          Score'
FROM students
WHERE absences-2 > 0
ORDER BY absences DESC
```

That query produces the output:

```
first_name          last_name          Absence Score
---------------     ---------------     -------------
Edward              Sorin              12
Mike                Abrams             6
Susan               Davis              4
Christopher         Murphy             3
Richard             Jones              1

(5 row(s) affected)
```

This output is much more useful for the principal. It now contains the names of only those students exceeding the absence quota and rank orders them using the ORDER BY clause (discussed in Chapter 7).

Transact-SQL supports dozens of additional functions that you can use to manipulate data. Some of the more common ones appear in Table 8-4.

Table 8-4	Common Transact-SQL Functions
Function	*Description*
ABS()	Returns the absolute value of numeric input
DATEADD()	Adds an amount of time to a date and time value
DATEDIFF()	Determines the difference between two date and time values
DATEPART()	Returns the specified part of a date and time value
LEFT()	Returns the specified number of characters from the left side of a string
LEN()	Returns the number of characters in a string
LOWER()	Converts a string to lowercase
PI()	Returns the value 3.14159265358979
RAND()	Returns a pseudo-random number between 0 and 1
RIGHT()	Returns the specified number of characters from the right side of a string
ROUND()	Rounds a number to a specified precision
SQRT()	Returns the square root of a number
SQUARE()	Returns the square of a number
UPPER()	Converts a string to uppercase

For a complete list of Transact-SQL functions, consult SQL Server Books Online.

Managing complexity with subqueries

You can dramatically simplify complex SQL statements by nesting queries within each other. For example, suppose you wanted to retrieve a list of teachers who don't have any assigned students. You can easily accomplish this by combining two SELECT queries:

```
SELECT first_name, last_name
FROM teachers
WHERE teacher_id NOT IN ( SELECT teacher
                          FROM students
                          WHERE teacher IS NOT NULL)
```

This query builds upon the list condition queries I discussed in Chapter 7, but uses the results of another SQL query (the subquery) as the source of the list. It produces the output you probably expect:

```
first_name       last_name
---------------  ---------------
Ann              Edwards

(1 row(s) affected)
```

Dealing with different cases

The CASE statement allows you to perform different actions based upon the value of a database column. For example, suppose the principal of the school wanted to expand the absence scoring system I discussed earlier to include ratings for each student, based upon the following criteria:

- Students with two or fewer absences receive a rating of "Good."
- Students with three to five absences receive a rating of "Warning."
- Students with six or more absences receive a rating of "Violation."

You could implement these three cases by using the following SELECT statement:

```
SELECT first_name, last_name, absences, 'Absence Rating' =
         CASE
             WHEN absences IS NULL THEN 'Unknown'
             WHEN absences > 5 THEN 'Violation'
             WHEN absences > 2 THEN 'Warning'
             ELSE 'Good'
         END
FROM students
ORDER BY absences DESC
```

This produces the desired report:

```
first_name       last_name         absences Absence Rating
---------------  ---------------   -------- --------------
Edward           Sorin             14       Violation
Mike             Abrams            8        Violation
Susan            Davis             6        Violation
Christopher      Murphy            5        Warning
Richard          Jones             3        Warning
Renee            Smith             2        Good
Mary             Keenan            0        Good
Matthew          Jones             NULL     Unknown

(8 row(s) affected)
```

Notice a few things about the CASE statement:

✔ Cases are processed from top down and each row only matches one case. For example, Mike Abrams had more than five absences, so he received a rating of "Violation." SQL Server then ignored the remaining two conditions.

✔ Cases begin with the CASE keyword and end with the END keyword.

✔ You should handle the NULL case explicitly in a CASE statement, as I did with the "Unknown" rating.

✔ You can use the ELSE keyword as a catch-all for any cases you don't explicitly list.

For more details on constructing CASE statements, see *SQL For Dummies,* 6th Edition, by Allen G. Taylor (Wiley Publishing, Inc.).

Using Database Views

Database views allow you to create virtual tables based upon query results. There are two major reasons you might want to use views instead of providing users with access to the underlying database table(s) themselves:

✔ **Views allow you to limit the data users can access.** For example, you can create a view that returns only certain rows from a table and then grant users permission to access the view. They won't be able to access rows in the table that don't meet the criteria of the view.

✔ **Views reduce complexity for end users.** If end users aren't comfortable writing complex SQL queries, you can write the query for them and then hide the complexity in a view.

Creating a view

In the previous section, I provide you with a complex query that uses a CASE statement to create an absence report. If you won't be the only one retrieving that report, you probably want to hide the complexity of the query from the end user.

Here's the SQL command that you can use to create a view called absence_ report that uses the earlier query:

```
CREATE VIEW absence_report AS
SELECT first_name, last_name, absences, 'Absence Rating' =
        CASE
            WHEN absences IS NULL THEN 'Unknown'
            WHEN absences > 5 THEN 'Violation'
            WHEN absences > 2 THEN 'Warning'
        ELSE 'Good'
        END
FROM students
```

When you execute this statement, you see the simple result:

```
Command(s) completed successfully.
```

You can now access the view just as you would any other SQL Server database table. For example, the query

```
SELECT * FROM absence_report
ORDER BY absences desc
```

returns the same results as my original query:

```
first_name       last_name        absences Absence Rating
---------------  ---------------  -------- --------------
Edward           Sorin            14       Violation
Mike             Abrams           8        Violation
Susan            Davis            6        Violation
Christopher      Murphy           5        Warning
Richard          Jones            3        Warning
Renee            Smith            2        Good
Mary             Keenan           0        Good
Matthew          Jones            NULL     Unknown

(8 row(s) affected)
```

That's certainly a lot simpler than rewriting the original query repetitively, isn't it?

Modifying a view

After you've created a view, you can change the underlying SQL statement by using the ALTER VIEW command. Suppose you wanted to provide the teacher Richard Allen with access to the absence report, but you don't want him to see the absence records from students not in his class. You can rewrite the view as

```
ALTER VIEW absence_report AS
SELECT first_name, last_name, absences, 'Absence Rating' =
          CASE
              WHEN absences IS NULL THEN 'Unknown'
              WHEN absences > 5 THEN 'Violation'
              WHEN absences > 2 THEN 'Warning'
              ELSE 'Good'
          END
FROM students
WHERE teacher = (SELECT teacher_id
                   FROM teachers
                   WHERE first_name = 'Richard' AND
                   last_name = 'Allen')
```

Now, if you issue the same command I used earlier to retrieve all records from the view, as follows:

```
SELECT * FROM absence_report
ORDER BY absences desc
```

your view of the results is limited to those students in Richard Allen's class, as shown in the following output:

```
first_name        last_name          absences Absence Rating
---------------   ----------------   -------- --------------
Susan             Davis              6        Violation
Richard           Jones              3        Warning
Renee             Smith              2        Good

(3 row(s) affected)
```

Deleting a view

You may find it necessary to delete an existing view based upon changing business needs. You can delete a view using the DROP VIEW command. For example, if you wanted to delete the absence report view, you would issue the command:

```
DROP VIEW absence_report
```

SQL Server confirms the successful deletion of the view with the following result message:

```
Command(s) completed successfully.
```

Chapter 9

Turning Data into Information with SQL Server Reporting Services

In This Chapter

▶ Configuring SQL Server Reporting Services with Reporting Services Configuration Manager

▶ Designing reports

▶ Publishing and viewing reports

QL Server Reporting Services (SSRS) is one of SQL Server 2008's advanced features. SSRS provides database administrators and developers with a built-in mechanism for designing and publishing data-driven reports to end users. Microsoft gave SSRS a significant overhaul with the release of SQL Server 2008. Most notably, SSRS no longer requires Internet Information Server (IIS) as it did in earlier SQL Server versions. It's now a stand-alone service.

SSRS offers a wide variety of reporting functionality and is the subject of many entire books. In this chapter, I provide you with a basic introduction to SQL Server Reporting Services. I discuss how to set up and configure SSRS, create and publish a basic report, and manage SSRS reports.

If you're interested in learning more after reading this chapter, I suggest you read *Professional SQL Server 2008 Reporting Services,* by Paul Turley, Thiago Silva, Bryan C. Smith, and Ken Withee (Wiley Publishing, Inc.)

Setting up SQL Server Reporting Services

Before you can create and publish reports with SSRS, you need to configure it to meet the requirements of your business environment. You may do this using the Reporting Services Configuration Manager.

To use SQL Server Reporting Services, you must have it installed on your SQL Server instance. (I discuss installing SQL Server components in Chapters 1 and 2.) Follow these steps to set up SSRS:

1. **From the All Programs menu, choose Microsoft SQL Server 2008⇨ Configuration Tools⇨Reporting Services Configuration.**

2. **Provide the connection details for your Report Server in the Reporting Services Configuration Connection window and click the Connect button.**

   If you're running the configuration tool on your SQL Server computer, the window will most likely pop up preconfigured with the correct server name and instance. If you're connecting to a remote SSRS server, you need to provide the server name. Additionally, you need to select the report server instance if more than one exists on that system.

3. **Review the details on the Report Server Status screen.**

   The status screen, shown in Figure 9-1, provides basic information about your Report Server. You may use the Start and Stop buttons on this screen to change the status of the SSRS instance.

4. **Click the Service Account page and confirm that SSRS is running under the correct account. If you decide to make changes, click the Apply button when you're finished.**

   The Server Account page, shown in Figure 9-2, allows you to select the account used to run SSRS. You may choose to use a domain account (as shown in the example) or a built-in account.

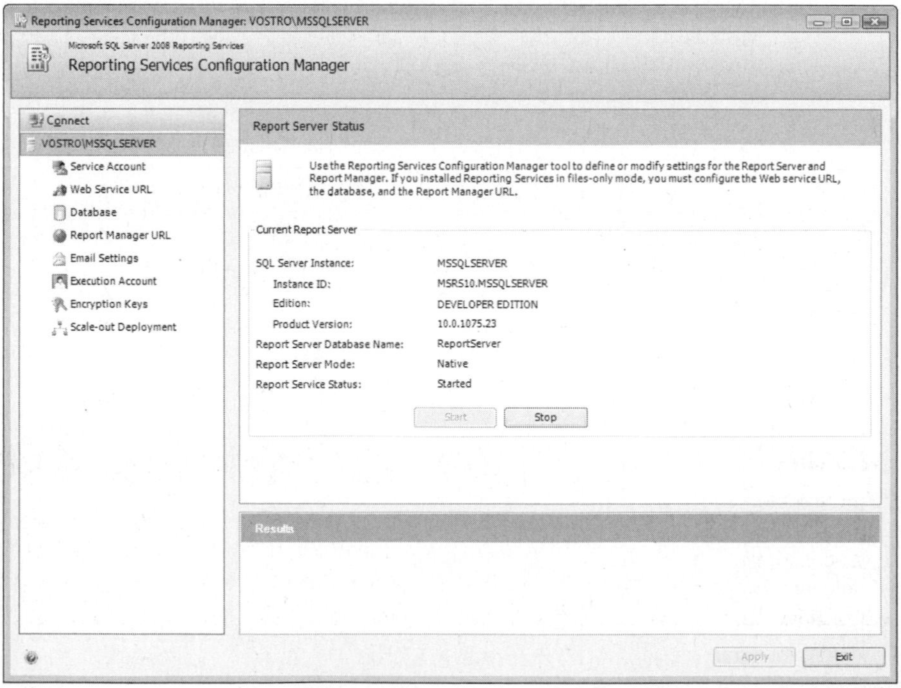

Figure 9-1: Report Server status.

5. **Click the Web Service URL page to review the Web server configuration and make any desired changes. When you finish, click the Apply button.**

   SSRS distributes reports through the use of a Web server. On this screen, shown in Figure 9-3, you may modify the IP address(es) and TCP port assigned to SSRS. This is especially important if your server fills multiple roles in your organization, because you may have only one server listening on the default HTTP port (80) for each IP address.

   This screen also allows you to choose an SSL certificate to use if you want to provide HTTPS secure encrypted access to your reports. This protects them against eavesdropping as they travel across the network from the server to the client. Your server administrator will need to install an SSL certificate on your server before it will appear in the SSL Certificate drop-down menu.

   Make note of the URL(s) shown in the Report Server Web Service URLs section of this window. You should provide these URLs to users who need to access SSRS.

6. **Review the other pages in the Configuration Manager and customize any settings you want.**

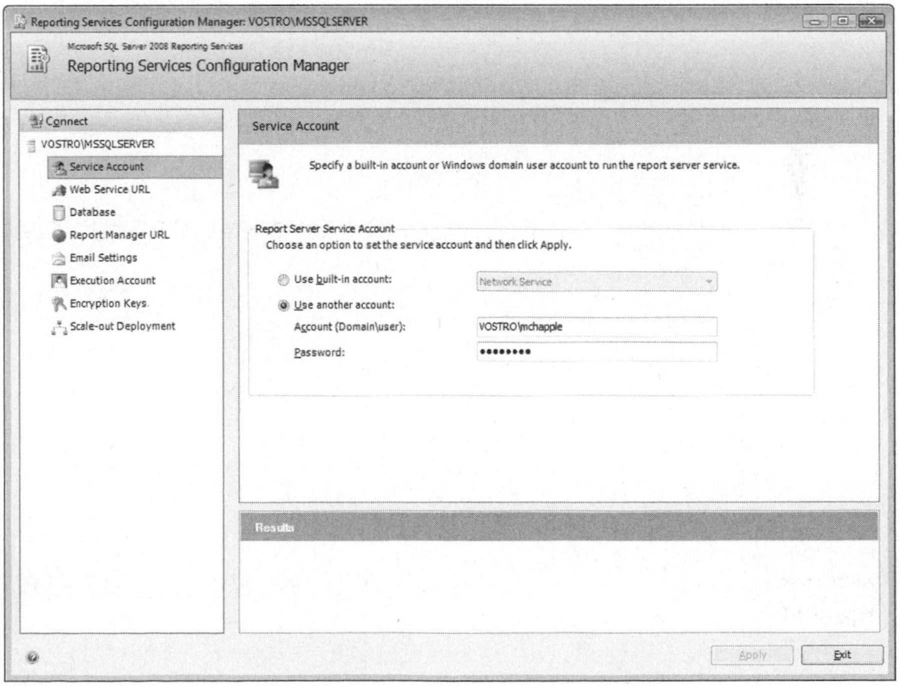

Figure 9-2:
Selecting
a service
account.

I return to the Configuration Manager later in this chapter when I discuss Report Manager (see the "Working with Deployed [Published] Reports" section, later in this chapter). In the meantime, you should take a few minutes to familiarize yourself with the other configuration settings offered in the tool.

 7. **Click the Exit button to close the Reporting Services Configuration Manager.**

After you've set your basic configuration settings with Configuration Manager, you're ready to begin designing reports for distribution on your Report Server.

Creating an SSRS Report with Report Builder

Report Builder allows you to create reports for distribution on an SSRS server. It provides a graphical interface that allows you to visually design reports, dropping in data-driven elements as needed. Report Builder allows you to include tables, images, matrices, lists, and charts in your reports and to populate those elements with data from your SQL Server database, and a variety of other data sources.

Installing and starting Report Builder 2.0

With the release of SQL Server 2008, Microsoft also planned to introduce a new stand-alone reporting tool: Report Builder 2.0.

Unfortunately, immediately before this book went to press, Microsoft removed Report Builder from the product and announced plans to release it separately in late August 2008. The material on Report Builder in this chapter is based on a beta version of that tool. When Microsoft releases the final version of Report Builder, I will update this chapter and make the new download available on the Web at:

```
www.dummies.com/go/sqlserver2008fd
```

Downloading and installing Report Builder is easy: Just walk through the wizard and accept all the default options. When you've installed Report Builder, you may start it by choosing SQL Server 2008 Report Builder⇨ Report Builder 2.0 from the All Programs menu.

Choosing a data source and data set

After you start Report Builder, it opens with a new blank report, ready for your design, as shown in Figure 9-4. Before you begin, you need to configure a data source using the following process:

1. **With Report Builder open, choose New⇨Data Source from the drop-down list in the Data pane.**

   Report Builder displays the Data Source Properties window, shown in Figure 9-5.

2. **Provide a name for your data source by typing it in the Name textbox.**

3. **Choose the Embedded connection radio button and select the appropriate connection type from the drop-down menu.**

   If you already have a shared data source you would like to use instead, you may select the "Use Shared Data Source Reference option instead. For SQL Server database connections, choose Microsoft SQL Server from the Type drop-down menu.

   Report Builder allows you to pull in data from non-SQL Server data sources. Some of those include:

   - Oracle databases
   - SAP NetWeaver
   - OLE DB and ODBC data sources
   - XML data sources
   - Hyperion Essbase

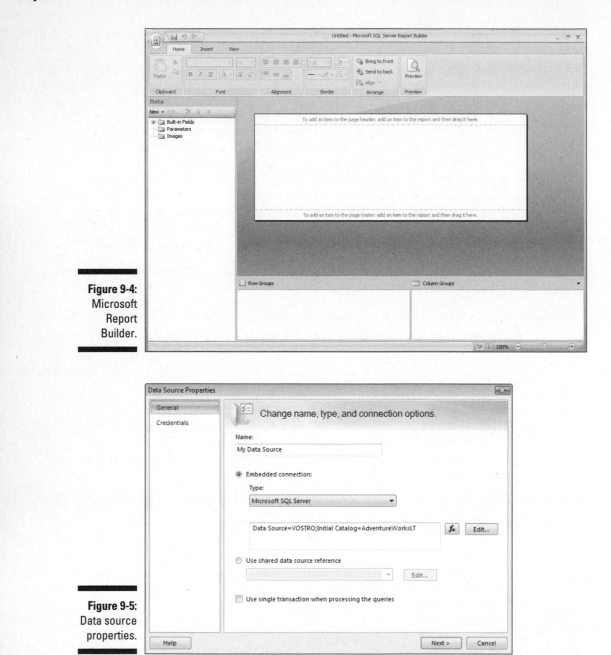

Figure 9-4:
Microsoft
Report
Builder.

Figure 9-5:
Data source
properties.

4. Click the Edit button.

The Connection Properties screen for your selected connection
type appears. Figure 9-6 shows the screen for Microsoft SQL Server
connections.

5. Provide the connection details for your database and click the OK button to continue.

I recommend that before you click OK, you click the Test Connection button to verify that you have provided correct connection details.

6. Click the Next button to continue.

7. Type the SQL Query you want to use for your data source in the Query Editor window.

You need to provide a SQL query that produces the data you want included in your report in the Query Editor window, as shown in Figure 9-7. If you don't want to enter the query manually, you may open an existing query (.sql) file or import a query from another report using Query Editor's toolbar icons.

8. Click the green triangle ("play") button to test your query.

When you click the green triangle, SQL Server executes your query and displays the results in the bottom pane of the Query Editor window. Use this pane to verify that your query produces the desired results. This pane is also where you can make any necessary modifications.

9. Click the Finish button to create your data source.

You return to Report Builder. Note that the dataset you created now appears as an expandable folder in Report Builder's Data pane.

Figure 9-6:
The
Connection
Properties
screen.

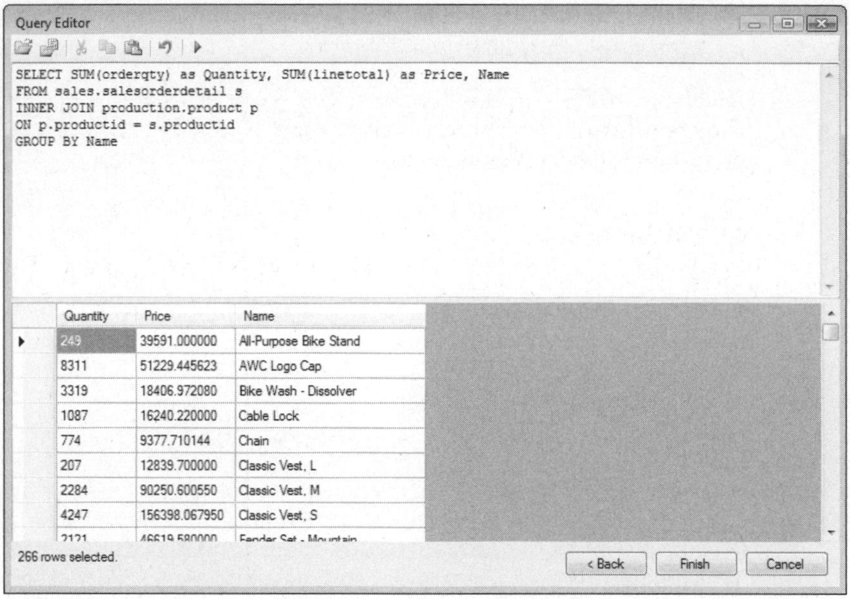

Query Editor

```
SELECT SUM(orderqty) as Quantity, SUM(linetotal) as Price, Name
FROM sales.salesorderdetail s
INNER JOIN production.product p
ON p.productid = s.productid
GROUP BY Name
```

Quantity	Price	Name
249	39591.000000	All-Purpose Bike Stand
8311	51229.445623	AWC Logo Cap
3319	18406.972080	Bike Wash - Dissolver
1087	16240.220000	Cable Lock
774	9377.710144	Chain
207	12839.700000	Classic Vest, L
2284	90250.600550	Classic Vest, M
4247	156398.067950	Classic Vest, S
2121	46619.580000	Fender Set - Mountain

266 rows selected.   < Back   Finish   Cancel

Figure 9-7:
Type your
query in
the Query
Editor.

Laying out the report

After you've added a data source for your report, you may use the various
items on the Insert Ribbon of Report Builder to add elements to your report.
Report Builder allows you to simply drag and drop elements where you'd
like them to appear.

Adding a text box

You may add static (unchanging) text to your report using the Text Box control within Report Builder. Here's the process:

1. **Ensure that you're viewing the Insert menu on the Report Builder
   Ribbon, as shown in Figure 9-8.**

2. **Click the Text Box icon in the Report Items section of the Insert menu.**

3. **Drag the text box to the desired spot on your report.**

   For example, you may want to place the text box in the header or footer
   section of your report.

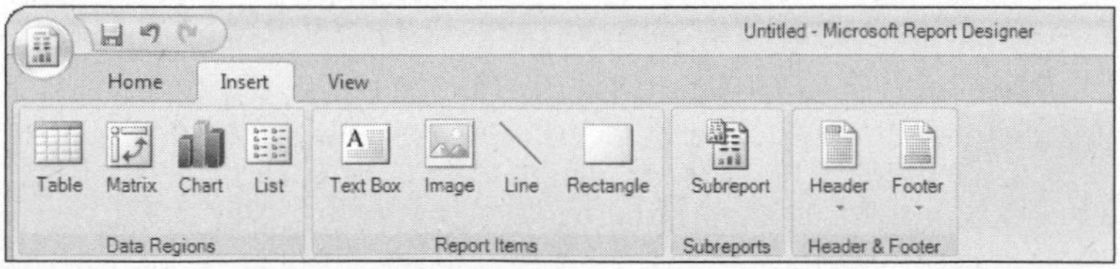

Figure 9-8:
Click Insert
on the
Ribbon.

Untitled - Microsoft Report Designer

Home   Insert   View

Table Matrix Chart List   Text Box Image Line Rectangle   Subreport   Header Footer

Data Regions   Report Items   Subreports   Header & Footer

4. **Use the mouse to click inside the text box and type the text that you would like to appear in the report.**

As with any other document, be sure to save your report periodically to avoid losing your work. You can save your report by clicking the disk icon in the upper-left corner of Report Builder.

Adding a chart

Report Builder makes it easy to add a variety of charts to your SSRS reports. Available chart types include:

- ✔ Pie charts
- ✔ Line graphs
- ✔ Column graphs
- ✔ Funnel charts
- ✔ Bar graphs
- ✔ Area graphs
- ✔ Range graphs
- ✔ Scatter plots

To add a chart to your report, follow these steps:

1. **Click the Chart icon on the Ribbon's Insert menu.**

   Report Builder displays the Select Chart Type window, shown in Figure 9-9.

2. **Select the type of chart you want to include in your report and click OK.**

   Report Builder inserts a default chart of the type you selected, as shown in Figure 9-10.

3. **Choose the data field or fields for your chart and drag them from the Data pane onto the Drop Data Fields Here area above the sample chart.**

   The data fields contain the values to be plotted on your chart. (In the example shown later in Figure 9-12, the quantity field is the data field.)

4. **Choose the category field or fields for your chart and drag them from the Data pane onto the Drop Category Fields Here area above the sample chart.**

   The category fields contain the names corresponding to each of the data fields in your chart. In the example shown in Figure 9-12, the product name field is the category field.

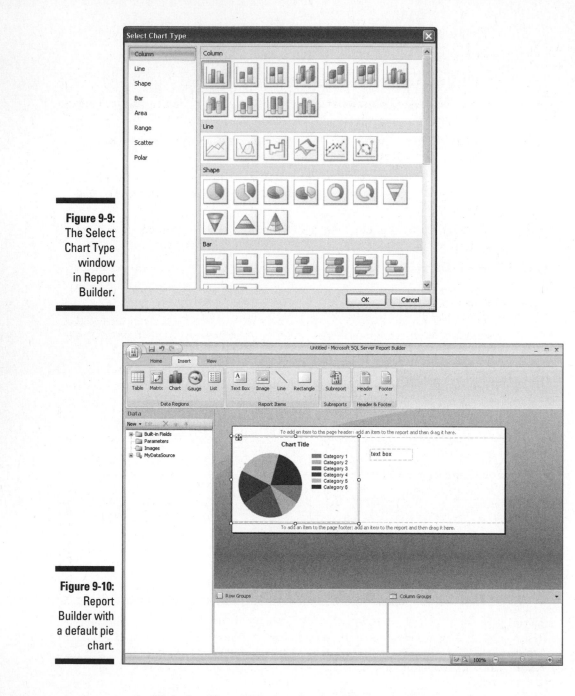

Figure 9-9:
The Select Chart Type window in Report Builder.

Figure 9-10:
Report Builder with a default pie chart.

5. **Click the Chart Title text box and enter the title you want to use for your chart.**

Adding a table

Adding a table to your report follows a similar process:

1. **Click the Table icon on the Ribbon's Insert menu.**

2. **Add or delete columns from your table by right-clicking the table and selecting the appropriate entries from the pop-up menu.**

3. **Click each cell in the Header row and type the text you want to appear in the table header.**

4. **Drag the data elements you would like to appear in each column from the Data pane to the appropriate column in the Data portion of the table.**

   You need to fill in only one row of the table. SSRS automatically creates the necessary number of rows when it generates your report.

Figure 9-11 shows a completed report in the Design view of Report Builder.

Preview your report

When you complete the layout of your report, you may preview it by switching to the Ribbon's View menu and selecting the Preview Report view. Doing so produces a report preview similar to the one shown in Figure 9-12.

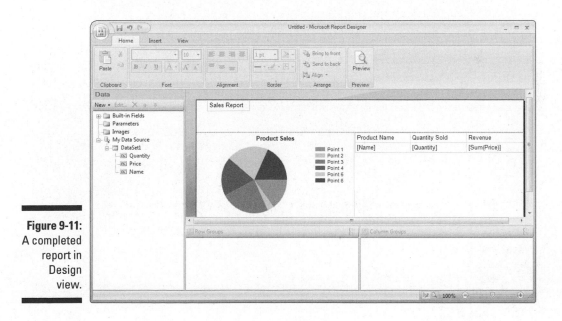

Figure 9-11:
A completed report in Design view.

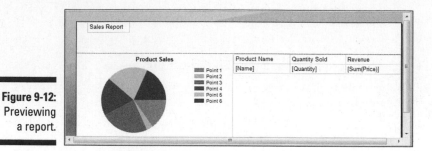

Publishing the report

After you've completed your report layout and previewed it to ensure that it meets with your satisfaction, you can publish the report to your Report Server for other users to view.

Here's how to publish a report to an SSRS server:

1. **Click the round report icon in the upper-left corner of the screen to activate the Report Builder pull-down menu and then choose Publish, as shown in Figure 9-13.**

2. **Confirm the deployment settings and click OK.**

   Confirm that the Report Server URL, report folder, and report name chosen by Report Builder are correct (as shown in Figure 9-14). The default settings should be acceptable, but you may make any necessary modifications.

   After clicking OK, you see a Report Deployed Successfully notification.

If you attempt to publish a report and receive an error message about improper permissions, verify that your account has membership in the Publisher role. For more information, see "Configuring report security," later in this chapter.

After you publish your report, it will be available to users accessing the reporting server with the appropriate permissions.

Working with Deployed (Published) Reports

You may access and modify your deployed reports using the URLs you provided in the Reporting Services Configuration Manager. In this section, I describe the basic concepts behind the SSRS Web interfaces.

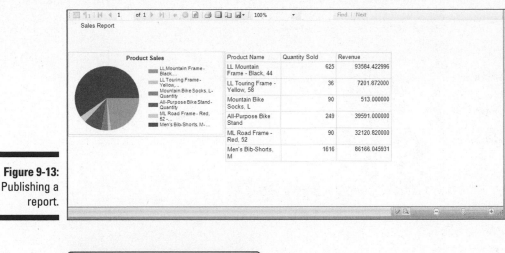

Figure 9-13:
Publishing a
report.

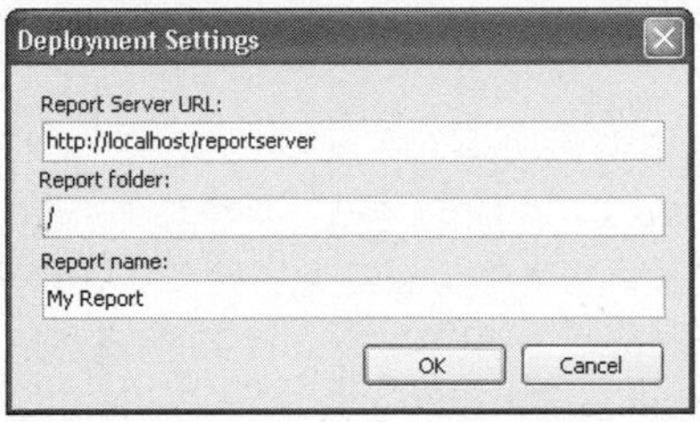

Figure 9-14:
Deployment
settings.

Viewing reports

The simplest way to view SSRS reports is to use the Web Services URL you provided in the Reporting Services Configuration Manager. Simply open a Web browser and type that URL into the address bar. SSRS will prompt you for your username and password and then display a report menu similar to the one shown in Figure 9-15.

Click the name of the report you want to view, and SSRS will generate the report dynamically and display it in your browser window, as shown in Figure 9-16.

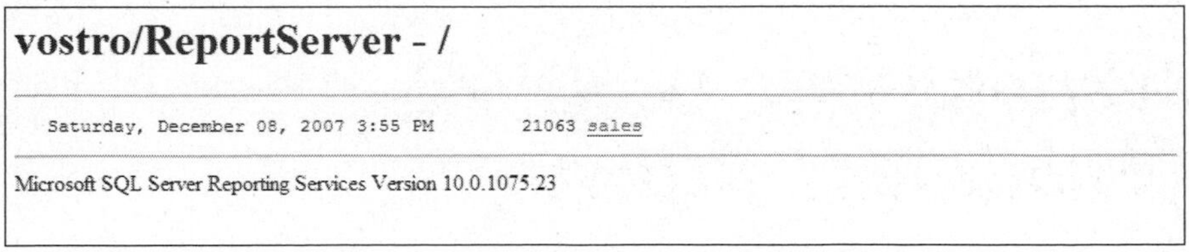

Figure 9-15:
SSRS Web
Service
menu.

vostro/ReportServer - /

Saturday, December 08, 2007 3:55 PM   21063 <u>sales</u>

Microsoft SQL Server Reporting Services Version 10.0.1075.23

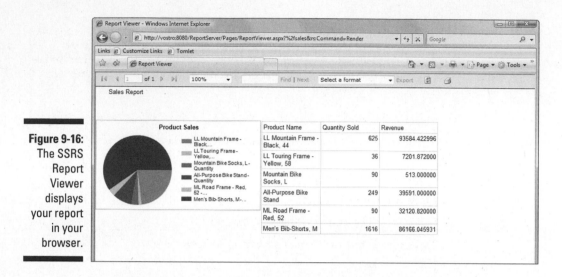

Figure 9-16:
The SSRS
Report
Viewer
displays
your report
in your
browser.

Configuring report security

You need to set up permissions for the users you want to administer and view SSRS reports. To do this, you first need to enable SSRS Report Manager and then use it to assign SSRS roles to the appropriate users and groups.

Setting up Report Manager

Report Manager is a Web application that allows you to modify SSRS settings through your Web browser. Before you can access Report Manager, you need to enable it using the following process:

1. **Open Reporting Services Configuration Manager.**

2. **Click the Report Manager URL page.**

3. **Click the Advanced button.**

4. **Click the Add button under Multiple Identities for Report Manager.**

5. **Click OK to accept the default options.**

6. **Click OK to close the Advanced Multiple Web Site Configuration.**

7. **Click the Apply button to start Report Manager.**

   Note the URL displayed in Configuration Manager. This is the URL required to access Report Manager.

Configuring site roles

Site-wide roles allow you to assign users permission to access Report Manager. By default, all users in the BUILTIN\Administrators local administrators group are Report Manager System Administrators. Here's how you can add additional users:

1. **Using Internet Explorer, open the URL for Report Manager.**

   You specified this URL when starting Report Manager in the previous section.

2. **Click the Site Settings link.**

3. **Click the Security page.**

4. **Click the New Role Assignment button.**

5. **Type the name of the user or group in the Group or User Name text box.**

6. **Select the box or boxes corresponding to any roles you would like to assign to the user or group.**

   The roles you may choose from are as follows:

   • System Administrator role members may perform all Report Manager administrative activities.

   • System User role members may view system properties and shared schedules only.

7. **Click the OK button to finish.**

Setting up content roles

In addition to creating site roles to access Report Manager, you may also create content roles that grant users varying levels of permission over SSRS content. You may create these permissions at the Home level, where they inherit downward to all newly created reports. Alternatively, you may set role membership for subfolders or individual items.

To set content roles at the Home folder level, follow this process:

1. **Click the Home link in Report Manager.**

2. **Click the Properties tab.**

3. **Click the New Role Assignment button.**

   You see the New Role Assignment screen, shown in Figure 9-17.

4. **Type the name of the user or group in the Group or User Name text box.**

5. **Select the box or boxes corresponding to any role you would like to assign to the user or group.**

   The roles you may choose from are as follows:

   - Publisher role members may publish and update reports on the Report Server.

   - Content Manager role members may manage folders, reports, and resources.

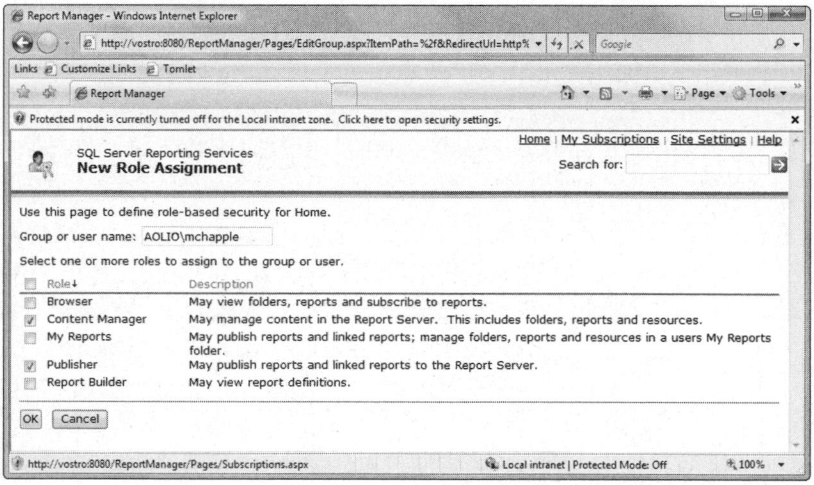

Figure 9-17:
Assigning
an SSRS
role.

   - My Reports role members may publish reports and manage folders, reports, and resources within their own My Reports folder.

   - Browser role members may view and subscribe to reports and folders.

   - Report Builder role members may view report definitions.

6. **Click the OK button to finish.**

Part IV

Inserting and Manipulating Your Data

The 5th Wave   By Rich Tennant

@RICHTENNANT

I told Russell he should data model before we go any further.

May I speak to Kate Moss, please.

In this part . . .

In this part, you find out how to go beyond simple retrieval of data and see how to get new data into a database. I also show you how to modify information that exists within a database table. Here, you discover how you can use SQL statements and bulk import tools to add information to your database tables. I also tell you about stored procedures, functions, and triggers — all great tools for making your life easier by automating those tedious database tasks.

Chapter 10

Inserting, Updating, and Deleting Data

Microsoft SQL Server 2008 provides you with a number of different ways to insert new data into your databases. Just as a carpenter has many different tools that can achieve the end goal of joining two pieces of wood, SQL Server offers different data insertion tools that are best suited for certain circumstances.

In this chapter, I explain each of those tools and provide advice on how you can determine the appropriate tool for a given situation. I begin by looking at the options available to you when you need to insert small numbers of rows into your database. I then expand the discussion to look at bulk import tools and techniques you can use to retrieve data from remote databases.

Inserting Small Quantities of Data

In many cases, you simply need to add a few new rows to your database, one at a time. Microsoft SQL Server provides you with two basic techniques for achieving this goal: data entry with SQL Server Management Studio's graphic interface and the SQL INSERT statement.

Understanding simple data entry

The easiest way to insert new data into your database is to use the graphic interface of SQL Server Management Studio (SSMS). SSMS provides a spreadsheet-style data entry format that allows you to simply access the table you'd like to insert data into and begin typing, just as you would in Microsoft Excel.

I use this technique in earlier chapters, so it may already be familiar to you if you've been following along. To insert data into a table, follow these steps:

1. **Open SQL Server Management Studio and connect to the SQL Server instance containing the database that you'd like to modify.**

   If you're not already familiar with this process, flip back to Chapter 3.

2. **Expand the Databases folder (click the plus icon next to the word Databases).**

3. **Expand the folder of the database you'd like to modify.**

4. **Expand the Tables folder for the database you'd like to modify.**

5. **Right-click the table name and choose Edit Top 200 Rows from the pop-up menu to open the table.**

   You should see the window shown in Figure 10-1.

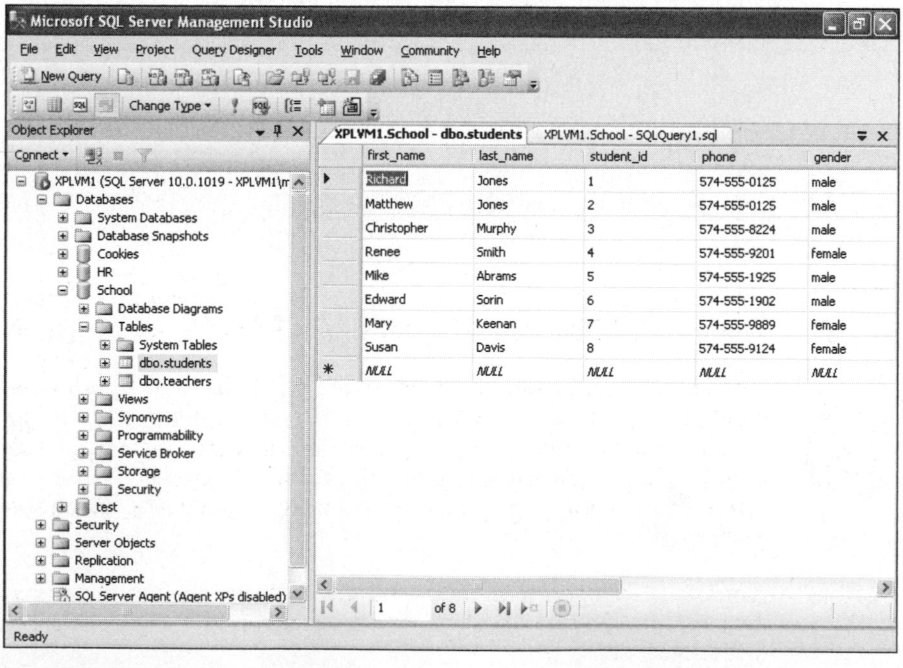

Figure 10-1: SSMS Data Entry window.

6. **Enter the data into the last row of the table to insert the new row into the table.**

   The last row of the table will contain NULL values for every column. Simply use the mouse to highlight those values and type over them with the data you'd like to insert into the table.

7. **Click the *X* in the upper-left corner of the window to close the data entry window.**

You must exit the line that you're editing by clicking into another line before exiting. SSMS does not save your data to the database until you've done so. SSMS indicates unsaved changes to a row with a circular red exclamation point icon, as shown in Figure 10-2.

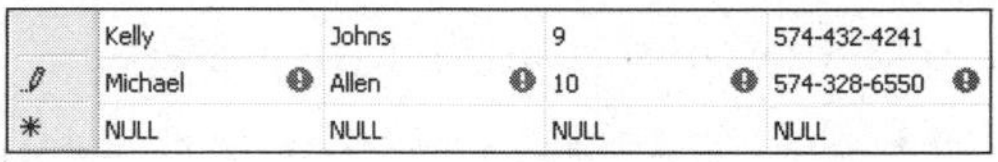

Figure 10-2:
The exclamation point indicates unsaved changes to a row in SSMS.

	Kelly		Johns		9		574-432-4241	
🖉	Michael	❶	Allen	❶	10	❶	574-328-6550	❶
✳	NULL		NULL		NULL		NULL	

Writing INSERT statements

You can also insert data into a SQL Server database using Transact-SQL. The INSERT statement allows you to add a row to a table and uses the following syntax:

```
INSERT INTO <table_name> (<columns>)
VALUES (<values>)
```

in which <columns> and <values> are comma-separated lists of the column names in the table and the values you'd like to insert, respectively.

The column list is actually an optional part of the INSERT statement. If you don't include the list of columns, SQL Server assumes that your list of values includes all columns in the correct order. However, I strongly recommend that you play it safe by specifying the column list in your INSERT statement. I've seen database users make far too many mistakes by taking shortcuts with their syntax.

You can also insert more than one row with the same INSERT statement by separating multiple rows (each enclosed in its own set of parentheses) with commas.

Here's how you would use the INSERT statement to add two new students into the students table from Chapter 7:

```
INSERT INTO students (first_name, last_name, student_id,
        phone, gender, birthdate, absences, teacher,
        city)
VALUES ('Mead', 'Remke', 11, '574-224-2312', 'male',
        2/12/1999, 5, 1, 'South Bend'),
       ('Calvin', 'Reynolds', 12, '574-482-2329', 'male',
        3/15/1999, 2, NULL, 'Granger')
```

In response, SQL Server offers a simple result:

```
(2 row(s) affected)
```

Modifying and Deleting Data

When it comes time to modify or remove data from your database, you have two options: use the graphical SSMS interface or write Transact-SQL statements. If you choose to use the SSMS interface, simply open the table as if you were going to add new rows and modify the table in Open Table view. In this section, I explain how to modify or remove data from your database using Transact-SQL.

Modifying data with UPDATE

SQL's UPDATE command allows you to modify data stored in a SQL Server table based upon data attributes. The basic syntax of this statement is as follows:

```
UPDATE <table_name>
SET <attribute> = <value>
WHERE <conditions>
```

For example, suppose you hire a new teacher, Ann Edwards, with a teacher ID of 3 and assign her all the students in your school not currently assigned to a teacher. You can update your student records to reflect these assignments by using the following UPDATE statement:

```
UPDATE students
SET teacher = 3
WHERE teacher IS NULL
```

which produces the following result:

```
(2 row(s) affected)
```

Notice that executing the query simply results in a statement showing the number of rows modified. This is normal. SQL Server will not display the contents of the modified rows.

The WHERE clause is optional. If you omit it, your change will affect *all* rows in the table. For example, if the principal wants to close the school for a day and assess all the students an absence, she can do so with the following statement:

```
UPDATE students
SET absences = absences + 1
```

This statement affects all rows in the table and produces the following output:

```
(12 row(s) affected)
```

The previous query computed a new value for the absences column by adding 1 to the existing value. Recall that NULL is a special value, so it is not changed. Adding 1 to NULL has no effect, and the result is still NULL.

Removing data from a database

You have several ways to remove data from a SQL Server database: deleting individual rows with the DELETE statement; deleting all rows with the TRUNCATE TABLE statement; and removing the entire table with the DROP TABLE statement.

Deleting rows with the DELETE statement

The SQL DELETE statement allows you to remove rows from your database that meet specified criteria. The format of the statement is as follows:

```
DELETE FROM <table_name>
WHERE <conditions>
```

Suppose that because of a school boundary realignment, you want to remove all students from your school who live in Granger. You can delete them from the students table using the following command:

```
DELETE FROM students
WHERE city = 'Granger'
```

SQL Server responds with the number of rows that were deleted:

```
(3 row(s) affected)
```

Deleting all rows from a table

If you want to delete all the rows from a table, you can simply use the DELETE statement with no WHERE condition. However, this method will take a long time for larger tables. SQL offers the TRUNCATE TABLE statement to make this process faster, using the following syntax:

```
TRUNCATE TABLE <table_name>
```

SQL Server responds with a simple

```
Command(s) completed successfully.
```

The TRUNCATE TABLE command removes all data from the table, but leaves the basic table structure intact for future use.

Deleting an entire table

To delete an entire table, including all data and the table structure itself, you can use the DROP TABLE statement, with the following syntax:

```
DROP TABLE <table_name>
```

Importing Large Quantities of Data

SQL Server also provides methods that you can use when you need to insert large quantities of data into a database at the same time. These automated techniques can help you insert data from the results of a SQL query, a text file, or another database.

Inserting query results

You can insert data into a table from the results of a SQL subquery by simply including it in place of the VALUES clause in an INSERT INTO statement. For example, when graduation time arrives and all students born in 1999 leave the school, you can copy their records into an alumni table using the following Transact-SQL statement:

```
INSERT INTO alumni
        SELECT * FROM students
        WHERE birthdate BETWEEN '12/31/1998' AND
        '1/1/2000'
```

In response to the alumni query shown previously, SQL Server will display the number of rows inserted:

```
(2 row(s) affected)
```

The preceding query assumes that the students and alumni tables share a common table structure (that is, they have the same columns).

Copying bulk data with BULK INSERT

If you need to insert data from a text file, the BULK INSERT command may be the best option for you. This Transact-SQL statement allows you to read a text file from your file system and insert the contents into a SQL Server table.

The basic syntax of the BULK INSERT statement is as follows:

```
BULK INSERT <table_name> FROM <file_name>
WITH <conditions>
```

For example, suppose you had a file called C:\classes.txt that contains information on all the courses taught at your school. The contents of that tab-delimited file appear below:

```
1        Mathematics    1        102
2        Science        3        204
3        History        2        213
4        Literature     2        102
5        Mathematics    1        114
6        Literature     2        119
7        Science        3        210
8        Science        3        221
9        Mathematics    1        125
10       Literature     2        102
11       Science        3        104
12       Mathematics    1        102
13       Literature     2        115
14       History        2        114
15       Mathematics    1        210
16       Science        3        221
17       Mathematics    1        205
18       Literature     2        208
```

You could insert these rows into your classes table with the following Transact-SQL statement:

```
BULK INSERT classes FROM 'C:\classes.txt'
```

SQL Server responds with the number of rows inserted:

```
(18 row(s) affected)
```

The BULK INSERT statement offers many options that help you insert different data types in a flexible manner. For example, you may specify how to handle constraints, how many rows to insert in each batch, the format of the file, and many other characteristics. These are beyond the scope of this book. For more information, see *SQL Server Books Online*.

Performing blk operations from the command line with bcp

SQL Server's bcp (bulk copy) command provides you with the ability to insert bulk data from the command line rather than use the BULK INSERT SQL statement. This approach is particularly useful if you need to insert data from within other programs or through batch files.

The basic format of the bcp command is as follows:

```
bcp <table_name> <direction> <file_name> <options>
```

in which

- ✔ table_name is the fully qualified name of a table, in the format database_name.owner.table_name.
- ✔ direction is either in (for data import) or out (for data export).
- ✔ file_name is the full path to a file.
- ✔ options are the arguments to the command. Common options include:
    - −c to specify a text file containing tab-delimited columns with a newline character at the end of each row
    - −T to specify a trusted connection using Windows authentication

There are many more options designed to make the bcp command a flexible, powerful data import and export utility. For more information, see SQL Server Books Online.

Importing bulk data with bcp

You can use the following command to import the same text file that I use as an example in the previous section's BULK INSERT command:

```
bcp school.dbo.classes in "C:\classes.txt" -c -T
```

Here's what it looks like from the DOS prompt:

```
C:\>bcp school.dbo.classes in "C:\classes.txt" -c -T

Starting copy...

18 rows copied.
Network packet size (bytes): 4096
Clock Time (ms.) Total     : 16      Average : (1125.00
          rows per sec.)C:\>
```

Exporting bulk data with bcp

You can also use bcp to export bulk data by simply changing the in operator to an out operator. If you want to create a tab-delimited file containing all the records in your classes table, you can use the following command:

```
bcp school.dbo.classes out "C:\classes_output.txt" -c -T
```

At the DOS prompt, you see

```
C:\>bcp school.dbo.classes out "C:\classes_output.txt" -c
          -T

Starting copy...

18 rows copied.
Network packet size (bytes): 4096
Clock Time (ms.) Total     : 1      Average : (18000.00
          rows per sec.)
```

```
C:\>
```

And you now have a file stored on your hard drive called classes_output.txt that contains exactly the same contents as the classes.txt input file used earlier.

The major difference between the bcp and BULK INSERT commands is where you execute them. BULK INSERT is a SQL statement issued from within SSMS, whereas bcp is a command-line utility used at the DOS prompt.

Working with SQL Server Integration Services

SQL Server Integration Services (SSIS) offers a clean, graphic interface that allows you to easily import or export data from your SQL Server databases. Microsoft first introduced SSIS with the release of SQL Server 2005, as a replacement to the Data Transformation Services (DTS) found in earlier versions of the product.

To import data into your database with SSIS, use the following process:

1. **With SSMS open, right-click the name of the database into which you will import data.**

2. **Choose Import Data from the Tasks menu. (See Figure 10-3.)**

3. **Click Next to advance past the Welcome screen.**

   The Welcome screen, shown in Figure 10-4, appears when SSIS starts.

4. **Click the Data Source drop-down list and choose Flat File Source. (See Figure 10-5.)**

   Notice that you have many other options for data sources. SSIS allows you to import data from Microsoft Access, Microsoft Excel, other SQL Server or Oracle databases, and many other data sources.

5. **Enter a valid filename or click the Browse button to locate a file; then, click the Next button to continue.**

   At this step, you can also change file format options, if necessary.

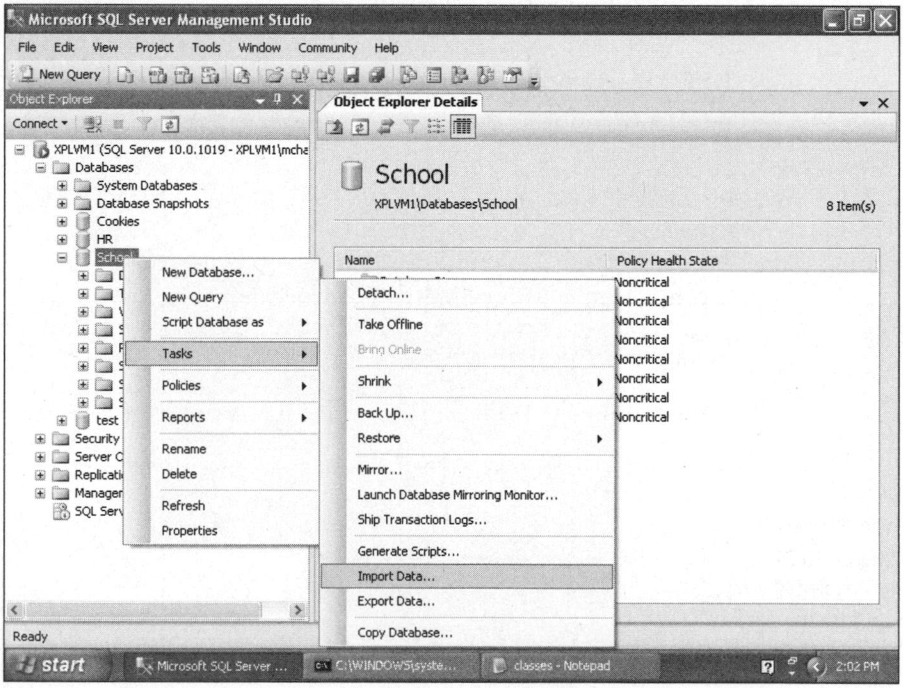

Figure 10-3:
Invoking
SSIS.

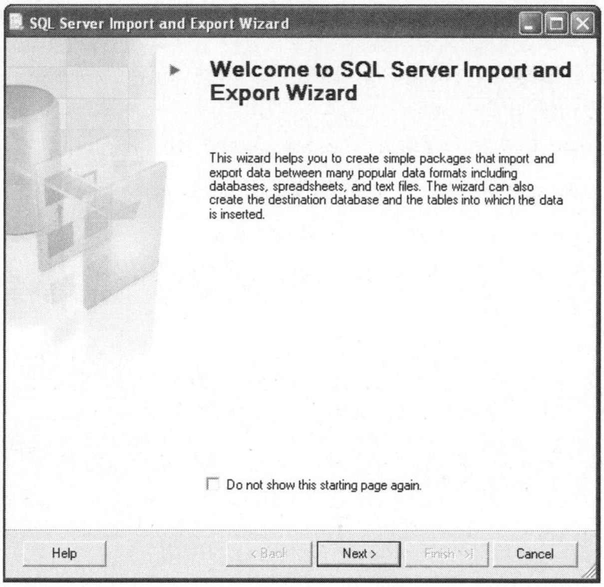

Figure 10-4:
SSIS
Welcome
screen.

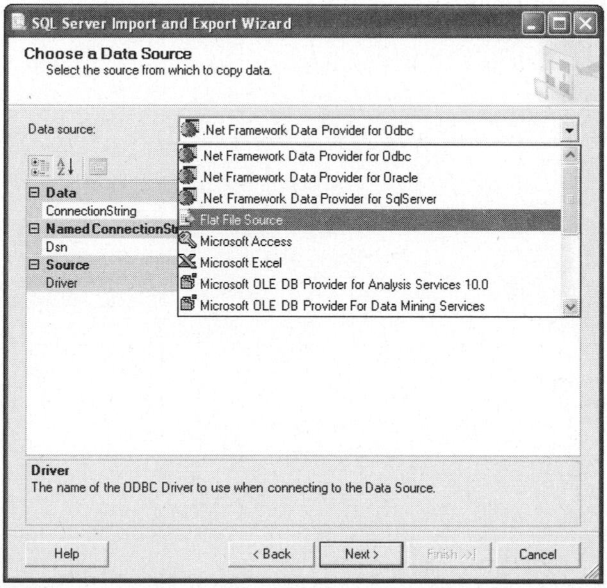

Figure 10-5:
Choosing a
data source.

6. **View the preview on the next screen and confirm that the import appears to be functioning properly. Click the Next button to continue when you are satisfied.**

7. **Click the Destination drop-down list and choose SQL Server Native Client.**

   This choice indicates that you want to import data into a SQL Server database table.

8. **Choose the destination database for your import operation by selecting it from the Database drop-down list and then click Next. (See Figure 10-6.)**

9. **Verify the destination table and variable mappings; then click Next to continue.**

   SQL Server will attempt to guess the correct destination table and variable mappings based upon the filename and attributes. If the destination table is not correct, use the drop-down list under Destination to choose the correct table. You can verify the mapping of text file columns to database variables by clicking the Edit Mappings button.

10. **Click the Finish button.**

    You may also elect to save the steps you performed as an SSIS Package. Saving these steps will allow you to repeat this operation in the future without repeating the wizard process.

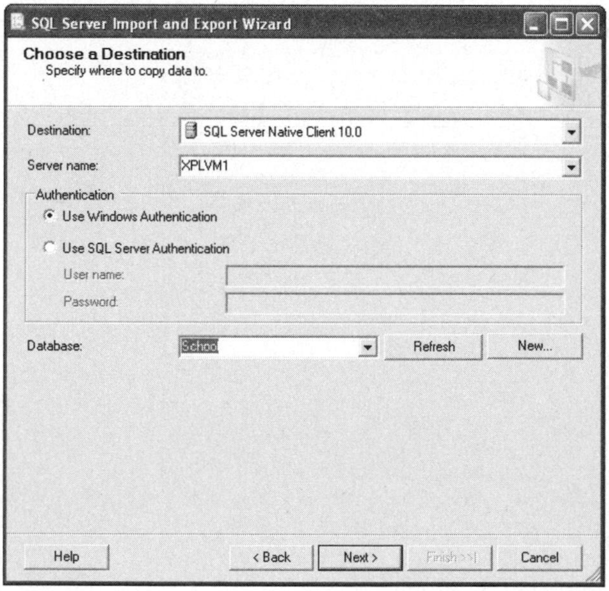

Figure 10-6:
Choosing
the import
destination.

11. Click Finish again to begin the import.

SQL Server presents the screen shown in Figure 10-7, which updates you on the import progress.

Reversing the process to export data is straightforward: Simply switch Steps 4 and 7 to choose a SQL Server database as your source and a Flat File as your destination.

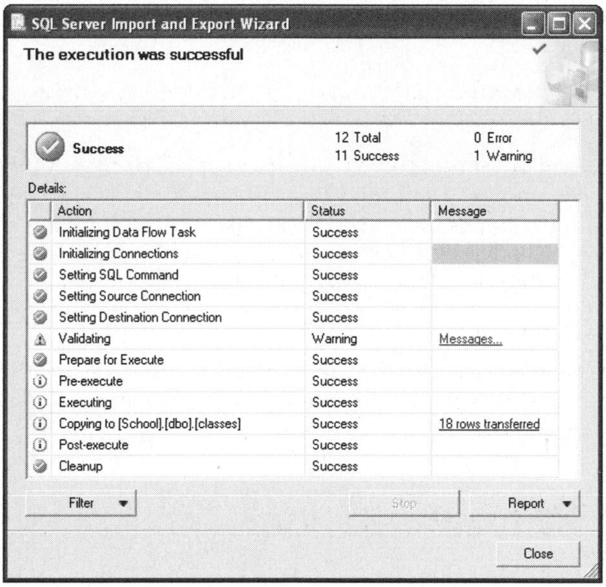

SQL Server Import and Export Wizard

The execution was successful

✓ Success	12 Total	0 Error	
	11 Success	1 Warning	

Details:

	Action	Status	Message
	Initializing Data Flow Task	Success	
	Initializing Connections	Success	
	Setting SQL Command	Success	
	Setting Source Connection	Success	
	Setting Destination Connection	Success	
⚠	Validating	Warning	Messages...
	Prepare for Execute	Success	
ⓘ	Pre-execute	Success	
ⓘ	Executing	Success	
ⓘ	Copying to [School].[dbo].[classes]	Success	18 rows transferred
ⓘ	Post-execute	Success	
	Cleanup	Success	

Filter ▼   Stop   Report ▼

Close

Figure 10-7:
SSIS import status.

Chapter 11

Saving Time with Functions, Stored Procedures, and Triggers

In This Chapter

▶ Use SQL Server functions to simplify your queries

▶ Write stored procedures to reuse code and improve application security

▶ Use triggers to update tables automatically

*1*n Chapters 4 through 6, I describe many of the powerful features of SQL Server and Transact-SQL. That discussion focuses on writing Transact-SQL statements that explicitly tell SQL Server how you'd like the database to react. In the real world, SQL statements can become quite complex, taking dozens of lines (or longer!) to fully express a complex query.

SQL Server provides several features to help you manage this complexity and simplify your Transact-SQL statements. In this chapter, I describe how you can use functions, stored procedures, and triggers to streamline your SQL statements, reuse code, and improve database and application security.

Reusing Logic with Functions

Functions allow you to reuse common functionality, saving you the time and trouble of cutting and pasting (or rewriting!) SQL code that you use often. Before diving in to SQL Server's functions, I give you a brief example of the way you might use functions in the real world.

If you're a programmer, you're probably already familiar with the concept of a function. SQL Server functions are no different than those used by any other programming language.

Imagine that you're the supervisor at a vehicle depot and have several employees working for you who assist you in the management of a fleet of hundreds of vehicles. Before issuing a vehicle to a customer, you send an employee to verify that the car has enough gas. That employee might take the following steps:

1. Obtain the keys for the vehicle from the key rack.

2. Walk to the vehicle's location in the garage.

3. Unlock the vehicle and open the door.

4. Insert the key into the ignition and start the vehicle.

5. Check the gas gauge and write the fuel level down on a piece of paper.

6. Walk back to the supervisor's desk.

7. Inform the supervisor of the fuel level.

This is a multistep process that employees repeat frequently to obtain a simple piece of information. You certainly wouldn't want to tell the employee all these steps every time you need to check a vehicle's fuel level. ("Hey Bill, go get the keys for vehicle #2, walk over to parking spot #2, unlock the door . . .") You'd spend your whole day repeating the same thing over and over again, and your employees would think that you're insane.

Instead, you'd use the equivalent of a function. On the first day Bill reports for work, you'd explain the full seven-step process to him. On future days, the conversation would go like this:

You: "Bill, go check the fuel level on vehicle 2."

(Bill goes and follows the seven-step process.)

Bill: "It's half full."

SQL Server functions allow you to do the same thing with database queries. If you find yourself repeating the same SQL code over and over again, you've probably found a good candidate for a function.

In the following two sections, I describe two different types of SQL Server functions and how they can improve the efficiency of your database queries: built-in functions supplied as part of SQL Server, and user-defined functions that you can create yourself.

Understanding types of functions

You can use two different types of functions in SQL Server 2008: scalar functions and table-valued functions. They differ based upon the type of output they provide:

✔ **Scalar functions** return a single value. If you've used functions in other programming languages, these are the type of functions that you're probably most familiar with. They may have one, many, or no input parameters but always return a single value. For example, the `GETDATE()` function (built in to SQL Server) takes no arguments and always returns a `datetime` value containing the current date and time.

✔ **Table-valued functions** allow you to offer more complex output, in the form of a table. You might use a table-valued function to retrieve all the records in a table associated with a particular person. You'll often use table-valued functions in the `FROM` clause of a `SELECT` statement that further refines the output.

Leveraging SQL Server's built-in functions

To save you time, Microsoft included a large number of commonly used functions with SQL Server 2008. These function come in the following categories (among others):

✔ Aggregate (discussed in Chapter 7)

✔ Date and time

✔ Mathematical

✔ Security

✔ String

✔ Text and image

Providing a full description of each of SQL Server's built-in functions is beyond the scope of this book (it would take an entire book to do so!), but I give you the information you need to get started. In the next two sections, I show you how to call a built-in function and how to get a list of each function offered by SQL Server 2008.

I use the stock table from a fictional fruit wholesale company throughout this example. Here are the table contents:

```
item              warehouse         inventory    wholesale_price
----------------  ----------------  -----------  --------------------
Apples            New York          511          0.12
Apples            Seattle           412          0.13
Limes             Seattle           104          0.33
Oranges           New York          120          0.55
Oranges           Tampa             982          0.52
Pears             New York          9            0.39
```

You might have noticed that the stock table isn't very well designed. It violates several of the database normalization rules I discuss in Chapter 4. I designed the table this way intentionally, to keep this example simple.

Calling built-in functions

Using SQL Server's built-in functions is very straightforward. After you understand the function's inputs (if any), you simply use the function within your SQL statement, providing the appropriate input. I give you a few examples in the sections that follow.

Functions without input parameters

One of the simplest SQL Server functions is Pi(). As you might expect, this function provides you with an easy way to use the mathematical value π in your SQL statements. Pi() takes no arguments and returns a scalar value that approximates π. If you want to test it, you can issue the following SQL command:

```
SELECT Pi() AS 'Pi'
```

SQL Server returns simply

```
Pi
----------------------
3.14159265358979

(1 row(s) affected)
```

You can also use this value within a more complex SQL statement. For example, suppose (for some strange reason) that you wanted to increase the price of products in your Seattle warehouse by a factor of π. You could use the Pi() function, as follows:

```
SELECT item, warehouse, inventory, wholesale_price * Pi()
          AS 'Pi Price'
FROM stock
WHERE warehouse = 'Seattle'
```

This would produce the results:

```
item             warehouse        inventory   Pi Price
---------------  ---------------  ----------  ----------------------
Apples           Seattle          412         0.408407044966673
Limes            Seattle          104         1.03672557568463

(2 row(s) affected)
```

Functions with input parameters

Some functions use input parameters to provide information that the function will transform or use in its logic. For example, suppose you use the following query to retrieve a list of the warehouses owned by your company:

```
SELECT DISTINCT warehouse from stock
```

Normally, this would produce the following output:

```
warehouse
----------------
New York
Seattle
Tampa

(3 row(s) affected)
```

Perhaps you intend to provide this information directly to another program that requires input in all capital letters. You could use SQL Server's built-in upper() function to transform the warehouse column to an all-uppercase format. The upper() function takes a single input parameter of any text data type and returns an all-uppercase version of that parameter. Your new query would look like this:

```
SELECT DISTINCT upper(warehouse) AS 'WAREHOUSE' from stock
```

Your new query would also provide output in a format ready for the program that requires uppercase data:

```
WAREHOUSE
----------------
NEW YORK
SEATTLE
TAMPA

(3 row(s) affected)
```

Obtaining a list of built-in functions

You can find out more information about SQL Server's built-in functions using SQL Server Management Studio. To do so, follow these steps:

1. **Open SQL Server Management Studio and connect to your SQL Server.**

2. **Expand the Databases folder by clicking the plus (+) icon to the left of the word Databases.**

3. **Expand the folder for any database on your server.**

The built-in functions are available in any SQL Server database, so for exploration purposes, it doesn't matter which database you choose in this step.

4. **Expand the Programmability folder under the database folder.**

5. **Expand the Functions folder.**

6. **Expand the System Functions folder.**

   You see a series of category folders used to organize the SQL Server built-in functions.

7. **Expand the category folder of your choice.**

   A list of the built-in functions appears within the category that you selected.

8. **Expand the function folder of your choice.**

   Select a function that interests you and expand its folder.

9. **Using the mouse, hover over the name of the function.**

   SQL Server displays a pop-up window that offers a brief description of the function's purpose.

10. **Click the Parameters folder.**

    When you click the Parameters folder, the SSMS Object Explorer window provides information about the function's parameters, including the parameter names and types.

Figure 11-1 shows SSMS displaying the explanatory pop-up window and parameters for the Datediff() function.

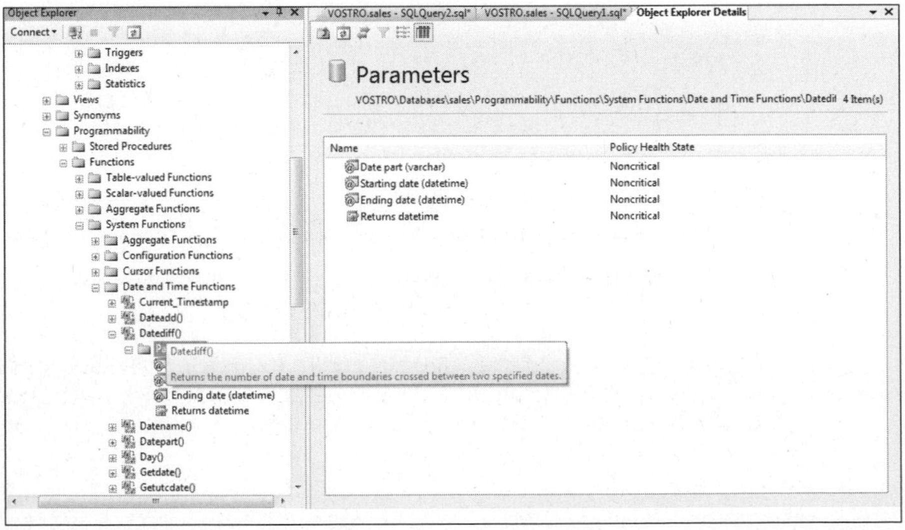

Figure 11-1:
Exploring SQL Server's built-in functions.

Creating Your Own Functions

Although SQL Server's built-in functions are powerful and useful, they're not always sufficient to meet your customized needs. Fortunately, SQL Server allows you to create your own user-defined functions using the CREATE FUNCTION command.

The structure of the CREATE FUNCTION statement is as follows:

```
CREATE FUNCTION <owner>.<function_name> (<parameters>)
RETURNS <type>
AS
BEGIN
          <SQL code>
END
```

The following list describes the user-defined elements in this statement.

- ✔ *owner* is the SQL Server account that owns the function. In many cases, this will be the database owner (dbo) account.

- ✔ *function_name* is the name you select for your function.

- ✔ *parameters* consist of zero, one, or more input parameters that must be supplied when the function is executed. You provide them in the form @parameter_name datatype, and you separate multiple parameters with commas.

- ✔ *type* is the datatype of the function's output value.

- ✔ *SQL code* is the "meat" of the function, where you perform whatever actions are necessary to create the output value. Here are some tips:

  - • Separate multiple SQL statements by ending each one with a semicolon.

  - • Create working variables (used within the function or returned as output) using the DECLARE <variable_name> <datatype> SQL statement.

  - • Set variable values using the SET <variable_name> = <value> SQL statement.

  - • When finished, provide the return value using the RETURN(<value>) SQL command.

Suppose you wanted to create a function for use in your business that takes a wholesale price as input and computes the sales price based upon two business rules:

✔ All wholesale prices are marked up 20 percent to cover the business' operating expenses and profit margin.

✔ The business is required to collect 6.5 percent sales tax on all purchases.

You could create a function called `GetSalesPrice` to perform this computation for you, as follows:

```
CREATE FUNCTION dbo.GetSalesPrice (@wholesale_price smallmoney)
RETURNS smallmoney
AS
BEGIN
  -- Declare a temporary value to hold our sales price
    DECLARE @salesprice smallmoney;

  -- Add on a 20% markup to the wholesale price
    SET @salesprice = @wholesale_price + @wholesale_price * 0.2;

  -- Add on 6.5% sales tax
    SET @salesprice = @salesprice + @salesprice * .065;

    RETURN (@salesprice);
END;
```

You should be able to correlate each part of the preceding CREATE FUNCTION statement with the general syntax I provide earlier in this section.

After you create the `GetSalesPrice` function, you can call it from within any other SQL statement. Here's a simple example in which I ask SQL Server to tell me the sales price corresponding to a wholesale price of $1:

```
SELECT dbo.GetSalesPrice(1.00) AS 'Sales Price'
```

SQL Server responds with the new value, including the 20 percent markup and 6.5 percent sales tax:

```
Sales Price
--------------------
1.278

(1 row(s) affected)
```

You can also use the function within the context of a more complicated statement. Suppose you wanted to retrieve the wholesale and selling price for each item in your database. You could use this statement:

Comments

Note that in the preceding statement, I do introduce one new item, however: the SQL comment. You use a comment when you want to add some explanatory text so that people can understand the purpose of each SQL statement in the function, but you don't want SQL Server to think that it's part of the function itself.

Comments are a critical part of any type of programming, whether you're using SQL or any other programming language. They allow you to leave notes within your code explaining how it works so that when another person comes across your work, he or she can easily interpret your syntax. In fact, I've found myself grateful that I left comments in my own SQL statements when I've needed to look back at them years later!

You can make an entire line a comment by beginning the line with two dashes (−−) or comment out multiple lines of the statement by inserting a line with the text /* before the first line and ending it with a last line of */. This comment syntax works in any SQL statement, not just function definitions.

```
SELECT item, warehouse, wholesale_price, dbo.
          GetSalesPrice(wholesale_price) AS 'sales price'
FROM stock
```

which provides the output

```
item              warehouse         wholesale_price        sales price
---------------   ---------------   --------------------   --------------------
Apples            New York          0.12                   0.1534
Apples            Seattle           0.13                   0.1661
Limes             Seattle           0.33                   0.4217
Oranges           New York          0.55                   0.7029
Oranges           Tampa             0.52                   0.6646
Pears             New York          0.39                   0.4984

(6 row(s) affected)
```

Reusing SQL Code with Stored Procedures

SQL Server stored procedures are precompiled bundles of SQL statements that are stored within a SQL Server database. Stored procedures may have zero, one, or more input parameters and may return a scalar value, a table, or nothing at all.

Why use stored procedures? There are two great reasons to include them in your SQL Server repertoire:

- ✔ Stored procedures offer the same code reuse benefits provided by functions.

- ✔ Stored procedures allow you to enhance the security of your database. You may grant users permission to execute a stored procedure (which in turn inserts, updates, retrieves, or removes data from your tables) without granting them full access to the underlying table.

At this point, you may be asking yourself, "Gee, stored procedures sure sound a lot like functions. What's the difference?" There are actually two significant differences between stored procedures and functions:

- ✔ Functions must always return a value to the caller. Stored procedures do not have this requirement. They may simply execute and complete silently.

- ✔ You commonly use functions within another expression, whereas you often use stored procedures independently.

As I do with functions earlier in this chapter, in this section I first explain the system stored procedures included with SQL Server 2008 and then cover how you can create your own stored procedures.

Saving time with system stored procedures

SQL Server offers dozens of built-in system stored procedures. Most of these allow you to obtain or modify information about SQL Server or your database. One very helpful system stored procedure is sp_helptext, which retrieves the SQL statement associated with a function, stored procedure, trigger, CHECK constraint, or database view (among other SQL Server objects). This ability to retrieve a statement is very useful when you want to verify or modify the functionality of one of these objects.

You can execute a system stored procedure (or any stored procedure, for that matter) using the EXEC command. If you wanted to use sp_helptext to retrieve the text of the GetSalesPrice function I describe earlier in the chapter, you would use the following SQL statement:

```
EXEC sp_helptext GetSalesPrice
```

SQL Server then provides the statement used to create the function. SQL Server will include comments and formatting, as shown in the following code:

```
Text
-------------------------------------------------------------------------
CREATE FUNCTION dbo.GetSalesPrice (@wholesale_price smallmoney)
RETURNS smallmoney
AS
BEGIN
-- Declare a temporary value to hold our sales price
          DECLARE @salesprice smallmoney;

-- Add on a 20% markup to the wholesale price
          SET @salesprice = @wholesale_price + @wholesale_price * 0.2;

-- Add on 6.5% sales tax
          SET @salesprice = @salesprice + @salesprice * .065;

          RETURN (@salesprice);
END;
```

Notice that SQL Server provides the text of the function in CREATE FUNCTION format. You could recreate this function by simply cutting and pasting the text into SSMS and executing it. Similarly, you could change the words CREATE FUNCTION to ALTER FUNCTION and use this SQL statement to modify the function's behavior. (I discuss ALTER FUNCTION more at the end of this chapter.)

You can obtain information about system stored procedures using the same process I describe in the "Obtaining a list of built-in functions" section of this chapter. However, rather than expand the Functions and System Functions folders, you expand the Stored Procedures and System Stored Procedures folders.

Writing your own stored procedures

It's very likely that at some point in your SQL Server career, you'll want to create your own stored procedure. I do this constantly and I encourage you to embrace the reusability and security benefits of stored procedures in your own databases.

Creating your stored procedures

You can create stored procedures using a syntax very similar to that used to create a function. Simply change the CREATE FUNCTION statement to CREATE PROCEDURE. You don't need to include the RETURNS clause if your stored procedure has no output.

Suppose you wanted to write a stored procedure that removes an item from your inventory. Specifically, you want to

✔ Delete the item from the stock table.

✔ Send an e-mail to the supervisor alerting him or her of the change.

You can accomplish these tasks with the following stored procedure:

```
CREATE PROCEDURE dbo.RemoveProduct(@item varchar(16), @warehouse varchar(16))
AS
BEGIN
-- Delete the item from the stock table
   DELETE
   FROM stock
   WHERE item = @item AND warehouse = @warehouse;

-- Send an e-mail to the supervisor
   EXEC msdb.dbo.sp_send_dbmail
     @profile_name = 'Inventory Mail',
     @recipients = 'supervisor@foo.com',
     @body = 'Stored procedure RemoveProduct altered the inventory.',
     @subject = 'Inventory Deleted' ;
END
```

Executing your stored procedures

after you create the stored procedure, you execute it using the same syntax used for a system stored procedure, except that you must also include the name of the stored procedure's owner (dbo, in this case):

```
EXEC dbo.RemoveProduct 'Pears', 'New York'
```

My stored procedure doesn't include any return value, so the output is quite simple:

```
(1 row(s) affected)
Mail queued.
```

The "1 row(s) affected" statement is the result of the DELETE SQL statement, and the "Mail queued" statement is the result of sending the message to the supervisor.

Notice that I'm calling a system stored procedure (msdb.dbo.sp_send_dbmail()) from within my own stored procedure. Calling one stored procedure from within another is known as "nesting" stored procedures, and it's perfectly acceptable.

SQL Server allows you to have up to 32 levels of nesting.

The send_dbmail() stored procedure uses SQL Server's Database Mail functionality, which I discuss in Chapter 2.

TECHNICAL STUFF

Performing complex database interactions with SQLCLR technology

Functions and stored procedures provide a sophisticated way to hide the complexity of your SQL statements and improve security. However, they're not always the best way to achieve your goal. If you need to perform very complex operations, you can improve their performance by using Microsoft's SQL Common Language Runtime (SQLCLR).

SQLCLR allows programmers to use advanced programming languages to create SQL Server objects, including:

✔ User-defined functions

✔ Stored procedures

✔ Triggers

✔ User-defined types

✔ Aggregates

You can use any of the following Microsoft .NET programming languages with SQLCLR:

✔ Microsoft Visual Basic

✔ Microsoft Visual C++

✔ Microsoft Visual C#

Creating SQLCLR objects requires programming skills in one of these languages and is beyond the scope of this book.

Updating Data Automatically with Triggers

Triggers are actions that take place when a series of conditions are met. You see them in everyday life all the time. Consider the dreaded Internal Revenue Service (IRS). It depends on a complex series of triggers to help it in collecting taxes and keeping us honest. Here are some examples:

✔ When it receives a W-2 from an employer stating your annual wages, it checks to make sure that you reported that income on your 1040 form. If you didn't, the IRS sends you a notice that you must correct your taxes.

✔ When you claim a dependent on your tax return, the IRS checks the Social Security number of that dependent against other forms in its database to ensure that only one taxpayer claims each dependent. If it detects duplication, it opens an investigation.

✔ When you file a form with itemized deductions, it compares your deductions to those of similar taxpayers and flags your return for an audit if your deductions seem excessive.

Each of these triggers consists of a condition ("if there is duplication of SSNs") and an action ("open an investigation"). SQL Server provides similar functionality for database users, allowing you to automatically take specified actions when certain conditions are met.

Creating a trigger

SQL Server triggers consist of four major components:

- ✔ Trigger name
- ✔ Trigger scope (the database, server, table, or view affected by the trigger)
- ✔ Trigger timing (determining whether the trigger should fire after [using the AFTER function] or instead of [using the INSTEAD OF function] the triggering action)
- ✔ Trigger condition (the conditions that cause the trigger to fire)
- ✔ Trigger action (the action SQL Server should take when the trigger condition is met)

The basic syntax used for creating a trigger is as follows:

```
CREATE TRIGGER <trigger_name>
ON <scope>
<trigger timing> <trigger condition>
AS
BEGIN
<trigger action>
END
```

Suppose you wanted to create a trigger that automatically notifies the supervisor whenever anyone changes your stock table. You would want this trigger to fire whenever an INSERT or UPDATE statement occurs on the table. Here's the way to make that happen:

```
CREATE TRIGGER inventory_minimum
ON stock
AFTER INSERT, UPDATE
AS
BEGIN
    EXEC msdb.dbo.sp_send_dbmail
    @profile_name = 'Inventory Mail',
    @recipients = 'supervisor@foo.com',
    @body = 'Someone changed the inventory.',
    @subject = 'Change Notification' ;
END
```

After you create the trigger, SQL Server automatically monitors the database every time an INSERT or UPDATE statement modifies the stock table.

Disabling a trigger

You may want to temporarily disable a trigger in certain circumstances using the DISABLE TRIGGER statement. For example, if you plan to make numerous changes to your inventory and don't want to clutter your e-mail with notifications from the inventory_minimum trigger, you can disable it with the following statement:

```
DISABLE TRIGGER inventory_minimum
ON stock
```

Re-enabling the trigger uses a similar statement:

```
ENABLE TRIGGER inventory_minimumON stock
```

Modifying and Deleting Functions, Stored Procedures, and Triggers

Throughout this chapter, I show you how to create programmable SQL Server objects: functions, stored procedures, and triggers. It's also sometimes necessary to change or remove those objects after you create them. The syntax for doing this is very similar for all three types of programmable objects.

Modifying objects

If you want to modify a function, stored procedure, or trigger, simply write a CREATE statement that contains the modified SQL and change the keyword CREATE to ALTER.

For example, to modify the GetSalesPrice stored procedure to charge a higher markup of 25 percent, use this SQL statement:

```
ALTER FUNCTION dbo.GetSalesPrice (@wholesale_price smallmoney)
RETURNS smallmoney
AS
BEGIN
  -- Declare a temporary value to hold our sales price
    DECLARE @salesprice smallmoney;
```

```
-- Add on a 20% markup to the wholesale price
   SET @salesprice = @wholesale_price + @wholesale_price * 0.25;

-- Add on 6.5% sales tax
   SET @salesprice = @salesprice + @salesprice * .065;


   RETURN (@salesprice);
END;
```

The `sp_helptext` command described earlier in this chapter comes in quite handy when you need to modify a function, stored procedure, or trigger. You can use `sp_helptext` to retrieve the CREATE command used to create the object and simply change the keyword CREATE to ALTER, modify the logic, and execute the statement to update your database.

Deleting objects

Deleting programmable objects is simple. Use one of the following DROP commands:

```
DROP FUNCTION <function_name>
```

```
DROP PROCEDURE <procedure_name>
```

```
DROP TRIGGER <trigger_name>
```

For example, you could delete the GetSalesPrice function using the following SQL statement:

```
DROP FUNCTION GetSalesPrice;
```

Part V

SQL Server Administration

The 5th Wave   By Rich Tennant

"Maybe your keyword search, 'legal secretary, love, fame, fortune,' needs to be refined."

In this part . . .

If you're responsible for administering SQL Server databases, this part is especially for you. Here you discover a variety of tips and tricks to help you keep your database operating at its best by tuning performance parameters and governing the best use of resources. You'll also find advice on using SQL Server's administration tools to make the server do the routine work for you.

The final chapters in this part are dedicated to helping you troubleshoot SQL Server problems and administer multiple servers in the same environment.

Chapter 12

Keeping Your SQL Server Running Smoothly

*A*ny complex mechanism you deal with requires some type of routine maintenance. You probably bring your car in for service every 3,000 miles to verify that it's functioning properly. You may have an air conditioning specialist perform preventive maintenance on your HVAC system before the warm summer months arrive. SQL Server databases also require maintenance to stay in tip-top shape and deliver optimal performance.

In this chapter, I describe a number of ways you can improve the performance of your SQL Server databases. I begin by discussing the use of indexes and partitioning to speed up database queries. Then I show you how you can optimize disk utilization by automatically or manually shrinking files. Finally, I give you some advice on verifying the integrity of your database and placing limits on the use of resources by individual users.

Indexing Data to Improve Query Performance

Here's a challenge for you: Pick up this book and identify every page that contains information about SQL Server's use of transactions. You have two basic options for meeting my challenge:

✔ Read every page in the book and report each page that contains a reference to transactions.

✔ Turn to the index in the back of the book and look up "transactions."

Obviously, it's a whole lot faster to consult the index. If I didn't include one in this book, you would have much more trouble quickly finding information on a particular topic. It's obviously a good idea for my publisher to hire a specialist to create an index that allows you easy access to the information you need.

SQL Server databases use indexes for a similar purpose. When you want to retrieve data from a database, SQL Server could check every single row to see if it matches your query, but that would be horribly inefficient. Instead, SQL Server builds and maintains indexes that allow it to quickly locate commonly used fields.

The catch is that building and maintaining indexes requires both computing time (to develop the index) and space (to store the index). You need to decide what indexes are appropriate for your database based upon the types of queries that you perform.

SQL Server allows you to create indexes on single or multiple columns. Generally speaking, an index will speed up query performance for queries based upon the column(s) in the index.

Using clustered indexes

Each database can (and should!) have only one *clustered index,* which is an index that defines how SQL Server sorts the data stored in the table. The data in the table may be sorted in only one way, hence the reason that having two clustered indexes on the same table isn't possible.

In almost all cases, the best clustered index for a table is the table's primary key. This isn't always true, but the rule is general enough that you can rely upon it. The good news is that SQL Server automatically creates an index when you define a primary key for a table and, by default, makes that index a clustered index. SQL Server does all the work for you!

Creating nonclustered indexes

You can create your own nonclustered indexes to improve the performance of queries against your SQL Server databases. Nonclustered indexes are similar to the index in the back of this book: They allow SQL Server to quickly locate information, but they don't change the sort order of data stored in a table.

The only decision you need to make when creating an index for a table is the column(s) you want to include in that index. If you're just getting started with indexes, it's generally best to stick to single-column indexes. However, you can gain some performance benefits by creating indexes that include multiple columns when those columns are found together in frequently executed queries.

Some excellent candidates for indexes are columns that are

- ✔ Commonly used in the WHERE or HAVING clauses of queries
- ✔ Frequently used for GROUP BY query results
- ✔ Used to sort results in an ORDER BY clause
- ✔ Used to reference another table as a foreign key
- ✔ Used to specify JOIN conditions

Follow these steps to create a nonclustered index in SQL Server, using SQL Server Management Studio:

1. **Start SQL Server Management Studio and connect to your SQL Server instance.**

2. **Click the plus (+) icon to the left of the Databases folder to expand it.**

   You see the contents of the folder: a subfolder for each database on the SQL Server instance.

3. **Click the plus (+) icon to the left of the database where you would like to create an index.**

   The subfolders for that database appear, containing groupings of database information.

4. **Click the plus (+) icon to the left of the Tables folder to expand it.**

   A list of database tables appears.

5. **Click the plus (+) icon to expand the folder corresponding to the table upon which you would like to create an index.**

   SQL Server presents a series of subfolders containing information about the table.

6. **Right-click the Indexes folder and then select New Index from the pop-up menu that appears.**

   You see the New Index dialog box, as shown in Figure 12-1.

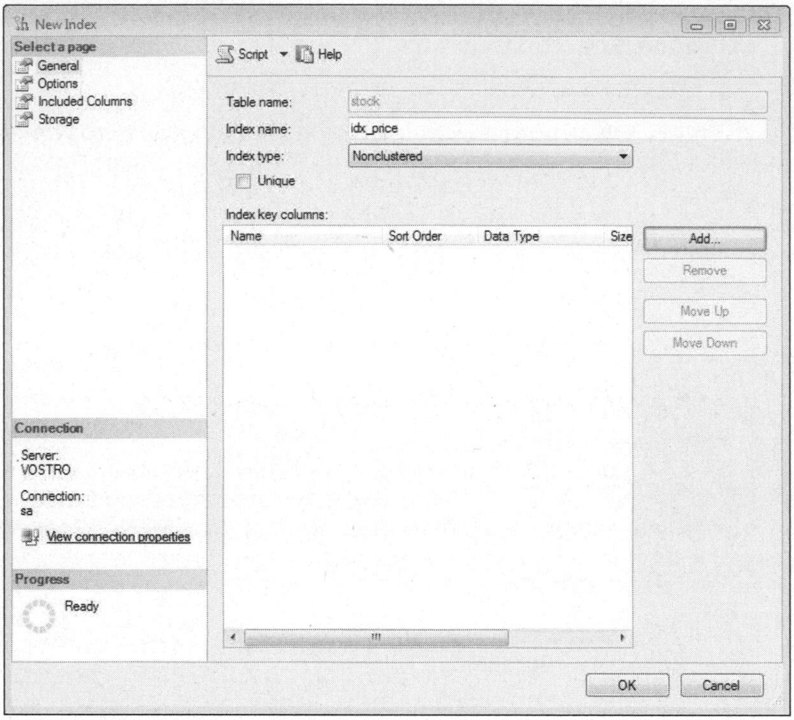

Figure 12-1:
Creating a
new non-
clustered
index.

7. **Type a name for your index in the Index Name text box and then click the Add button.**

The Select Columns dialog box appears, as shown in Figure 12-2.

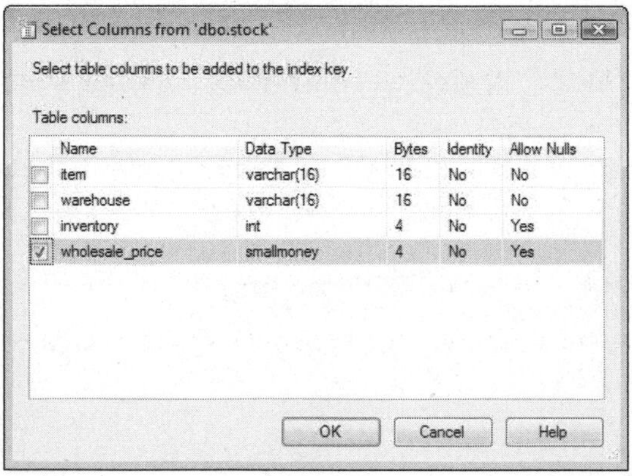

Figure 12-2:
Selecting
columns for
the nonclus-
tered index.

8. **Select the box(es) next to the column(s) you want to include in your nonclustered index.**

9. **Click OK to close the Select Columns window.**

10. **Click OK to close the New Index window and create your index.**

    SQL Server creates your index, which may take a considerable amount of time, depending upon the size of your table. When the index creation completes, you see the new index in SSMS Object Explorer. If it doesn't appear automatically, right-click the Indexes folder and choose Refresh from the pop-up menu.

Optimizing index performance

Over time, changes to indexes may cause them to become fragmented, which means they're not using disk space in an optimal fashion. You should periodically check the fragmentation level of your database indexes and reorganize or rebuild those indexes when the fragmentation reaches an unacceptable level.

Microsoft recommends reorganizing an index when the total fragmentation is between 5 and 30 percent, and rebuilding it if the total fragmentation is more than 30 percent. You don't need to worry about fragmentation levels below 5 percent because they have negligible impact on the performance of your database.

Here's how to check the fragmentation level of an index using SQL Server Management Studio:

1. **Open SSMS and navigate to the Indexes folder of the database and table in question.**

2. **Right-click the index and choose Reorganize or Rebuild, as appropriate.**

    You see a window similar to the one shown in Figure 12-3. Note the Total Fragmentation column, which indicates the current level of fragmentation in the index.

3. **Click OK to reorganize (or rebuild) the index.**

    This process may take hours if the index is large or complex.

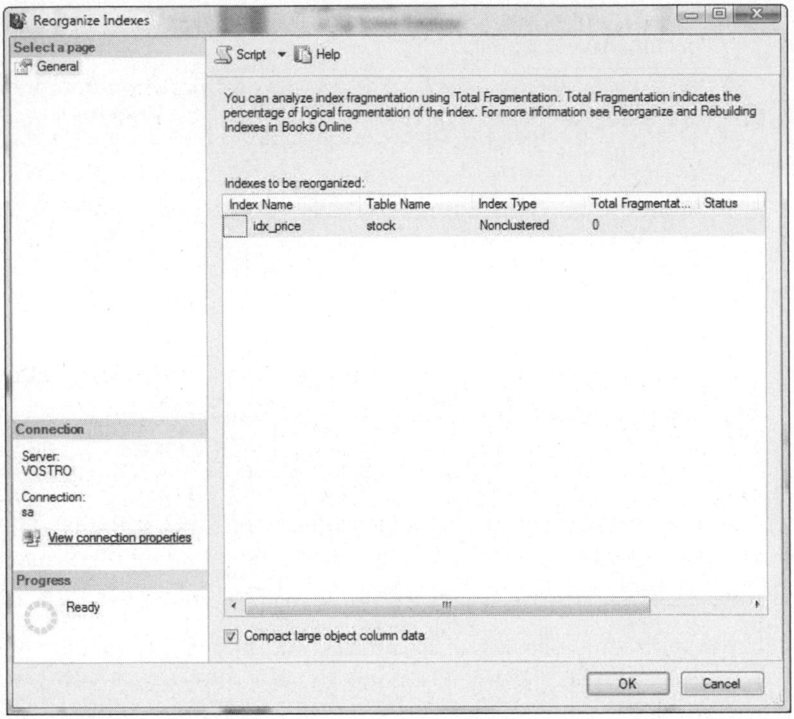

Figure 12-3:
Rebuilding/
reorganizing
an index.

Improving Performance with Partitions

In Chapter 5, I tell you how SQL Server allows you to create filegroups that you can use to separate tables for performance optimization. Partitions let you to go a step further and distribute the contents of individual tables or indexes on separate *filegroups,* which are collections of related files. One way to efficiently manage large databases is by placing parts that change frequently (volatile data) on one filegroup and parts that change infrequently (nonvolatile data) on another filegroup.

To create a partition, you first need to define the partition function, which describes how SQL Server should separate the data. Next, you must create a partition scheme that defines how SQL Server will place the partitions on filegroups. Finally, you create the table or index and specify the appropriate partition scheme.

Creating a partition function

The first step in partitioning a table is to write a partition function describing how you want SQL Server to partition your data. You create a partition function using the following Transact-SQL syntax:

```
CREATE PARTITION FUNCTION partition_function_name ( input_parameter_type )
AS RANGE [ LEFT | RIGHT ]
FOR VALUES ( [ boundary_value [ ,...n ] ] )
```

in which:

- ✔ *partition_function_name* is the name you want to assign to the function.

- ✔ *input_parameter_type* is the data type you will partition on. It may be any data type other than `text`, `ntext`, `image`, `xml`, `timestamp`, `varchar(max)`, `nvarchar(max)` and `varbinary(max)`.

- ✔ The `RANGE` statement specifies either the `LEFT` or `RIGHT` keyword, indicating the "side" into which each boundary condition should fall.

- ✔ *boundary_value* is a series of values of type *input_parameter_type* that identify the partition boundaries.

Here's an example to help clarify. Suppose you administer a school database that holds a table containing records on all graduates. One logical way to partition that table would be to base it upon year of graduation. Doing so would place recent graduates on one partition and older graduates on a series of other partitions. You might want to break the table up as shown in Table 12-1.

Table 12-1	Partitions for an Alumni Table Using **RANGE RIGHT**
Partition Number	*Years of Graduation*
1	earlier than 1960
2	1960–1969
3	1970–1979
4	1980–1989
5	1990–1999
6	2000 and later

You can create a partition function (I call it `alumni_partfunct`) using the following Transact-SQL:

```
CREATE PARTITION FUNCTION alumni_partfunct (int)
AS RANGE RIGHT
FOR VALUES (1960, 1970, 1980, 1990, 2000)
```

Note that the values clause specifies the "boundary" years that correspond to the partition boundaries specified in Table 12-1. The RANGE RIGHT clause indicates that SQL Server should include values that fall on the boundary itself in the partition on the "right" side. Alternatively, if I had used RANGE LEFT, the partitions would have been slightly different, as shown in Table 12-2.

Table 12-2	Partitions for an Alumni Table Using RANGE LEFT
Partition Number	**Years of Graduation**
1	1960 and earlier
2	1961–1970
3	1971–1980
4	1981–1990
5	1991–2000
6	2001 and later

Creating a partition scheme

When you create a partition function, it merely describes a way that you might separate data into hypothetical partitions. It does not, however, define the specific filegroups that will store the partitions. That's where a partition scheme comes into play.

You create a partition scheme using the CREATE PARTITION SCHEME command with the following syntax:

```
CREATE PARTITION SCHEME partition_scheme_name
AS PARTITION partition_function_name
[ ALL ] TO ( { file_group_names | [ PRIMARY ] })
```

The elements of this command are as follows:

- ✔ *partition_scheme_name* is the name you want to assign to the partition scheme.

- ✔ *partition_function_name* is the name of a partition function (see the previous section) that defines your partition boundary conditions.

- ✔ *file_group_names* is a comma-delimited list of filegroup(s) on which you wish to store the partitions. Alternatively, you may use the ALL keyword and specify a single filegroup name to place all partitions on the same group. You may also use the PRIMARY keyword in place of a filegroup name to specify that you wish to place the partitions on the primary filegroup.

Before creating a partition scheme, you need to create the filegroups. If you aren't familiar with the filegroup creation process, you can read about it in Chapter 5.

Continuing the alumni example that I use to create a partition function in the previous section, here I create a partition scheme named `alumni_partscheme` that specifies six different file groups (which I creatively named `filegroup1` through `filegroup6`) for the data. Here's the Transact-SQL:

```
CREATE PARTITION SCHEME alumni_partscheme
AS PARTITION alumni_partfunct
TO (filegroup1, filegroup2, filegroup3, filegroup4,
        filegroup5, filegroup6)
```

Creating a partitioned table

In the previous two sections, I show you how to create a partition function specifying how to divide data into partitions and to create a partition scheme describing how to store the partitions on different filegroups. However, you still haven't actually partitioned any data!

Actually, after you've created the partition function and partition scheme, partitioning a table is easy. You simply add the following clause to your `CREATE TABLE` statement:

```
ON { partition_scheme_name ( partition_column_name )
```

In this clause, the *partition_scheme_name* is the name of a partition scheme you created earlier (if you followed along in the previous section of this chapter). Your partition scheme already links to a specific partition function, (remember, you specified it in the AS PARTITION clause), so you don't need to include it in the CREATE TABLE statement.

You also need to specify the *partition_column_name,* that is, the column that contains the values referenced by the partition function. For example, you could create a simple alumni table using the partition function and scheme I build in the previous sections with the following CREATE TABLE statement:

```
CREATE TABLE alumni (FirstName nvarchar(40), LastName
        nvarchar(40), GraduationYear int)
ON alumni_partscheme (GraduationYear)
```

For more information on the CREATE TABLE statement, see Chapter 5.

I mention earlier in this chapter that you can also partition an index. The process for creating a partitioned index is exactly the same as that for creating a partitioned table. Add an ON clause to the CREATE INDEX statement specifying the partition scheme and partition column.

Updating Database Statistics

SQL Server uses a query optimizer to determine the most efficient execution plan for database queries. This powerful tool works behind the scenes to improve the performance of your database. You may choose to either let SQL Server automatically update statistics or you can update them manually.

Automatically updating statistics

In most cases, letting SQL Server automatically create and update database statistics is fine. This is the default behavior of SQL Server. If you've already disabled it on your database, you may reenable the automatic creation and updating of statistics by executing the following Transact-SQL statements in SSMS:

```
ALTER DATABASE database_name
SET AUTO_CREATE_STATISTICS ON;
```

```
ALTER DATABASE database_name
SET AUTO_UPDATE_STATISTICS ON;
```

Also, you may verify the current status of automatic statistics creation or updating for a table by executing the following stored procedure in SSMS (see Chapter 3 for more about SSMS):

```
sp_autostats 'table_name'
```

Manually updating statistics

If you're not using automatic statistics updating, you may periodically update statistics for a table manually using the following Transact-SQL statement:

```
UPDATE STATISTICS table_name
```

To view the statistics used by the query optimizer, you can access them using the DBCC SHOW_STATISTICS command. This command takes two parameters: the name of the table or view and the name of the statistics "target" — that is, the index name, statistics name, or column name.

For example, to view information about the PK_stock primary key index on a hypothetical stock table, you use the following Transact-SQL statement:

```
DBCC SHOW_STATISTICS ('stock', PK_stock)
```

There's much more to the creation and updating of statistics than I can discuss within the limited scope of this chapter. If you're really trying to eke out that last bit of performance from SQL Server, you may want to explore this subject in further detail.

Managing File Sizes

As with any other data file, SQL Server database files consume space on your disk that could be used for other purposes. By default, SQL Server will "grow" database files as you add data to them to ensure that you don't run out of space. However, SQL Server does not have a corresponding default shrinking action to reduce the amount of unused space consumed by database files.

In most cases, this behavior is fine; databases tend to grow over time as you add more and more data. However, if you remove a large quantity of data from a database, you may wind up unintentionally "hogging" a large amount of disk space that you're not actually using to store data. SQL Server allows you to reclaim this unused space by automatically or manually shrinking your database files.

Automatically shrinking database files

You can have SQL Server can automatically shrink the files associated with a database by using the following Transact-SQL statement:

```
ALTER DATABASE database_name
SET AUTO_SHRINK ON
```

After you set this option, SQL Server periodically checks the database files to determine whether they contain excess free space. If they do, it begins a background process to shrink the database's files.

Automatically shrinking database files may have a significant negative impact on database performance, especially if the size of your database files tends to fluctuate on a regular basis. I generally don't recommend using the AUTO_SHRINK option unless you have a unique situation that requires it.

If you're not sure whether a database is set to automatically shrink, you can check it by issuing the following Transact-SQL statement:

```
SELECT DATABASEPROPERTYEX('database_name',
         'IsAutoShrink');
```

This statement returns a value of 1 if the database is configured to automatically shrink and a value of 0 otherwise.

Manually shrinking a single database file

If you want to manually shrink a single database file that contains a large amount of unused space (perhaps after you've deleted a large amount of data from the database), you may use the following Transact-SQL command:

```
DBCC SHRINKFILE (file_name, target_size)
```

in which *file_name* is the name of the file you want to shrink and *target_size* is the desired size (in megabytes) after the shrinking operation.

For example, to shrink the file dbfile to a size of 10MB, you use the following statement:

```
DBCC SHRINKFILE (dbfile, 10)
```

Manually shrinking all files associated with a database

SQL Server also allows you to shrink all the data and log files associated with a single database. You can do this using the DBCC SHRINKDATABASE command, as follows:

```
DBCC SHRINKDATABASE ('database_name', target_percent)
```

in which *database_name* is the name of the database and *target_percent* is the amount of free space that you'd like to leave in the file for future use.

Many people confuse the *target_percent* parameter with the percent of the database that you want to shrink. If you specify a *target_percent* of 10, you're stating that you want 10 percent free space remaining in the database file after the shrinking completes. You are *not* saying that you want to shrink the database by 10 percent.

For example, if you wanted to shrink all files in the sales database so that they had 10 percent free space, you would use the following Transact-SQL command:

```
DBCC SHRINKDATABASE ('sales', 10)
```

You should note an important difference between the SHRINKFILE and SHRINKDATABASE commands. SHRINKDATABASE never shrinks a file below its original size (when you created it). If you need to shrink a file below its original size, you must use the SHRINKFILE command.

Checking Database Integrity

Databases are complex structures and, as with any complex information system, can become corrupt over time. As a database administrator, you should periodically check the integrity of your database using the DBCC CHECKDB command.

Running DBCC CHECKDB

If you simply execute the Transact-SQL statement DBCC CHECKDB, SQL Server checks the integrity of the current database. Otherwise, you can specify the name of a database using the following format:

```
DBCC CHECKDB ('database_name')
```

For example, to check the integrity of the sales database, issue the following command:

```
DBCC CHECKDB ('sales')
```

Completing the execution of this command can take quite a long time, even as long as several hours, depending upon the size of your database and its structural complexity. Therefore, you should always plan to run a consistency check during periods of low demand.

If your database is so large that you can't reasonably run DBCC CHECKDB without negatively impacting performance, you might want to consider other options. DBCC CHECKDB actually executes a number of other DBCC commands behind the scenes. Among other activities, it

 ✔ Checks the database disk structure integrity using the DBCC CHECKALLOC command.

 ✔ Checks the consistency of each table and view individually using the DBCC CHECKTABLE command.

 ✔ Checks the database catalog consistency using the DBCC CHECKCATALOG command.

If you need to minimize disruptions, you can create your own integrity verification schedule by using the commands in the list above. Simply run each one at different times to consume resources in a more manageable fashion.

Here's an example of DBCC CHECKDB output from a database table named sales:

```
DBCC results for 'sales'.
Service Broker Msg 9675, State 1: Message Types analyzed: 14.
Service Broker Msg 9676, State 1: Service Contracts analyzed: 6.
Service Broker Msg 9667, State 1: Services analyzed: 3.
Service Broker Msg 9668, State 1: Service Queues analyzed: 3.
Service Broker Msg 9669, State 1: Conversation Endpoints analyzed: 0.
Service Broker Msg 9674, State 1: Conversation Groups analyzed: 0.
Service Broker Msg 9670, State 1: Remote Service Bindings analyzed: 0.
DBCC results for 'sys.sysrscols'.
There are 567 rows in 6 pages for object "sys.sysrscols".
DBCC results for 'sys.sysrowsets'.
There are 81 rows in 1 pages for object "sys.sysrowsets".
DBCC results for 'sysallocunits'.
There are 92 rows in 1 pages for object "sysallocunits".
DBCC results for 'sys.sysfiles1'.
There are 2 rows in 1 pages for object "sys.sysfiles1".
DBCC results for 'sys.sysfgfrag'.
There are 2 rows in 1 pages for object "sys.sysfgfrag".
DBCC results for 'sys.sysphfg'.
There are 1 rows in 1 pages for object "sys.sysphfg".
DBCC results for 'sys.sysprufiles'.
There are 2 rows in 1 pages for object "sys.sysprufiles".
DBCC results for 'stock'.
There are 4 rows in 1 pages for object "stock".
DBCC results for 'sys.queue_messages_1977058079'.
There are 0 rows in 0 pages for object "sys.queue_messages_1977058079".
DBCC results for 'sys.queue_messages_2009058193'.
There are 0 rows in 0 pages for object "sys.queue_messages_2009058193".
DBCC results for 'sys.queue_messages_2041058307'.
There are 0 rows in 0 pages for object "sys.queue_messages_2041058307".
CHECKDB found 0 allocation errors and 0 consistency errors in database 'sales'.
DBCC execution completed. If DBCC printed error messages, contact your system
                    administrator.
```

I have to omit part of the results. Even for a simple database, the full results would consume a good part of this chapter!

The key is to look at the second-to-last line of the output, where SQL Server reports the results of the integrity check. My example contains neither allocation errors nor consistency errors. This is the sign of a perfectly healthy database.

Correcting integrity errors

If you do detect errors, you'll want to repair them. You have three options for repairing database integrity errors:

✔ **Use the `REPAIR_REBUILD` option.** This options performs nonrisky repairs to your database that don't jeopardize your data. For example, to use this option on a database named "sales," you issue the following sequence of commands:

```
ALTER DATABASE sales SET SINGLE_USER;
DBCC CHECKDB ('sales', REPAIR_REBUILD);
ALTER DATABASE sales SET MULTI_USER;
```

Note that before running DBCC CHECKDB with a repair option, I place the database into single-user mode. Doing so prevents other users from accessing the database while SQL Server is in the middle of the repair. When the repair completed, I put the database back into standard multiuser mode.

✔ **Restore from backup.** If you have serious database integrity errors, restoring from backup is often best. In fact, this is Microsoft's recommended practice. I discuss options for creating and restoring database backups in Chapter 18.

✔ **Use the REPAIR_ALLOW_DATA_LOSS option.** This option sounds scary, and there's good reason behind the menacing name. Running DBCC with this option may correct your integrity errors, but it might destroy portions of your database in the process! As with REPAIR_ REBUILD, if you decide to use this option, you need to first put the database into single-user mode, as follows:

```
ALTER DATABASE sales SET SINGLE_USER;
DBCC CHECKDB ('sales', REPAIR_ALLOW_DATA_LOSS);
ALTER DATABASE sales SET MULTI_USER;
```

Because of the risky nature of this command, I *strongly* recommend that you back up your database immediately before executing it.

Governing Resource Consumption

SQL Server 2008 includes a new feature, Resource Governor, that allows you to limit the server resources consumed by various types of connection. For example, you can use Resource Governor to place limits on the CPU time and memory used by particular users, applications, and systems.

You should understand a little terminology before reading more about Resource Governor:

✔ **Resource pools** contain portions of the total CPU time and memory available to SQL Server.

✔ **Workload groups** are collections of similar SQL Server sessions that make use of server resources. When you create a workload group, you assign it a resource pool.

✔ **Classifier functions** help SQL Server assign new sessions to workload groups based upon connection attributes (such as the user, application, or host initiating the connection).

Each time a new session starts on a SQL Server instance, Resource Governor (if activated) uses a classifier function to analyze the connection attributes of that session and assign it to a workload group based upon those attributes. SQL Server then allows the session to use the CPU and memory resources allocated to its resource pool on a shared basis with other sessions in that workload group (or other workload groups assigned the same resource pool).

Resource Governor only classifies a session once: when it is created. If you change the classifier function, the change will only affect new sessions. Existing sessions will retain their original classification.

Microsoft will very likely add new features to Resource Governor in the near future. Be sure to check the release notes for future SQL Server 2008 service packs to identify any new capabilities.

In the remainder of this chapter, I walk you through an example of configuring Resource Governor with the goal of limiting SSMS users to a maximum of 50 percent of available CPU time and memory.

Creating resource pools

SQL Server comes with two resource pools preconfigured:

✔ The *internal* resource pool (which uses the internal workload group) handles the resource needs of SQL Server itself. There are no limitations on the use of resources within the internal pool, and you can't modify this behavior.

✔ The *default* resource pool has minimum values of 0 and maximum values of 100 for both memory and CPU time by default. You may modify these characteristics if you wish.

You can create your own user-defined resource pools using the CREATE RESOURCE POOL Transact-SQL statement, which has the following syntax:

```
CREATE RESOURCE POOL resource_pool_name
WITH ( [ MIN_CPU_PERCENT = value ]
      [ [ , ] MAX_CPU_PERCENT = value ]
      [ [ , ] MIN_MEMORY_PERCENT = value ]
      [ [ , ] MAX_MEMORY_PERCENT = value ] )
```

In this statement, *resource_pool_name* must be a unique alphanumeric name of no more than 128 characters. Each *value* should be specified as an integer between 0 and 100. The resource pool parameters are as follows:

- ✔ MIN_CPU_PERCENT indicates the guaranteed average CPU percentage for the resource pool.

  The sum of the MIN_CPU_PERCENT values for all resource pools in an instance may not exceed 100 percent.

- ✔ MAX_CPU_PERCENT provides the maximum average CPU percentage that queries assigned to this resource pool will receive when other queries compete for CPU time.

- ✔ MIN_MEMORY_PERCENT indicates the guaranteed minimum portion of memory dedicated to this resource pool.

  The sum of the MIN_MEMORY_PERCENT values for all resource pools in an instance may not exceed 100 percent.

- ✔ MAX_MEMORY_PERCENT provides the maximum amount of memory that a resource pool may use.

Recalling our example from the previous section, I wanted to use Resource Governor to limit SSMS users to 50 percent of available CPU and memory resources. You can create a resource pool named SSMS pool containing those resources with the following Transact-SQL statement:

```
CREATE RESOURCE POOL SSMSpool
WITH (MAX_CPU_PERCENT = 50,
MAX_MEMORY_PERCENT = 50)
```

If you wish to modify a resource pool, the ALTER RESOURCE POOL statement uses a similar syntax:

```
ALTER RESOURCE POOL {resource_pool_name | "default"}
WITH ( [ MIN_CPU_PERCENT = value ]
      [ [ , ] MAX_CPU_PERCENT = value ]
      [ [ , ] MIN_MEMORY_PERCENT = value ]
      [ [ , ] MAX_MEMORY_PERCENT = value ] )
```

For example, if you wished to modify the default pool so that it can only consume a maximum of 75 percent of CPU time and 25 percent of memory, you would use the following Transact-SQL statement:

```
ALTER RESOURCE POOL "default"
WITH ( MAX_CPU_PERCENT = 75,
       MAX_MEMORY_PERCENT = 25)
```

As demonstrated in the preceding example, if you want to alter the resources assigned to the default pool, you must enclose the word *default* in quotation marks.

Creating workload groups

SQL Server 2008 also comes preconfigured with two workload groups, internal and default. These workload groups use the resource pools of the same names, as I discussed in the previous section.

You can create new workload groups using the CREATE WORKLOAD GROUP statement, with the following syntax:

```
CREATE WORKLOAD GROUP workload_group_name
WITH ( [ IMPORTANCE = { LOW | MEDIUM | HIGH } ]
          [ [ , ] REQUEST_MAX_MEMORY_GRANT_PERCENT = value ]
          [ [ , ] REQUEST_MAX_CPU_TIME_SEC = value ]
          [ [ , ] REQUEST_MEMORY_GRANT_TIMEOUT_SEC = value ]
          [ [ , ] MAX_DOP = value ]
          [ [ , ] GROUP_MAX_REQUESTS = value ] )
[ USING { resource_pool_name | "default" } ]
```

The parameters to the CREATE WORKLOAD GROUP command are:

- ✔ IMPORTANCE reflects the relative importance of the workload group and may have a value of HIGH, MEDIUM or LOW. Resource Governor uses this value to allocate resources when different workload groups using the same resource pool compete for CPU time or memory.

- ✔ REQUEST_MAX_MEMORY_GRANT_PERCENT is a value between 0 and 100 specifying the maximum amount of memory that a query may take from the resource pool. This number is a percentage of the memory assigned to the pool, rather than a percentage of the total system memory.

- ✔ REQUEST_MEMORY_GRANT_TIMEOUT_SEC is the maximum amount of time (in whole seconds) that a query may wait for resources used by other queries.

- ✔ MAX_DOP is a number between 0 and 64 indicating the maximum degree of parallelism.

✔ GROUP_MAX_REQUESTS is an integer specifying the maximum number of queries that may execute simultaneously in the group.

✔ *resource_pool_name* is the name of the resource pool available to the workload group.

You can create a simple workload group for my SSMS example with a medium relative importance using the following command:

```
CREATE WORKLOAD GROUP SSMSworkload
WITH (IMPORTANCE = MEDIUM)
USING SSMSpool
```

You may modify an existing workload group using the ALTER WORKLOAD GROUP command, which has the same syntax as the CREATE WORKLOAD GROUP command.

Creating classifier functions

The classifier function is a user-defined function that assigns new sessions to workload groups based upon connection attributes. I fully describe the creation of user-defined functions in Chapter 11 but will provide an example of a classifier function in this section.

Here are a few important characteristics of classifier functions:

✔ You should create classifier functions in the master database.

✔ The classifier function should return the name of a workload group. If the classifier function does not return the name of a valid workload group, Resource Governor will assign the session to the default group.

✔ The classifier function must be schema-bound. You create a schema-bound function by including the WITH SCHEMABINDING clause in your function definition.

✔ You may only have one active classifier function at any time.

Here's a classifier function that implements the scenario I described earlier: placing all SSMS sessions in the SSMS workload group:

```
CREATE FUNCTION dbo.SSMSClassifier()
RETURNS SYSNAME
WITH SCHEMABINDING
AS
BEGIN
     DECLARE @wkldgroup SYSNAME
     IF (APP_NAME() = 'Microsoft SQL Server Management Studio')
```

```
            SET @wkldgroup = 'SSMSgroup'
      ELSE
            RETURN NULL
      RETURN @wkldgroup
END
```

Activating and deactivating Resource Governor

When you're ready to activate Resource Governor, you must first assign it a classifier function, as shown in the Transact-SQL command below:

```
ALTER RESOURCE GOVERNOR
WITH (CLASSIFIER_FUNCTION = dbo.SSMSClassifier)
```

Of course, you'll want to replace dbo.SSMSClassifier with the name of your classifier function. Finally, you need to apply your changes by instructing SQL Server to reconfigure Resource Governor with your modifications. The following Transact-SQL statement accomplishes this:

```
ALTER RESOURCE GOVERNOR RECONFIGURE
```

You must issue the RECONFIGURE command any time you make a change to the Resource Governor configuration or SQL Server won't apply your change.

If you'd like to deactivate Resource Governor on a SQL Server instance, use the following command:

```
ALTER RESOURCE GOVERNOR DISABLE
```

Chapter 13

Automating SQL Server 2008 Administration

S QL Server database administration is full of mundane, repetitive tasks such as log reviews and preventive maintenance. Fortunately, SQL Server offers techniques to alleviate much of this boring work through the use of SQL Server Agent and maintenance plans. As does any other agent, SQL Server agent acts on your behalf to assist with database maintenance and monitoring tasks.

In this chapter, you discover how to automate your database administration tasks using these tools. I show you how you can get rid of the burden of regularly implementing the techniques discussed in Chapter 12 through the power of automation.

Scheduling Tasks with SQL Server Agent

SQL Server Agent is the core of SQL Server's automation capabilities. It allows you to instruct SQL Server to perform actions on a scheduled, automated basis, alleviating you of many of the tedious demands of database administration.

In this section, I provide you with the information you need to start SQL Server Agent running on your database server, create jobs that you would like to run in an automated fashion, and schedule those jobs to occur on a periodic basis.

Starting SQL Server Agent

Before you can schedule tasks with SQL Server Agent, you need to make sure that the SQL Server Agent service is running on your database server. To do so, follow these steps:

1. **Start SQL Server Configuration Manager.**

   I discuss the process for starting SQL Server Configuration Manager in Chapter 3.

2. **Select SQL Server Services from the menu in the left pane.**

   You see the service list shown in Figure 13-1. Locate the service named SQL Server Agent (MSSQLSERVER) and examine the current service state. If it reads Running, SQL Server Agent is already running and you can continue to the next section, "Creating a SQL Server Agent job." Otherwise, you need to start SQL Server Agent.

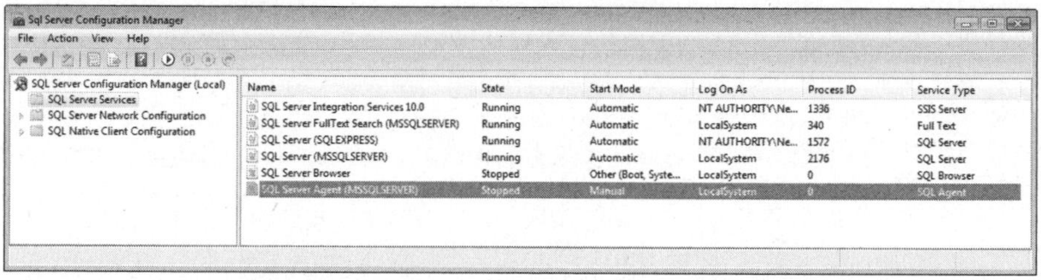

Figure 13-1:
SQL Server 2008 Service Status.

3. **Right-click SQL Server Agent and select Start from the pop-up menu.**

   SQL Server Configuration Manager starts the service, a process that may take a minute or longer to complete. While you wait, SQL Server displays the status window shown in Figure 13-2.

Following this process starts SQL Server Agent only a single time. If you want to ensure that SQL Server Agent will run every time your system starts, you need to set it to use the automatic start mode. I discuss service start modes in Chapter 3.

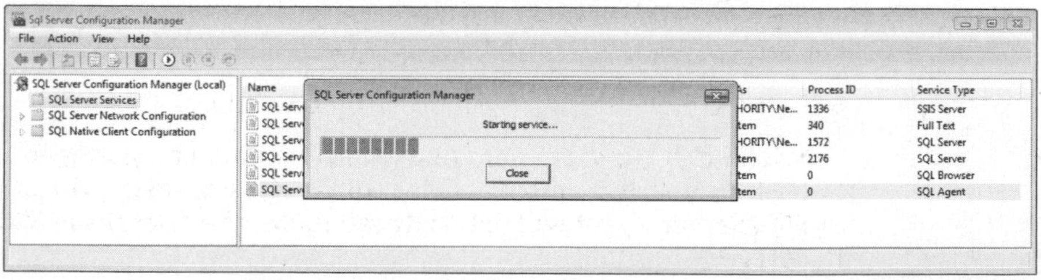

Figure 13-2:
Starting a SQL Server 2008 Service.

4. Close SQL Server Configuration Manager.

Creating a SQL Server Agent job

SQL Server Agent uses the concept of a job to group related tasks. Each job consists of a series of job steps that you may schedule to run on a periodic basis. In this section, I describe the process for creating a SQL Server Agent job. A job establishes the shell in which you may define job steps for SQL Server Agent to carry out on your behalf.

1. Connect to a SQL Server instance using SQL Server Management Studio.

2. Expand the SQL Server Agent folder in Object Explorer.

You see the options shown in Figure 13-3.

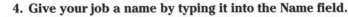

Figure 13-3:
The SQL
Server
Agent folder
in SSMS.

- SQL Server Agent
  - Jobs
  - Job Activity Monitor
  - Alerts
  - Operators
  - Proxies
  - Error Logs

3. Right-click the Jobs folder and select New Job from the start-up menu.

SSMS then presents the New Job creation window, shown in Figure 13-4.

4. Give your job a name by typing it into the Name field.

You may choose any name you like, but I recommend using a descriptive name. Doing so makes identifying the job in the future much easier.

5. Specify the job owner in the Owner text box.

You may either type in the name of the account that you want to designate as the job owner, or search for and select it by clicking the ellipses (. . .) to the right of the text box.

The owner of the job is the only account (other than members of the sysadmin role) that may modify the job after you create it. When the job runs, it does so with the same permission settings that apply to the owning account.

6. Select a job category from the drop-down list.

SQL Server provides a number of predefined categories to help you classify your jobs. Many of the administrative tasks you facilitate with SQL Server Agent will naturally fall under the "Database Maintenance" category.

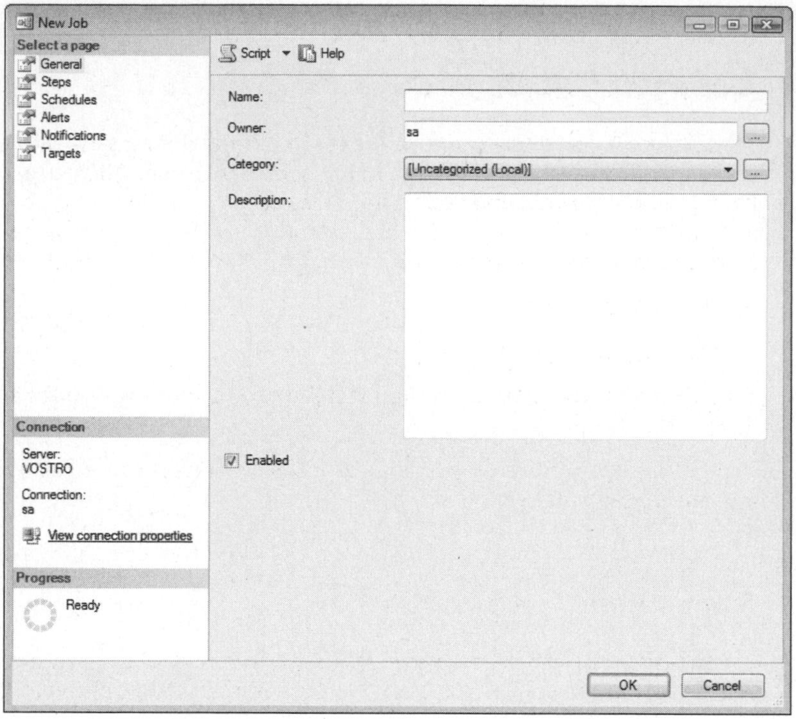

Figure 13-4:
The SSMS
New Job
creation
window.

7. **Type a plain-English description of your job in the Description textbox.**

   This textbox gives you the opportunity to record a written description of your job's purpose to help other administrators understand your job. It's also a great way to remind your future self of what you intended to do months or years ago!

8. **Ensure that the Enabled box is selected.**

   In order to run according to a schedule (I show you how to define one later in this section), you must enable the job by selecting the Enabled check box on this screen.

At this point, you've created an empty SQL Server Agent job. In the next section, I describe how you can add steps to this job, defining the actions that you want SQL Server to carry out each time the job executes. When that's complete, I show you how to schedule the job to execute on a periodic basis.

Note that the series of steps I use to create the job don't end by clicking OK to close the New Job window. You should keep this window open to add job steps in the next section.

Adding job steps to a SQL Server Agent job

SQL Server Agent allows you to create job steps defining the individual actions you would like included in the job. SQL Server 2008 supports a number of different job step types, including:

- ✔ Transact-SQL scripts
- ✔ ActiveX scripts
- ✔ Operating system (CmdExec) scripts
- ✔ Replication-related scripts (see Chapter 15 for more information on replication)
- ✔ SQL Server Integration Services (SSIS) packages (see Chapter 10 for more information on SSIS)
- ✔ SQL Server Analysis Services (SSAS) commands and queries

SSAS is beyond the scope of this book.

In the following steps, I walk you through the process of creating a single-step job designed to run the DBCC CHECKDB command, discussed in Chapter 12:

1. **Within the New Job window, click the Steps icon under Select a Page.**

   You see the blank Job Step list shown in Figure 13-5.

2. **Click the New button.**

   SQL Server presents the New Job step window, shown in Figure 13-6.

3. **Name the step by typing a descriptive name in the Step name text box.**

4. **Choose the step type from the Type drop-down list.**

   Here, I assume that you're using a Transact-SQL script step type. Other step types support advanced functionality and are beyond the scope of this book.

5. **Select a database context using the Database drop-down list.**

   Your selection here tells SQL Server which database it should execute the script against. SQL Server allows you to specify the database at the step, rather than the job, level. Specifying it at this level permits you to run scripts against multiple databases within the same job. For example, you might create a job that executes database consistency checks against several databases that you administer.

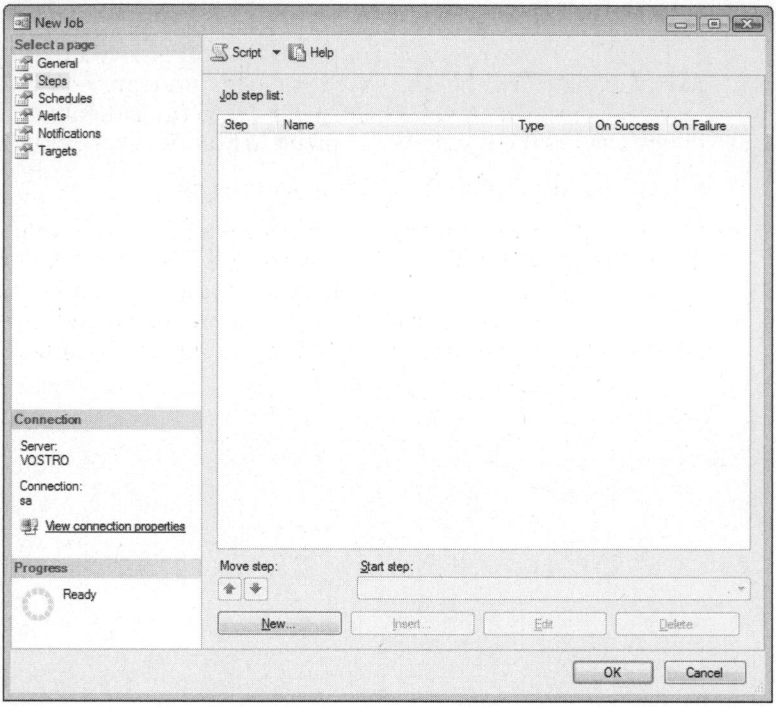

Figure 13-5:
The SQL
Server
Agent Job
Step list.

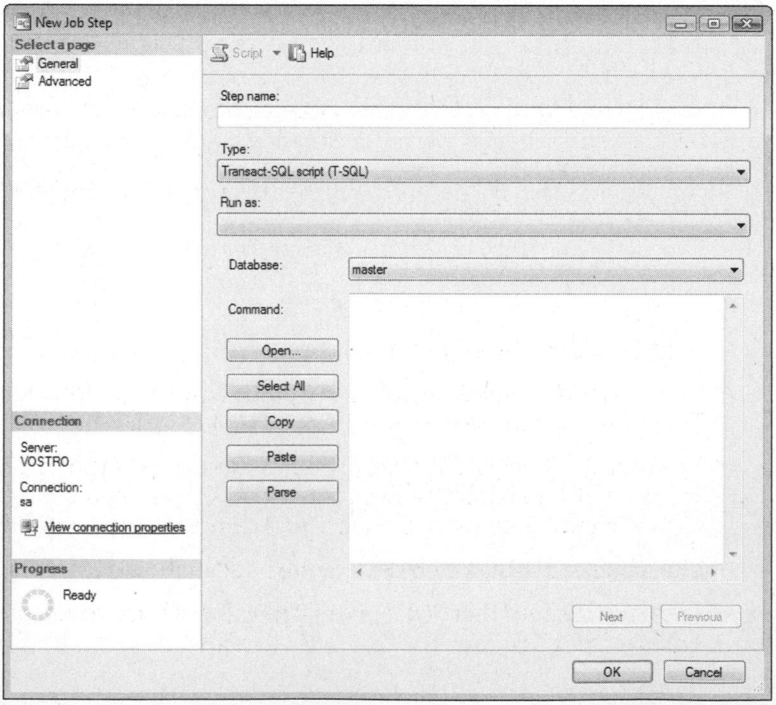

Figure 13-6:
Creating
a new job
step with
SSMS.

6. **Enter your Transact-SQL script in the Command text box.**

   You may include any valid Transact-SQL statements that you want to execute against the database specified in the previous step. For example, enter the text **DBCC CHECKDB** to run a database consistency check against the database specified in Step 5.

7. **Click the Parse button to validate your input.**

   This step gives you the opportunity to have SQL Server validate your Transact-SQL script before creating the job. It's a good opportunity to perform a quick syntax check before scheduling the job to run. If your syntax is correct, you see the pop-up window shown in Figure 13-7. Otherwise, correct your syntax and click the Parse button again.

Figure 3-7:
Parse
Command
Text.

Parse Command Text

The command was successfully parsed.

OK

8. **Click the OK button to create the step.**

   You may repeat this process as many times as necessary to create your job. You may customize your job steps even further by using the Advanced page of the Job Step Properties sheet, shown in Figure 13-8. This page allows you to specify the following:

   - ✔ The number of times SQL Server Agent should attempt to retry the step if it fails and the time interval it should wait between retry attempts.

   - ✔ The action SQL Server Agent should take if the step ultimately fails. These actions include:

     - • Go to the next step

     - • Quit the job and report success

     - • Quit the job and report failure

   - ✔ The action SQL Server Agent should take if the step ultimately succeeds. These are the same options you have for step failure.

   - ✔ The output file where SQL Server Agent should record the results of the Transact-SQL command and whether the results should overwrite the file's current contents or be appended to the current contents.

   - ✔ The name of a table where SQL Server Agent should store log results.

   - ✔ The user account that SQL Server Agent should use to execute the Transact-SQL statement.

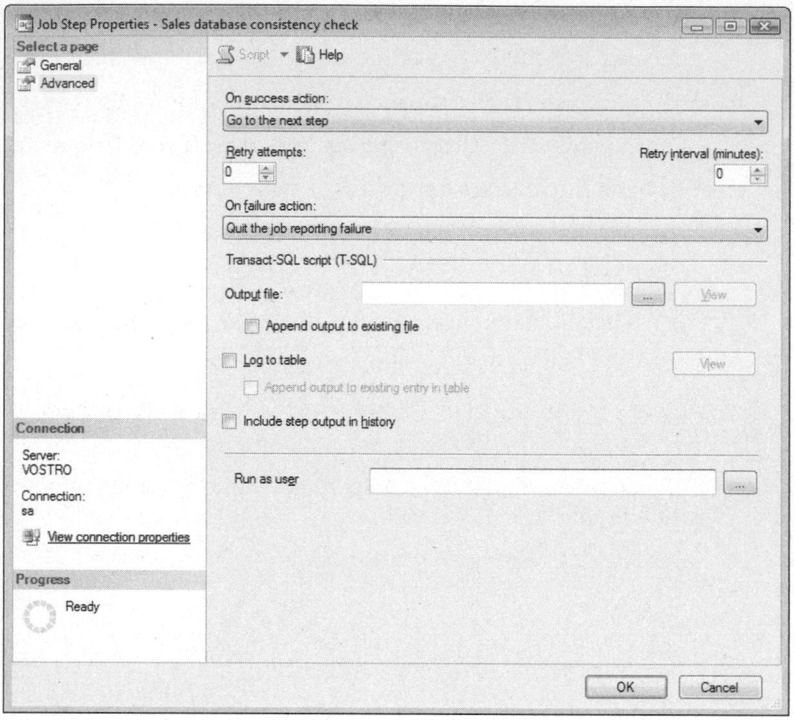

Figure 13-8:
Job Step
Advanced
page.

When you've finished creating your job steps, you can use the Move Step arrows at the bottom of the list to rearrange the order of job steps, as necessary.

Scheduling a SQL Server Agent job

One of the most powerful features offered by SQL Server Agent is the ability to schedule jobs to occur in the future on a one-time or repetitive basis. SQL Server Agent offers a number of flexible job-scheduling options, thereby allowing you to select the mix appropriate for your environment.

To add a schedule to your SQL Server Agent job, follow these steps:

1. **Click the Schedule icon in the Select a Page portion of the New Job window.**

   I'm assuming that you're still in the New Job window opened earlier in this section. If you're not, simply open the Properties sheet associated with the job from within the SQL Server Agent folder of SSMS.

2. **Click the New button at the bottom of the window.**

   You see the New Job Schedule window, which is shown in Figure 13-9.

3. **Provide a descriptive name for your schedule in the Name text box.**

4. **Choose a schedule type from the Schedule Type drop-down box.**

   You have the following options:

   - One Time
   - Recurring
   - Start Automatically when SQL Server Agent Starts
   - Start Whenever the CPUs Become Idle

5. **Provide the appropriate details for the schedule frequency and duration.**

   SQL Server Agent allows you to specify the frequency of the schedule with a great degree of detail.

6. **Click the OK button to add the schedule to the job.**

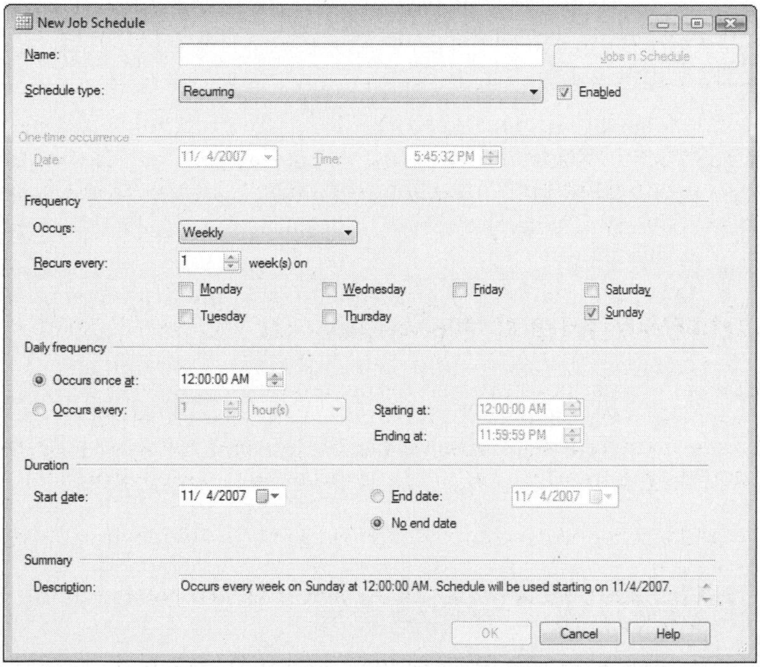

Figure 13-9:
Creating
a new job
schedule.

Notifying someone when the job completes

Schedule SQL Server Agent jobs run on an unattended basis. Therefore, it's often advisable to notify database administrators when a job completes. Here's how you can configure job completion notification:

1. **Click the Notifications icon in the Select a Page portion of the New Job window.**

   I'm assuming that you're still in the New Job window opened earlier in this section. If you're not, simply open the Properties sheet associated with the job from within the SQL Server Agent folder of SSMS.

2. **Select the box(es) corresponding to the notification actions you want SQL Server Agent to perform when the job completes.**

   Your options include the following:

   - Send an e-mail to a database operator
   - Send a pager message to a database operator
   - Send a "net send" message to a database operator
   - Write a message to the Windows Application Event Log
   - Delete the job

3. **Choose the notification target from the drop-down box next to each option, if applicable.**

   You need to select a database operator to notify for the e-mail, page, or net send notification options. I discuss creating database operators later in this chapter.

4. **Select the notification condition(s) from the drop-down box(es) next to the selected notification type(s).**

   You may choose from the following notification options:

   - Execute the option any time the job completes
   - Execute the option when the job completes successfully
   - Execute the option when the job fails to complete

Implementing Database Maintenance Plans

SQL Server 2008 also offers another way (in addition to SQL Server Agent jobs) to automate administrative tasks: the use of database maintenance plans. The primary advantage of these plans over SQL Server Agent jobs is their ease of creation: You can use a graphical wizard to create them and you can add many common maintenance tasks without writing Transact-SQL statements.

Identifying the tasks to include in a maintenance plan

Before you begin the process of creating a database maintenance plan, you should think carefully about the actions the plan will perform and the frequency with which you desire each to occur. The maintenance plan tasks supported by SQL Server 2008 include:

- ✔ Back up a database
- ✔ Check the integrity of a database
- ✔ Execute a SQL Server Agent job
- ✔ Execute a Transact-SQL statement
- ✔ Clean up historical database information
- ✔ Clean up leftover files from maintenance plan execution
- ✔ Perform an operator notification
- ✔ Rebuild or reorganize an index
- ✔ Shrink a database
- ✔ Update database statistics

After you've selected the appropriate mix of maintenance tasks, you can move on to creating the maintenance plan itself.

Creating a maintenance plan

The easiest way to create a database maintenance plan is by using the Maintenance Plan Wizard provided with SQL Server 2008. This wizard guides you through the process step-by-step using a graphical interface. Here's how you can use it to create your own plan:

1. **With SSMS open, expand the Management folder.**

2. **Right-click the Maintenance Plans folder and select Maintenance Plan Wizard from the pop-up menu.**

   You see the welcome screen shown in Figure 13-10.

Figure 13-10:
The
Database
Main-
tenance
Plan Wizard.

3. **Click the Next button to advance to the next wizard screen.**

4. **Provide a Name and Description for your maintenance plan by typing each in its appropriate text box.**

   Figure 13-11 shows the Plan Properties page of the wizard. You should provide an understandable name and clear description of your maintenance plan's purpose to help future administrators understand your work.

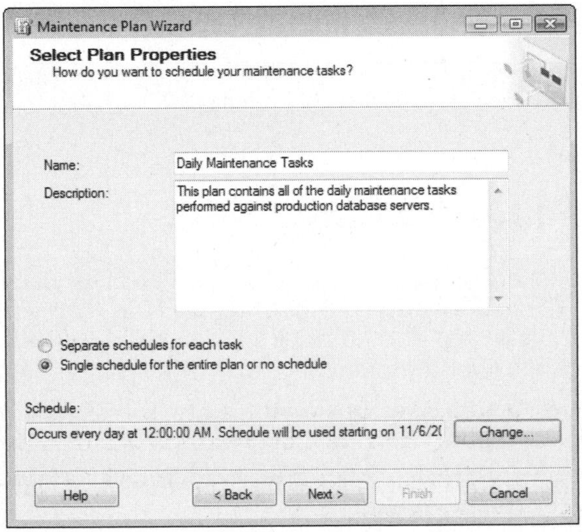

Figure 13-11:
Setting the
Database
Main-
tenance
Plan
properties.

5. **Choose to use a single schedule for the entire plan or separate schedules for each task.**

   For simplicity's sake, you probably want to choose a single schedule for each task in your maintenance plan. However, if you desire more scheduling flexibility, you may choose the Separate Schedules for Each Task option and then configure each task individually.

6. **Click the Change button, fill out the schedule options in the screen that appears, and click OK.**

   Note that this is the same New Job Schedule screen that's used for SQL Server Agent jobs and is shown previously in Figure 13-9.

7. **Click the Next button to advance to the task selection window.**

8. **Select the check box(es) next to the task(s) you want to include in your maintenance plan. Then click the Next button to continue.**

   The Select Maintenance Tasks screen, shown in Figure 13-12, allows you to select the tasks you'd like to include in your plan. Don't worry about the details at this point; you'll be asked to provide further configuration options for each task at a later step in the process.

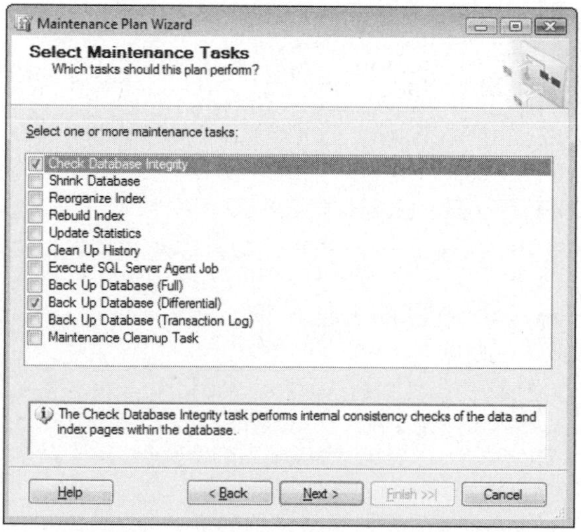

Figure 13-12: Selecting tasks to include in the maintenance plan.

9. **Click the Move Up and Move Down buttons to provide the correct order of task execution. Then click the Next button to continue.**

   You may rearrange the order of tasks by using the Move Up and Move Down buttons, as shown in Figure 13-13.

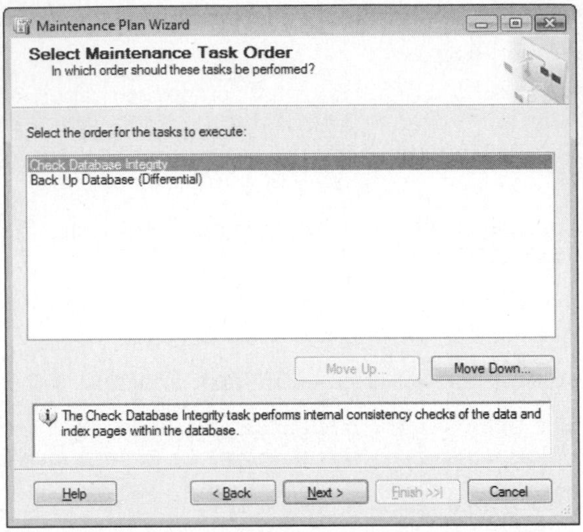

Figure 13-13:
Configuring
the mainte-
nance task
order.

10. **Configure the details of each maintenance plan task and click the Next button to continue.**

   The wizard then presents a series of screens asking you to provide details for each task that you selected in Step 8. These screens vary from task to task. For example, the Differential Backup screen is shown in Figure 13-14. I provide more information on the configuration details necessary for each task elsewhere in this book. Information on backup tasks appears in Chapter 18.

   These task configuration screens also contain a Change button to configure a per-task schedule. This button is unavailable (greyed out) if you selected a single schedule for the entire plan in Step 5.

11. **Select the check box(es) corresponding to the reporting option(s) you want and click the Next button to continue.**

   You have two options for reporting the results of maintenance plan execution, as shown in Figure 13-15: writing the output to a text file and e-mailing the report to a SQL Server database operator. You can choose them both, if you want.

12. **Click Finish to create the maintenance plan.**

Only members of the sysadmin server role may view, create, or modify SQL Server maintenance plans. I discuss managing server roles and user permissions in Chapter 16.

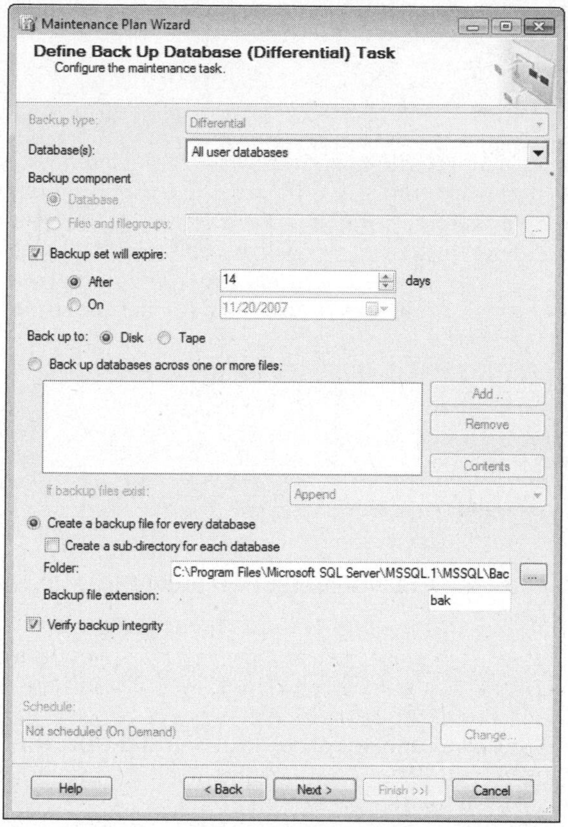

Figure 13-14:
Configuring
a differential
backup
mainte-
nance plan
task.

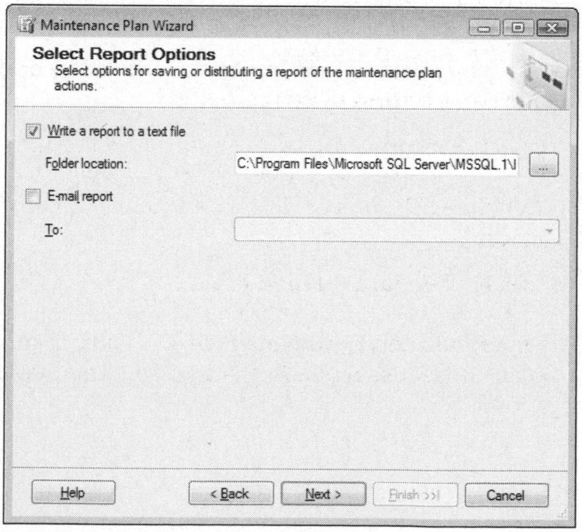

Figure 13-15:
Configuring
mainte-
nance plan
reporting
options.

Alerting Administrators about Database Events

Database monitoring is one of the most important tasks facing SQL Server administrators. Vigilant monitoring of database resource utilization and performance issues will help you stay in control of your database and prevent significant problems from occurring. Constant monitoring of these issues without the use of automated tools is quite difficult. Fortunately, SQL Server provides an alerting facility that monitors the database status on your behalf and notifies you when issues requiring your attention occur.

Configuring database operators

You can use database operators in SQL Server to define individuals who should receive alert notifications. Here's how to create a new database operator:

1. **Open SSMS and expand the SQL Server Agent folder.**

2. **Right-click the Operators icon and choose New Operator from the pop-up menu.**

3. **Provide a useful name for the operator (usually the person's first and last name).**

4. **Provide an e-mail address, net send address, or pager address for each operator.**

    You can provide all three addresses if you want.

5. **Provide details of the operator's on-call schedule, if applicable.**

    If you want an operator to receive notifications only during specified time periods or on specified days, configure those options on this screen as well. This is a useful function when you have rotating on-call schedules, because you can create different operators with notification schedules corresponding to your on-call schedule.

    An example of a completed New Operator screen appears in Figure 13-16.

6. **Click the OK button to create the operator.**

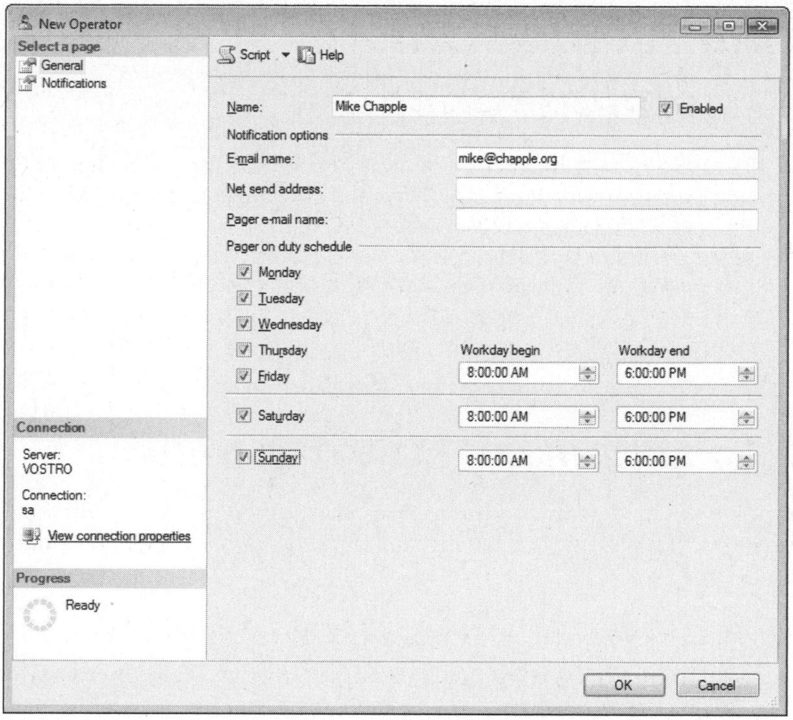

Figure 13-16:
Creating
a new
database
operator.

Creating SQL Server alerts

SQL Server allows you to create automated administrator alerts based upon three types of conditions:

- SQL Server events defined by a combination of a database name and SQL Server error code or severity. For example, you can create an alert that occurs when an error of severity 23 (a fatal error where the integrity of the entire database is in jeopardy) occurs.

- SQL Server performance conditions defined by an object, counter, instance, and threshold value. For example, you can create an alert when the log file uses 85 percent of its capacity for a particular database.

- Windows Management Instrumentation (WMI) events. WMI is an interface that allows Windows components to share performance information. The topic of WMI is beyond the scope of this book.

You can create a new alert using SQL Server Management Studio, as follows:

1. **With SSMS open, expand the SQL Server Agent folder.**

2. **Right-click Alerts and select New Alert from the pop-up menu.**

3. **Choose a name for your alert and type it in the Name text box.**

4. **Choose a type for your alert (SQL Server event, SQL Server performance condition, or WMI event).**

5. **Provide the appropriate details for the alert type you chose.**

   The configuration details you need to provide in this step will vary based upon the type of alert selected. Figure 13-17 shows a SQL Server event alert configured to alarm when fatal hardware errors occur. Figure 13-18 shows a SQL Server performance condition alert configured to alarm when the server login rate rises above three logins per second.

6. **Ensure that a checkmark appears in the Enabled check box.**

7. **Choose the Response page from the Select a Page portion of the New Alert window.**

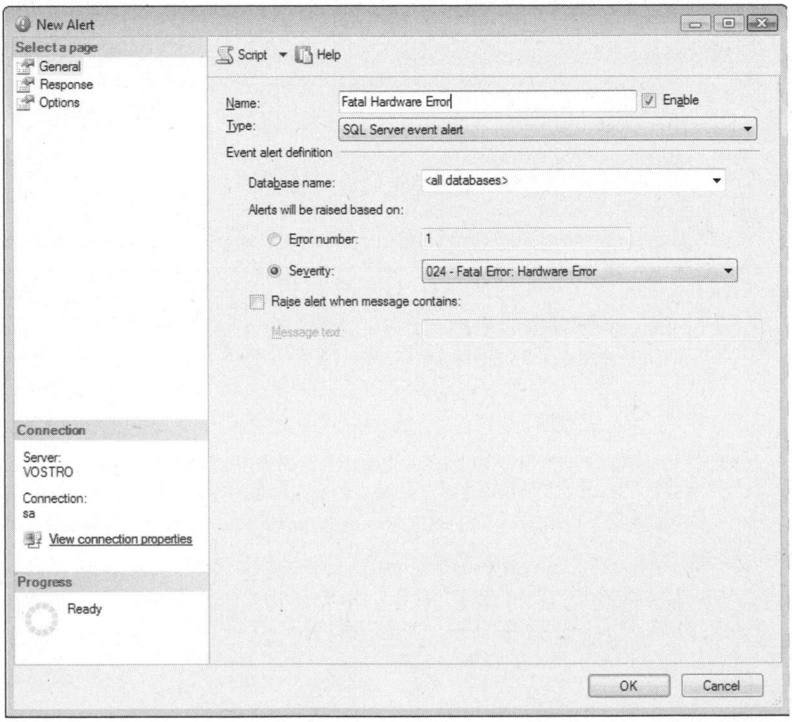

Figure 13-17: Creating a SQL Server alert for fatal hardware errors.

8. **Select the Notify Operators check box and then select the notification method(s) you want to use (if any) for each database operator in the list.**

9. **Click OK to create the alert.**

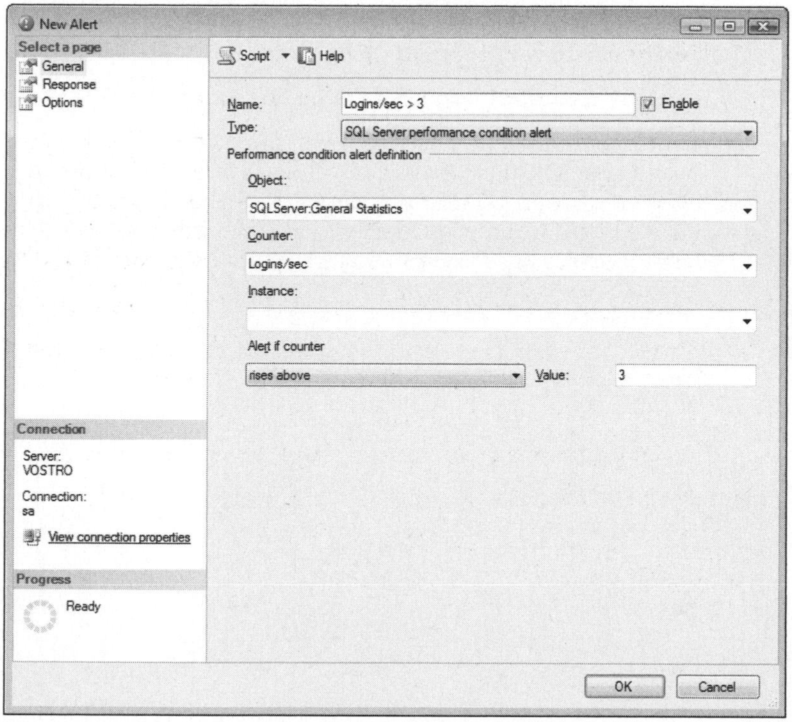

Figure 13-18: Creating a SQL Server Alert based upon the logins/sec rate.

Chapter 14

Troubleshooting SQL Server 2008 Problems

*F*rom time to time, you may encounter problems with your SQL Server databases. These issues may come as the result of poorly written database queries, hardware/software performance issues, or the physical failure of hardware components.

When performance issues arise, troubleshooting often requires a joint effort between database administrators and server administrators. In this chapter, I describe some of the tools available to SQL Server 2008 DBAs to assist in the detection and troubleshooting of database problems.

Understanding the Inner Workings of SQL Server Queries

SQL Server allows you to capture quite a bit of information about queries in progress. Some commonly used data elements include:

- ✔ Transact-SQL statements executed
- ✔ Stored procedures invoked

✔ Query execution time (in CPU time or clock time)

✔ Physical disk activity

✔ Login name responsible for each query

SQL Server provides this information through the use of the SQL Trace facility. This complex programming environment is accessible through an Application Programmer Interface (API). Alternatively, you can access this advanced functionality using the graphical user interface offered by SQL Server Profiler.

Creating a trace with SQL Server Profiler

If you'd like to capture detailed information about SQL Server performance using SQL Server Profiler, you must first create a trace. Each trace defines the events you would like to gather data about and the specific data elements you would like to capture.

Here's how to create a new trace using SQL Server Profiler:

1. **Open SQL Server Management Studio.**

2. **Choose Tools⇨SQL Server Profiler.**

   SQL Server Profiler opens in a new window.

3. **Choose File⇨New Trace.**

   A connection window (identical to the window used to connect to SSMS) opens.

4. **Fill in the details required to log in to your SQL Server instance and click the Connect button to continue.**

   If you need assistance determining the appropriate connection details, see Chapter 3. After you complete the connection, the Trace Properties window (shown in Figure 14-1) opens. This is where you perform the initial configuration of your new trace.

5. **Create a descriptive name for your trace and type it into the Trace Name text box.**

6. **Select a template for your trace from the drop-down list.**

   SQL Server Profiler includes a number of built-in templates to help you create new traces quickly. These include:

   • *Blank:* Exactly what the name implies: An empty template that allows you to define the exact events and columns you'd like to capture with your trace.

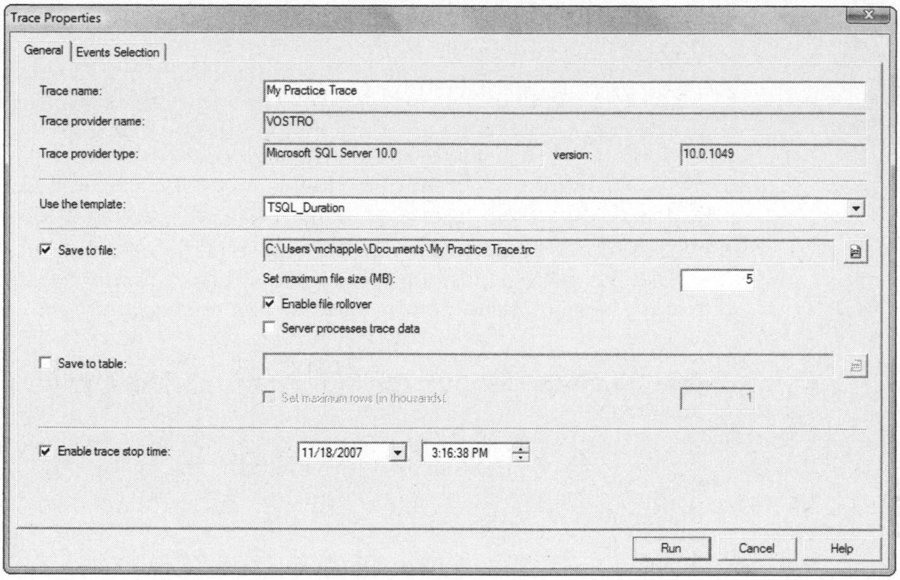

Figure 14-1:
The SQL
Server
Profiler
Trace
Properties
window.

- *SP_Counts:* Captures the number of times each stored procedure executes.

- *Standard:* The default template for SQL Server Profiler. It captures a variety of information about every connection, stored procedure, or Transact-SQL statement executed.

- *TSQL:* Collects all Transact-SQL batches and stored procedures executed against a database for troubleshooting purposes.

- *TSQL_Duration:* Records the Transact-SQL statements executed against a database along with the time (in milliseconds) required to complete each statement.

- *TSQL_Grouped:* Collects the same information as the Transact-SQL template but also groups the results by the user/application issuing the statement.

- *TSQL_Replay:* Gathers very detailed information about each Transact-SQL statement. This information is sufficient to replay the activity on the server in the future. It is commonly used for benchmark testing.

- *TSQL_SPs:* Records information about stored procedures executed against a database.

- *Tuning:* Provides detailed information required to tune a SQL Server database. The output of a Tuning trace may be used with the Database Engine Tuning Advisor that I describe in the last section of this chapter.

Remember that these templates are only a starting point and that you may modify them. If you want to develop a custom template, you don't have to use the Blank template as your starting point. You can save time by selecting the predefined template that most closely matches your needs and then customizing it to meet your specific requirements.

7. **Select the Save to File check box.**

SQL Server Profiler provides two options for capturing trace data: saving to a file or saving to a database table. I strongly recommend that you save trace data to files only. Saving this information to a database table may cause significant database performance degradation.

8. **Click the Save As icon to the right of the filename text box and select the location/name of the file where you'd like to store the results of your trace.**

9. **If you'd like to stop your trace automatically, select the Enable Trace Stop Time check box and choose an appropriate date and time from the drop-down lists.**

10. **Select the Events Selection tab in the Trace Properties window.**

This tab, shown in Figure 14-2, allows you to select the exact events and event columns you will capture with your trace. If you selected a template other than Blank in Step 6, this table will already contain some entries.

Figure 14-2:
The SQL
Server
Profiler
Events
Selection
screen.

Trace Properties

General | Events Selection |

Review selected events and event columns to trace. To see a complete list, select the "Show all events" and "Show all columns" options.

Events	TextD...	Applic...	NTUs...	Login...	CPU	Reads	Writes	Durati...	Client...	SPID	StartT...
Security Audit											
☑ Audit Login	☑	☑	☑	☑					☑	☑	☑
☑ Audit Logout		☑	☑	☑	☑	☑	☑	☑	☑	☑	☑
Sessions											
☑ ExistingConnection	☑	☑	☑	☑					☑	☑	☑
Stored Procedures											
☑ RPC:Completed	☐	☑	☑	☑	☑	☑	☑	☑	☑	☑	☑
TSQL											
☑ SQL:BatchCompleted	☑	☑	☑	☑	☑	☑	☑	☑	☑	☑	☑
☑ SQL:BatchStarting	☑	☑	☑	☑					☑	☑	☑

Security Audit
Includes event classes that are used to audit server activity.

☐ Show all events
☐ Show all columns

No data column selected.

Column Filters...
Organize Columns...

Run | Cancel | Help

11. **Select the Show all Events check box.**

    By default, the Events Selection tab will show only events included in your base template. If you'd like to include additional events, you need to first select this check box to display events not included in the current trace.

12. **Select the Show All Columns check box.**

    SQL Server Profiler allows you to capture quite a bit of information about each event. The Events Selection tab displays these data elements as table columns. If you want to include elements not already part of your trace, select the Show All Columns check box.

13. **Select the check boxes corresponding to any other data elements you'd like the trace to capture.**

    Be conservative when selecting the events to trace and the columns you wish to capture in your trace. Traces collecting too much data can quickly consume massive quantities of disk space and cause server performance issues. You don't want your troubleshooting efforts to create brand new problems!

14. **Click the Run button to start your trace.**

Reviewing trace results

When SQL Server Profiler begins executing your trace, it opens a trace window similar to the one shown in Figure 14-3.

Each line in the trace results window corresponds to a single event that you selected in the Events Selection tab. When you run your first trace against a database, you'll quickly understand the importance of being selective about the events and data elements you choose to capture; it's not unusual for a single trace to collect thousands of events per minute on a production database server.

You may navigate through the trace results using the scrollbar on the right side of the trace window. Additionally, if you click any individual row, you will see the Text Data element from that event occurrence in the large pane at the bottom of the window.

You may stop or pause a running trace using the stop, pause, and restart buttons at the top of the trace window. Figure 14-4 illustrates these buttons. The triangle icon is the restart button, the two parallel lines are the pause button, and the red square is the stop button.

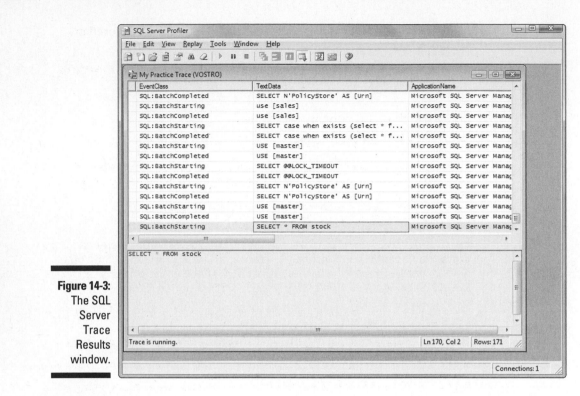

Figure 14-3:
The SQL
Server
Trace
Results
window.

Figure 14-4:
Trace
manipula-
tion buttons.

Reviewing Log Records

Let's face it: Reviewing server logs is a boring, thankless task. However, this mundane activity is one of the most important things you can do to keep your server running efficiently. It also provides valuable information that will assist you in your troubleshooting efforts.

SQL Server writes log data to two different locations during the course of normal activity:

✔ SQL Server's error log stores error information in a text file stored on the server.

✔ SQL Server also logs error information to the Windows Application Log, accessible through Event Viewer.

SQL Server error log

SQL Server uses a plain-text file to store error information reported by the SQL Server database engine. By default, the current SQL Server error log is stored in this location:

```
Program Files\Microsoft SQL Server\MSSQL.n\MSSQL\LOG\ERRORLOG
```

When the log becomes full, SQL Server closes the file and creates a new one. Old log files have a number appended to them indicating the sequence in which they occurred. SQL Server saves them as

```
Program Files\Microsoft SQL Server\MSSQL.n\MSSQL\LOG\ERRORLOG.n
```

In both cases, replace the n in the filenames with an integer number indicating the file/directory sequence number.

You may view these log files using any standard text file viewer, such as Windows Notepad.

Windows Application Log

Microsoft Windows operating systems provide their own native logging facility, accessed through the Windows Event Viewer. The three standard logs created by Windows are as follows:

✔ Application Log

✔ Security Log

✔ System Log

SQL Server writes error information to the Windows Application Log, as shown in Figure 14-5.

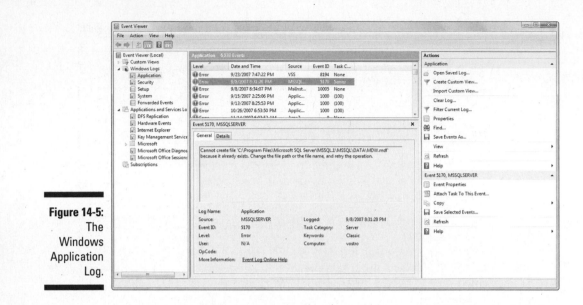

Figure 14-5:
The
Windows
Application
Log.

The exact process for starting Event Viewer varies slightly depending on the Windows operating system you use to run your SQL Server. Consult the documentation for that operating system if you're not familiar with Event Viewer.

SQL Server Management Studio Log File Viewer

In addition to the SQL Server error log and the Windows Application Log, SQL Server creates separate log files for SQL Agent activity and Database Mail events. As a SQL Server administrator, you may find it cumbersome to review and correlate records from all those locations. Fortunately, SSMS provides a Log File Viewer (shown in Figure 14-6) that consolidates all of this information in a single location.

Here's how to start Log File Viewer:

1. **Open SSMS and connect to the database server of your choice.**

2. **Expand the Management folder.**

3. **Right-click the SQL Server Logs folder.**

4. **Choose View⇨SQL Server and Windows Log from the pop-up menu.**

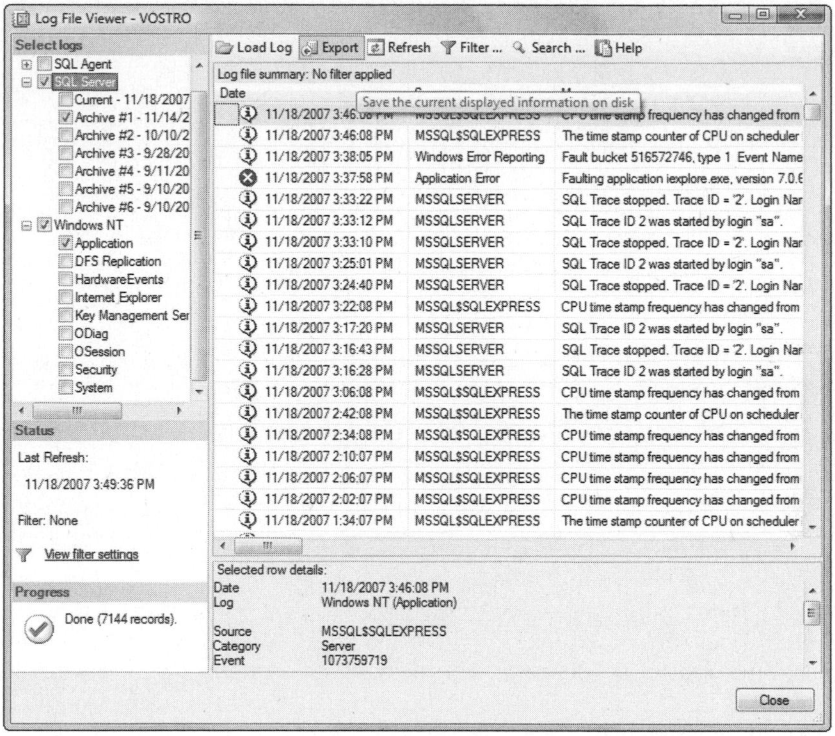

Figure 14-6:
The SSMS
Log File
Viewer.

Log File Viewer opens and displays a consolidated view of the SQL Server error log and the Windows Application Log, sorted by the time of each event's occurrence, which helps you identify related entries from different log files.

You can add different log files to this view by expanding the entries in the Select Logs pane and checking the boxes to the left of any files you'd like to import into Log File Viewer.

Monitoring Your Server with Performance Studio

SQL Server Performance Studio provides you with a data warehouse-driven way to monitor SQL Server performance. In this section, I explain how you can configure and use Performance Studio to monitor your SQL Server installations.

Configuring Performance Studio

Before you use Performance Studio for the first time, you must tell SQL Server that you want to begin collecting performance data. Here's how you configure the Management Data Warehouse to begin collecting this data:

1. **Open SQL Server Management Studio and connect to the SQL Server instance you want to monitor.**

2. **Click the plus (+) icon to the left of the Management folder to expand that folder.**

3. **Right-click Data Collection and select Configure Management Data Warehouse from the pop-up menu.**

   You see the Configure Management Data Warehouse Wizard's introductory screen.

4. **Click the Next button to advance past the Welcome screen.**

5. **Choose Create or upgrade a management data warehouse and click the Next button to continue.**

   You see the Configure Management Data Warehouse Storage screen, shown in Figure 14-7.

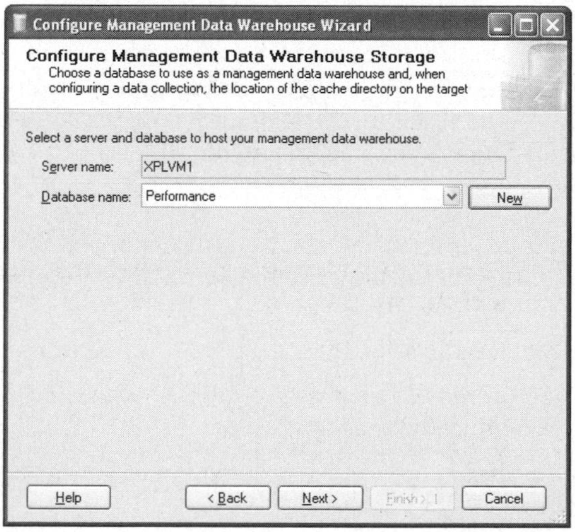

Figure 14-7:
Configuring Management Data Warehouse Storage.

6. **Click the New button to create a new database for the storage of performance data.**

   SQL Server opens the New Database window.

7. **Provide a name for the performance statistics database and click the OK button to create it.**

8. **Select the user accounts or groups you want to grant data warehouse permissions using the check boxes to the left of their names in the Users Mapped to This Login section of the Map Logins and Users window.**

   I show this process in Figure 14-8.

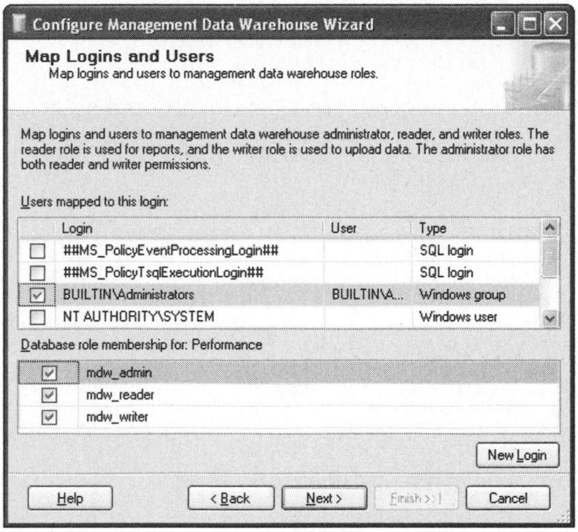

Figure 14-8: Mapping logins and users.

9. **Select the role(s) you want to grant each user in the Database Role Membership section of the window.**

   The available roles are the following:

   - *mdw_admin:* Grants the user/group full administrative control of the Management Data Warehouse.

   - *mdw_reader:* Grants the user/group read-only permission to the Management Data Warehouse.

   - *mdw_writer:* Grants the user/group write permission to the Management Data Warehouse.

10. **Click the Next button to continue.**

11. **Click the Finish button to create the Management Data Warehouse.**

    You see the status window shown in Figure 14-9 while SQL Server creates and enables the data warehouse.

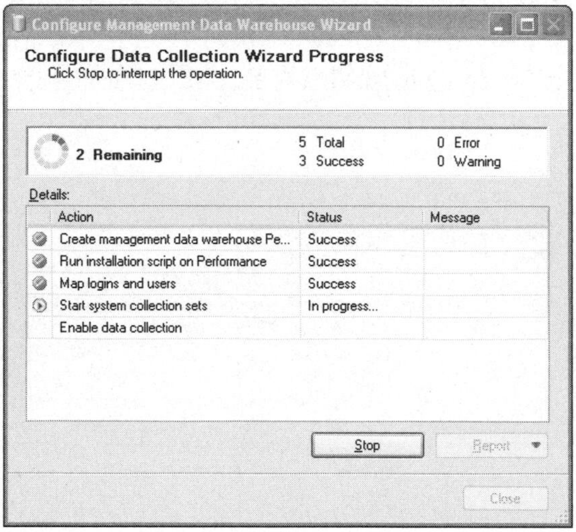

Figure 14-9:
Creating the
Manage-
ment Data
Warehouse.

12. **Click the Close button to exit the wizard.**

Reviewing performance data

You can review performance data collected in the Management Data Warehouse by viewing reports directly within SQL Server Management Studio. Here's how:

1. **Open SQL Server Management Studio and connect to the SQL Server instance you want to monitor.**

2. **Click the plus (+) icon to the left of the Management folder to expand that folder.**

3. **Right-click the Data Collection folder and select the Reports submenu from the pop-up menu. From this submenu, choose the Data Warehouse submenu. From that submenu, select the name of the report you want to view.**

SQL Server provides built-in reports covering the following areas:

- Disk Usage
- Query Statistics
- Server Activity

Figure 14-10 shows an example of the Disk Usage Summary report.

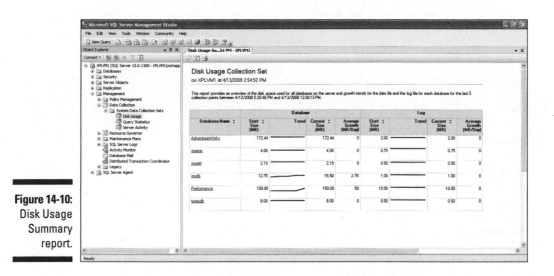

Figure 14-10:
Disk Usage
Summary
report.

Figure 14-11 shows an example of the Server Activity Summary report.

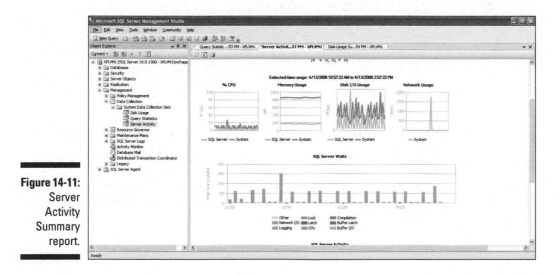

Figure 14-11:
Server
Activity
Summary
report.

Tuning Your Database with Database Engine Tuning Advisor

Every SQL Server deployment performs different tasks with a different mix of queries. Some may involve a large number of simple data lookup operations, whereas others may perform repetitive complex joins. Each of these instances requires unique configuration to achieve optimal performance. The configuration that works best for the server performing simple queries won't work well on the server performing complex join operations.

SQL Server includes the Database Engine Tuning Advisor (DTA) to help you optimally configure your database based upon your unique workload requirements. DTA makes recommendations to help you improve the physical structure of your database. It also allows you to immediately implement the recommendations or view the Transact-SQL statements required to implement the recommendations manually at a later time.

Here's how to run DTA:

1. **With SSMS open, choose Database Engine Tuning Advisor from the Tools menu.**

   DTA opens and displays a connection window.

2. **Fill in the connection details and click the Connect button.**

   DTA presents the tuning setup window shown in Figure 14-12.

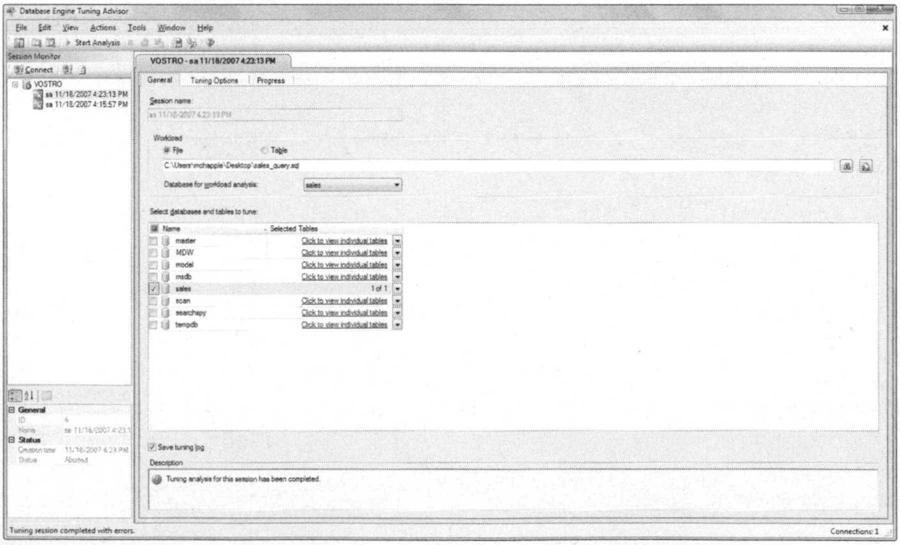

Figure 14-12:
The Database Engine Tuning Advisor.

3. **Select the File radio button in the Workload section and navigate to the file**

you'd like to use as your workload.

The workload tells DTA what tasks you'd like to optimize your database performance against. You may specify a SQL Trace file, an XML file, or an SQL file. You should ensure that you choose a workload file that corresponds to common activity on your database server. DTA will use this workload as the basis for all its recommendations.

TIP

I describe creating a SQL Trace workload in the section "Creating a Trace with SQL Server Profiler," earlier in this chapter. Be sure to use the Tuning template when creating a trace for use with DTA.

4. **Click the check box(es) to the left of the database(s) you'd like to tune.**

5. **Click the Start Analysis button.**

   DTA begins the analysis process and shows the status screen that appears in Figure 14-13.

6. **Review the recommendations presented and select the check boxes to the left of any you want to implement.**

   Figure 14-14 shows sample recommendations. If you want to apply any recommendations immediately, select the check boxes to their left.

7. **Select Apply Recommendations from the Actions menu.**

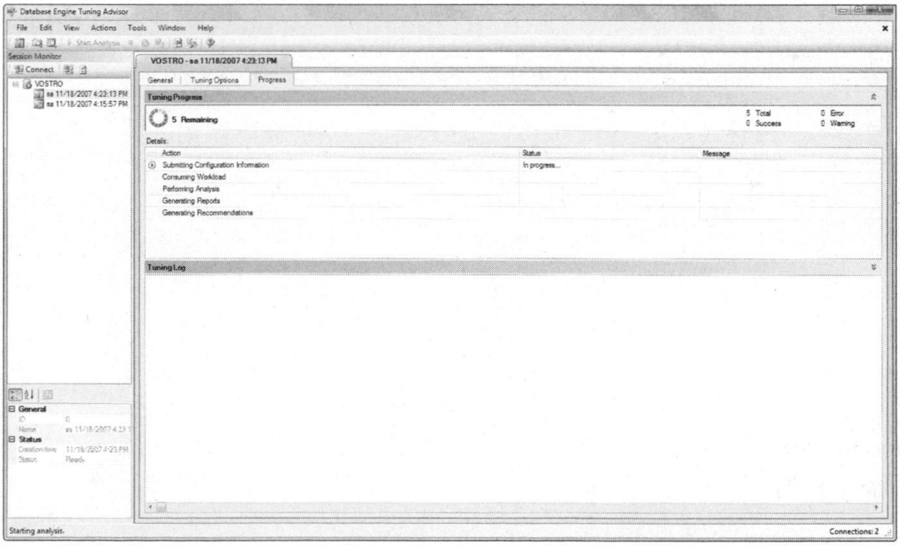

Figure 14-13:
The
Database
Engine
Tuning
Advisor
Status
Screen.

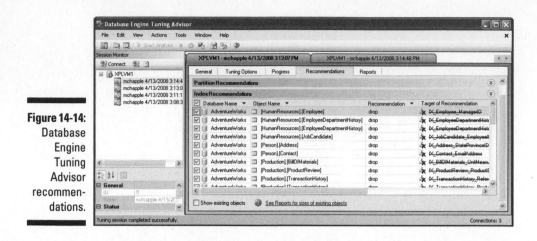

8. **Click the OK button to apply the recommendations immediately.**

   Alternatively, you may use the Schedule for later option to apply the recommendations at a future time.

9. **Review the status screen and click the Close button to complete the process.**

Chapter 15

Replicating Data across Multiple Servers

. . . .

In This Chapter

▶ Using replication to share SQL Server data across multiple servers

▶ Publishing data from the primary server

▶ Subscribing to published data

. . . .

Sometimes a single database server isn't sufficient to meet all your business requirements. You may need to distribute your data among multiple servers to meet growing demand. Fortunately, SQL Server provides several replication options to help you keep the contents of multiple databases synchronized.

Some scenarios in which you might want to employ replication include:

- ✔ You have multiple, geographically separated sites that need access to information on your SQL Server database. Connections between the sites are slow and expensive, so you want to host a local copy of the database at each site.

- ✔ You want to provide travelling users with an offline copy of a portion of your database for use on the road.

- ✔ Your organization has complex reporting needs, and you want to provide the reporting group with an offline copy of your database that the group can use without affecting the performance of your production SQL Server environment.

Understanding Replication

Replication allows you to transport copies of your databases between different SQL Server instances and keep those copies up-to-date as the database changes. SQL Server provides several different replication technologies, each of which uses different techniques to provide varying levels of currency in the data.

Server roles

In any SQL Server replication environment, there are three server roles that must be filled: the publisher, the distributor, and the subscriber.

Figure 15-1 illustrates the flow of data in this model from the publisher to the distributor and on to the subscribers.

Publisher

The publisher is the ultimate source of the data published in any replication scenario. It contains the "master" copy of the database and provides this data to the distributor.

Distributor

The distributor is responsible for managing the distribution of published data to the subscribers. In many cases, the publisher and distributor run on the same database server, referred to as a *local distributor*. In high-performance environments, DBAs often separate the distributor onto a separate database server, known as the *remote distributor*.

Subscriber

Subscribers are the end receivers of the published data. They may contact the distributor periodically to check for updates (known as the *pull* subscription model, shown in Figure 15-2). Alternatively, they may wait until the distributor contacts them with a notification that an update is available (known as the *push* subscription model, shown in Figure 15-3).

You should also be aware of the relationships between publishers, distributors, and subscribers. Each publication must have one and only one distributor. However, a single distributor may contain publications from multiple publishers. Each one of those publications may, in turn, serve multiple subscribers. This is the model illustrated in Figure 15-1, shown previously.

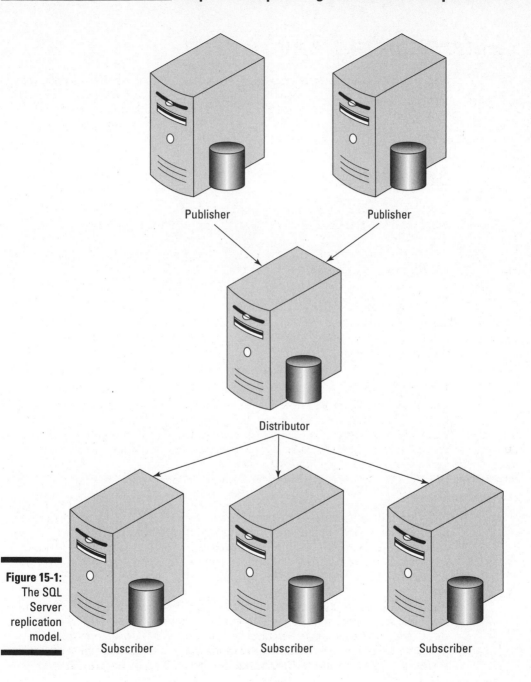

Figure 15-1:
The SQL
Server
replication
model.

Publisher   Publisher

Distributor

Subscriber   Subscriber   Subscriber

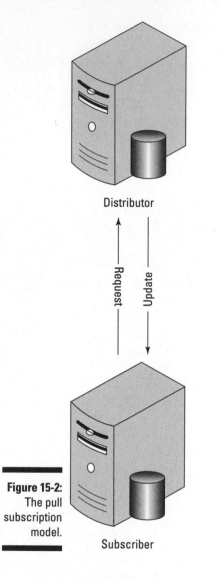

Distributor

Request   Update

Subscriber

Articles and publications

In the previous section, you probably noticed that the terminology used for replication is borrowed from the publishing industry. The publisher/distributor/subscriber model used for replication is exactly the same as that used to publish and distribute magazines.

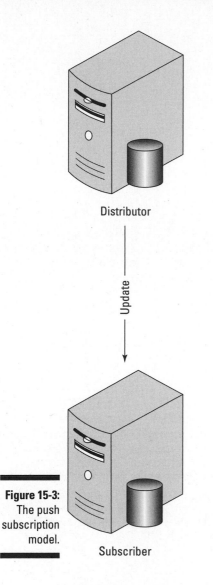

Distributor

Update

Figure 15-3:
The push
subscription
model.

Subscriber

You can continue with this analogy to describe the type of information that the publisher makes available to subscribers. The publisher selects various articles that it desires to publish and then bundles them together into a publication that it makes available to subscribers through the distributor.

SQL Server publishers may create articles that correspond to the following types of database object:

- ✔ Tables
- ✔ Views
- ✔ Stored procedures
- ✔ User-defined functions

Replication types

There's one more set of technologies I need to discuss before I move on to the process of creating and subscribing to publications: the types of replication supported by SQL Server 2008. Three options are available to you: snapshot replication, transactional replication, and merge replication.

Snapshot replication

Snapshot replication is the simplest form of SQL Server replication. In this scenario, the publisher periodically provides the distributor with a complete copy (or "snapshot") of the publication. The distributor, in turn, provides that copy to each one of the subscribers.

Snapshot replication may be simple to understand, but it can also be quite costly in terms of resources consumed, especially if your publication contains large amounts of data that are infrequently updated. Consider the case of a large product catalog that receives a massive update once per quarter but also receives minor price changes on a daily basis. If you use snapshot replication, you will need to transfer the entire product catalog to each subscriber during each update interval.

Snapshot replication also does not allow the subscriber to perform any updates to the database. It is strictly a one-way replication model, passing data from the publisher to the subscriber and not allowing any flow of data in the reverse direction.

Transactional replication

Transactional replication steps in where snapshot replication falls short. It begins by performing an initial snapshot replication to create a baseline at the subscriber. However, from that point forward, rather than transfer the entire publication, it transfers only update information. Here's how transactional replication works:

1. The subscriber receives an initial snapshot from the distributor and uses it to create a baseline database.

2. The Log Reader Agent running on the distributor monitors the publisher's transaction log.

3. When the Log Reader Agent detects an INSERT, UPDATE, or DELETE statement (or any other statement that modifies data), it stores them in the distributor's distribution database.

4. The Distribution Agent retrieves committed transactions from the distribution database and sends them to the subscriber.

The Distribution Agent runs in different places, depending upon the subscription model in use. In the case of a push subscription, the Distribution Agent runs on the distributor. This allows it to monitor the distribution database for changes continuously and push those changes out to subscribers when necessary. In the case of a pull subscription, the Distribution Agent runs at the subscriber, allowing it to reach out to the distributor when the subscriber wants to receive an update.

As does snapshot replication, the basic transactional replication model uses a one-way data flow; subscribers cannot make updates to the publisher. However, two variations on basic transactional replication exist that allow such exchanges: bidirectional transactional replication and peer-to-peer transactional replication. These approaches are beyond the scope of this book.

Some common scenarios that are particularly well-suited for transactional replication include:

✔ Business requirements dictate a very short period of time between when updates are made at the publisher and received at the subscriber (also known as "low latency").

✔ Applications require access to each intermediate state of a database, rather than just the final end state.

✔ One of the participants in the replication runs a DBMS other than SQL Server (such as Oracle).

Merge replication

Merge replication is designed to support the incorporation of data modifications made at either the publisher or a subscriber. In contrast to transactional replication, which relies upon the use of the transaction log, merge replication uses a series of triggers to detect changes in the database and propagate those changes to other participating databases.

You can use merge replication in any case in which the subscribers need to update data and want those changes reflected at the publisher. It's also quite useful when the subscribers need to take data offline, make changes, and then later synchronize with the publisher by applying those changes.

Here's the basic idea behind merge replication:

1. The Merge Agent applies the initial snapshot to all subscribers.

2. Triggers notify the Merge Agent each time a modification occurs to a published table.

3. The Merge Agent resolves any conflicts that may exist and propagates the changes to the publisher and other subscribers.

The trick with merge replication is that conflicts may occur that require resolution. For example, suppose that you're using merge replication to allow users to set the prices of items in a retail store. Also suppose that three different managers check out laptops at the beginning of the day and make pricing changes. Matthew changes the price of carrots at 2 p.m. and synchronizes his changes at 4 p.m. Renee changes the price at 10 a.m. but doesn't synchronize her changes until 5 p.m. Finally, Christopher changes the price at 3 p.m. and synchronizes immediately. Which price change should SQL Server retain?

The answer to that question is complex. You could argue that Renee's change was the last to synchronize, so it should be permanent. On the other hand, you could make a similar argument that Christopher was the last to change the price, so his change should be permanent.

By default, SQL Server uses the following merge replication conflict resolution protocol:

✔ If one of the changes is made on the publisher, that change is made permanent.

✔ If both changes are made on subscribers using client subscriptions (normally used in pull subscriptions), the change from the first subscriber to synchronize is made permanent.

✔ If both changes are made on subscribers using server subscriptions (normally used in push subscriptions), the change from the subscriber with the highest priority value is made permanent.

There isn't a single "correct" answer to this question. Therefore, SQL Server allows you to modify this default behavior by selecting a conflict resolver during the merge replication setup process. You select this conflict resolve on the Article Properties screen, shown in Figure 15-4.

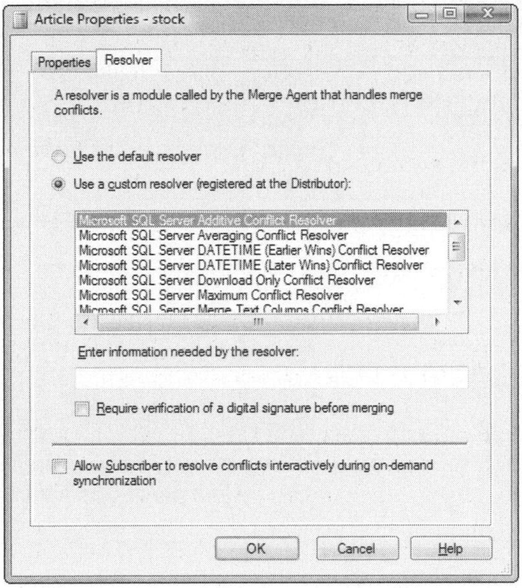

Figure 15-4:
Merge
replication
article
properties.

The Article Properties screen allows you to select from the COM Conflict Resolvers predefined by Microsoft and listed in Table 15-1. One of those resolvers, the Stored Procedure Resolver, allows you to create a stored procedure with user-defined logic specifying how SQL Server should resolve conflicts. Alternatively, if you're a developer with COM skills, you can create your own COM Conflict Resolver.

Table 15-1	Merge Replication COM Conflict Resolvers
Resolver Name	**Description**
Additive Conflict Resolver	Adds the conflicting values together to determine the winning value.
Averaging Conflict Resolver	Averages the conflicting values to determine the winning value.
DATETIME (Earlier Wins) Conflict Resolver	Works only with $DATETIME$ columns; the earlier value wins.
DATETIME (Later Wins) Conflict Resolver	Works only with $DATETIME$ columns; the later value wins.
Maximum Conflict Resolver	The mathematically larger value wins.
Minimum Conflict Resolver	The mathematically smaller value wins.

(continued)

Table 15-1 *(continued)*

Resolver Name	Description
Merge Text Conflict Resolver	Works only with text columns; the two columns are combined to form the winner.
Subscriber Always Wins Conflict Resolver	The value at the subscriber always wins.
Upload Only Conflict Resolver	Changes uploaded to the publisher win; changes on the publisher itself are ignored.
Download Only Conflict Resolver	Changes on the publisher win; changes uploaded to the publisher are ignored.
Stored Procedure Resolver	Allows you to specify a stored procedure containing custom conflict resolution logic.

Replication is a complex topic with many technical nuances. In the remainder of this chapter, I describe how to set up a simple snapshot replication scenario. My intention is to make sure that you have a basic understanding of SQL Server's replication capabilities and can recognize when replication might play a useful role in your organization. If you intend to implement replication in a production environment, I strongly recommend reading one of the many books dedicated to this topic alone.

Publishing Data with Snapshot Replication

The previous section covers the basics of replication; in this section, I turn to the actual implementation of replication in a SQL Server environment using snapshot replication. This is a three-step process. In this section, I explain the first two steps: creating a distributor and creating a publisher. The next section covers the third step: creating subscribers.

Creating a distributor

The first thing you must do when enabling snapshot replication is create a distributor. As mentioned earlier in this chapter, most small environments use the local distributor model, where the publisher and distributor reside on the same server. I assume that's the case as I walk you through the distributor creation process:

1. **Open SQL Server Management Studio and connect to the database server that you want to serve as the publisher/distributor.**

2. **Right-click the Replication folder and choose Configure Distribution from the pop-up menu.**

   The Configure Distribution Wizard begins.

3. **Click Next to advance past the wizard's welcome screen.**

4. **Select the option that this server will act as its own distributor and click the Next button to continue.**

   Figure 15-5 illustrates this step. If you want to use a remote distributor instead, you must first create the distributor and then return to this screen to select it from the list.

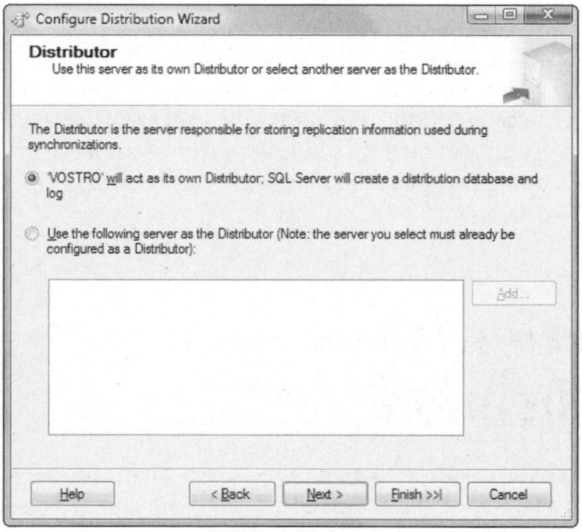

Figure 15-5:
Selecting the distributor.

5. **Accept the default selection — that SQL Server Agent should start automatically — and click the Next button to continue.**

   Replication requires SQL Server Agent, so it's a good idea to let it start automatically when the computer starts. If you don't select this option, you will need to manually start SQL Server Agent each time the computer restarts, or replication will fail.

6. **Type a UNC name or local file path for snapshot file storage into the Snapshot Folder field and click the Next button to continue.**

   If you're using only push subscriptions, you may provide either a local path (for example, `C:\Program Files\Microsoft SQL Server\MSSQL.1\MSSQL\ReplData`). If you want to support pull subscriptions, you must provide a UNC path (for example, `\\myserver\Program Files\Microsoft SQL Server\MSSQL.1\MSSQL\ReplData`).

7. **Accept the default name and paths for the distribution database and click Next to continue.**

8. **Select any other servers that may act as publishers to this distributor and click the Next button to continue.**

   Figure 15-6 illustrates this process. By default, the distributor may act as a publisher to itself. If you want to allow additional publishers, select them here.

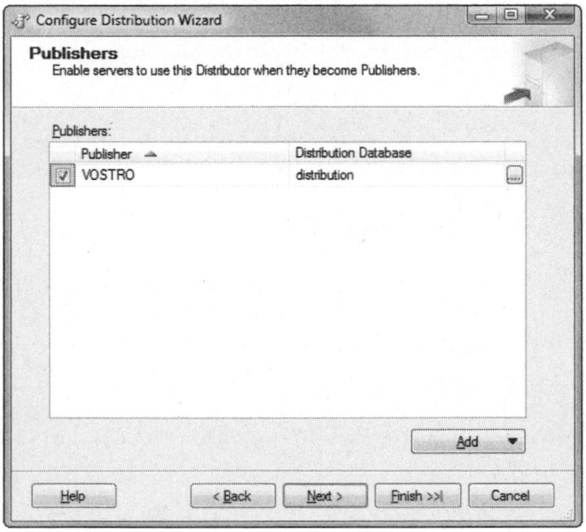

Figure 15-6: Selecting authorized publishers.

9. **Click the Next button to advance to the confirmation screen.**

   If you want to defer the distributor configuration to a later date, you may deselect the Configure Distribution check box and instead use the Generate a Script File with Steps to Configure Distribution check box. This option creates a reusable script.

10. **Review the choices presented in the Complete the Wizard screen and click Finish to configure your distributor.**

When you click Finish, SQL Server presents the status screen shown in Figure 15-7. It may take a few minutes for the configuration to successfully complete.

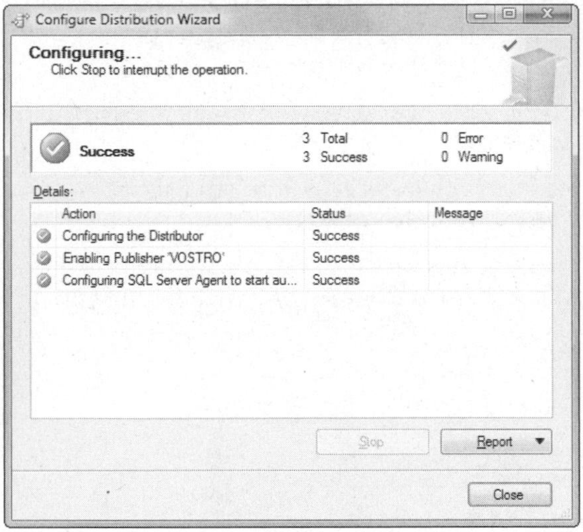

Figure 15-7:
Distributor configuration status.

Creating a publication

After you've successfully created a publisher/distributor, you next need to create a publication to which other servers may subscribe. The publication contains those articles (database objects) that you would like to replicate across servers. Here's how to create a publication:

1. **With SSMS open, expand the Replication folder of the server that will serve as the publisher.**

2. **Right-click Local Publications and select New Publication from the pop-up menu.**

   The New Publication Wizard starts.

3. **Click the Next button to launch the wizard.**

4. **Choose the publication database and click the Next button, as shown in Figure 15-8.**

5. **Choose the publication type and click the Next button.**

   In this example, I use the Snapshot publication type, as shown in Figure 15-9.

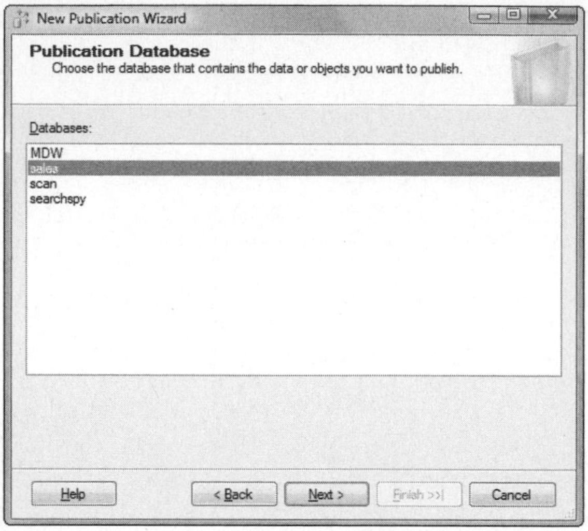

Figure 15-8:
Choosing a
publication
database.

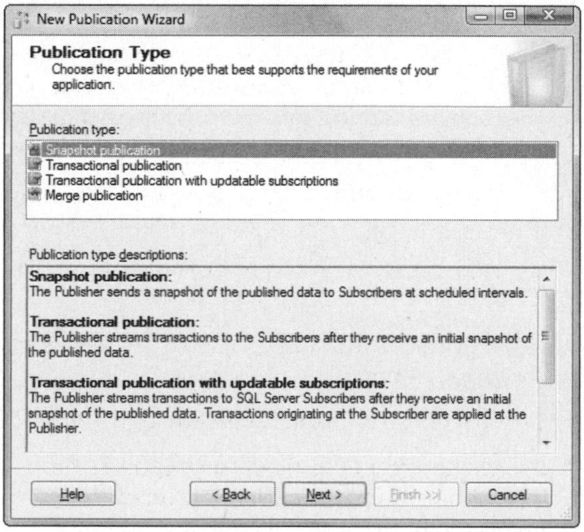

Figure 15-9:
Choosing a
publication
type.

6. **Choose the article(s) you wish to publish and click the Next button.**

You may select from any tables, stored procedures, or user-defined functions within the publication database, as shown in Figure 15-10. Optionally, you may click the Article Properties button to set advanced properties for each article.

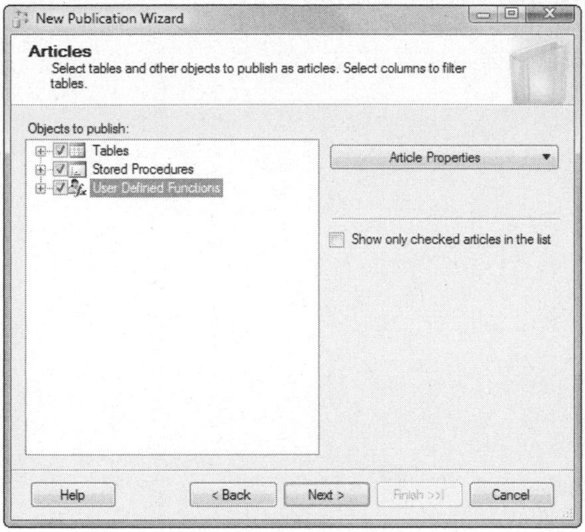

New Publication Wizard

Articles
Select tables and other objects to publish as articles. Select columns to filter tables.

Objects to publish:

☐✓ Tables
☐✓ Stored Procedures
☐✓ User Defined Functions

[Article Properties ▼]

☐ Show only checked articles in the list

[Help]   [< Back]   [Next >]   [Finish >>|]   [Cancel]

Figure 15-10:
Choosing
articles
for the
publication.

7. **Click Next to advance past the Filter Table Rows screen.**

   If you want, you may use a table filter to limit the rows that are repli-cated to subscribers for security or performance reasons. For example, if you're replicating a sales catalog to retail stores, you may want to filter out catalog entries for items not available at a particular store.

8. **Click the Create a Snapshot Immediately check box and click the Next button to continue.**

   You may also schedule the Snapshot Agent to run at future time(s) on this screen.

9. **Click the Security Settings button and provide the appropriate account details for the Snapshot Agent.**

   You must provide two items on the screen shown in Figure 15-11:

   • A domain or machine account used to run the Snapshot Agent. For security reasons, Microsoft does not recommend running the Snapshot Agent using the SQL Server Agent account.

   • A method for connecting to the publisher, either by impersonating the process account or using a specified SQL Server login.

10. **Click OK to close the Snapshot Agent Security screen and then click the Next button to continue.**

11. **In the next screen of the New Publication Wizard, click the Next button to accept the default option of creating the publication immedi-ately upon completion of the wizard.**

Figure 15-11:
The
Snapshot
Agent
Security
screen.

As with the creation of a publisher/distributor, you may also choose to create a script that you can use to generate the publication at a later date.

12. **Provide a publication name in the Publication Name text box and click the Finish button to create it.**

SQL Server presents the status screen shown in Figure 15-12. The process of creating the publication may take a few minutes to complete.

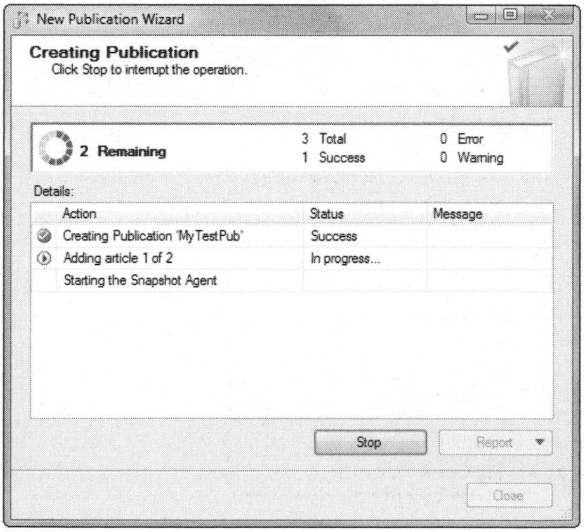

Figure 15-12:
Publication
status.

Subscribing to a Publication

The final step in setting up replication is configuring subscribers for the publication. You can do this at either the subscriber or the publisher, using the following process:

1. **With SSMS open, expand the Replication folder on the publisher.**

2. **Expand the Local Publications folder.**

3. **Right-click the publication to which you want to create a subscription and select New Subscriptions from the pop-up menu.**

   SQL Server starts the New Subscription Wizard.

4. **Click Next to advance past the Welcome screen.**

5. **Verify that the Publication pages shows the appropriate publisher and publication. Click the Next button to continue.**

6. **Choose either a push or pull subscription and click the Next button to continue.**

   The choice of a push or pull subscription (described earlier in this chapter, in the "Server roles" section) determines where the Distribution Agent runs. For push subscriptions, the Distribution Agent runs on the distributor. For pull subscriptions, the Distribution Agent runs on the subscriber. In this example, I choose a pull subscription, as shown in Figure 15-13.

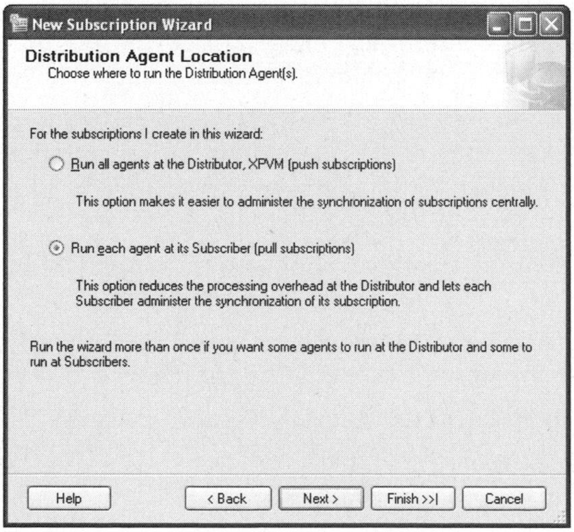

Figure 15-13: Selecting a pull subscription.

7. **Choose one or more subscribers using the check boxes, and choose subscription databases using the pull-down menus. When finished, click the Next button to continue.**

Figure 15-14 illustrates this process. If you want to add a subscriber not already shown, click the Add Subscriber button to configure the server.

You may use this wizard to configure subscribers running Microsoft SQL Server, Oracle, or IBM DB2 databases.

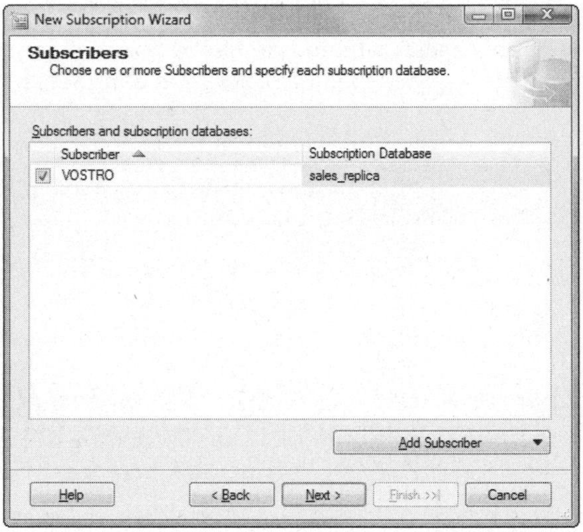

New Subscription Wizard

Subscribers
Choose one or more Subscribers and specify each subscription database.

Subscribers and subscription databases:

Subscriber	Subscription Database
☑ VOSTRO	sales_replica

Add Subscriber ▼

Help   < Back   Next >   Finish >>| Cancel

Figure 15-14: Selecting subscribers and subscription databases.

8. **Click the ellipses (. . .) button to configure Distribution Agent Security. After configuring the appropriate information, click the Next button to continue.**

You need to specify account information for the subscription connections. Doing so is similar to the process shown in Figure 15-11 for the Snapshot Agent.

9. **Choose a Distribution Agent schedule and click the Next button to continue.**

By default, the Distribution Agent synchronizes continuously. You may choose to make it synchronize on demand or define a custom schedule.

10. **Choose when to initialize the subscription and click the Next button to continue.**

Normally, you should accept the default option Immediately. If you set up a delayed synchronization schedule, you may opt to delay the subscription initialization until the first synchronization occurs.

11. **Click Next to accept the default option to create the subscription immediately upon exiting the wizard.**

As with other processes described in this chapter, you also have the option to create a script that will generate the subscription at a later time.

12. **Click the Finish button to create the subscription.**

SQL Server presents a status window similar to that shown previously in Figure 15-12 and notifies you when the operation completes.

Monitoring Replication

SQL Server provides a simple mechanism for viewing replication status: the Replication Monitor, shown in Figure 15-15.

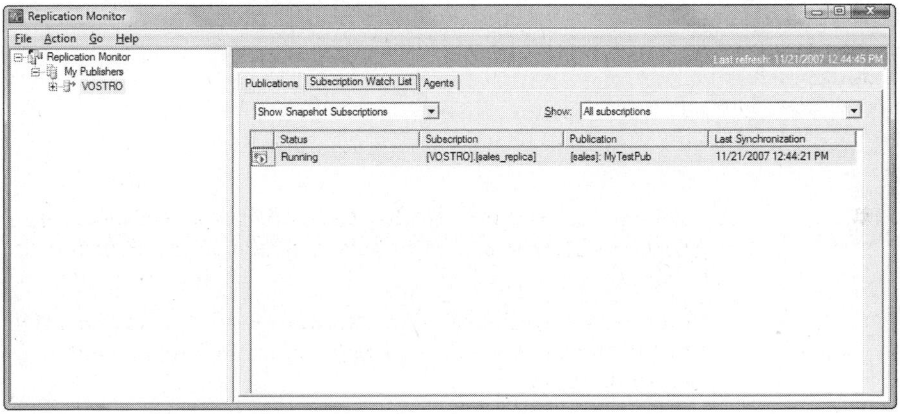

Figure 15-15: The SQL Server Replication Monitor.

Replication Monitor allows you to track the following:

✔ The status of each publication on a server, including

  • Number of subscriptions active

  • Number of subscriptions currently synchronizing

  • Average performance

  • Worst performance

✔ The status of each subscription, including

- The subscribing database

- The publication

- The date and time of the last synchronization

✔ The status of the following agents:

- Snapshot Agent

- Log Reader Agent

- Queue Reader Agent

- Maintenance Jobs

To invoke Replication Monitor, simply right-click the Replication folder in SSMS and select Launch Replication Monitor from the pop-up menu.

Part VI

Protecting Your Data

The 5th Wave
By Rich Tennant

Now maybe these folks got a decent disaster recovery plan and maybe they don't...

DANGER WILD RHINOCEROS

In this part . . .

Knowing how to protect your SQL Server data from unwanted intruders and natural or technical disasters is a critical requirement, and this part covers the basics of doing just that. You find out how to implement access controls to limit the rights of database users and how to use encryption to protect your information from unauthorized access. An entire chapter in this part is dedicated to introducing the concept of transactions and explaining how they can protect the integrity of data stored within your database. Finally, you discover techniques for backing up your database so that you can restore your data in the event of a disaster.

Chapter 16

Protecting Your Data from Prying Eyes

. . . .

In This Chapter

▶ Creating database logins and user accounts

▶ Using roles to manage user rights efficiently

▶ Protecting data with encryption in storage and transit

▶ Auditing SQL Server activity

. . . .

Databases often contain extremely sensitive information that is valuable to your organization and your customers. In many cases, laws, regulations, or good business practices dictate that you protect that information from disclosure to unauthorized individuals.

In this chapter, I discuss the mechanisms offered in SQL Server 2008 that help you protect your data from unauthorized access. I describe the process of managing database users and roles, grouping objects with schemas, using encryption to protect data in storage and transit, and enabling database auditing to meet compliance requirements.

Creating and Managing Logins

As I discuss in Chapter 2, SQL Server has two different authentication modes: Windows Authentication mode and SQL Server and Windows Authentication (mixed) mode. In either case, you may grant Windows users permission to connect to and manipulate SQL Server databases. If you use mixed mode authentication, you may also create dedicated SQL Server logins that exist only on the database server.

Creating server logins

Creating a database user follows the same basic process, whether you're granting SQL Server permissions to a Windows user or creating a SQL Server login account. Here are the basic steps:

1. **Open SQL Server Management Studio and connect to the SQL Server instance for which you want to create a new login.**

2. **Expand the Security folder.**

3. **Right-click the Logins folder and select New Login from the pop-up menu.**

    SSMS displays the Login - New window, shown in Figure 16-1.

4. **Click the radio button corresponding to the type of login you want to create: Windows authentication or SQL Server authentication.**

5. **Provide a login name in the appropriate text box.**

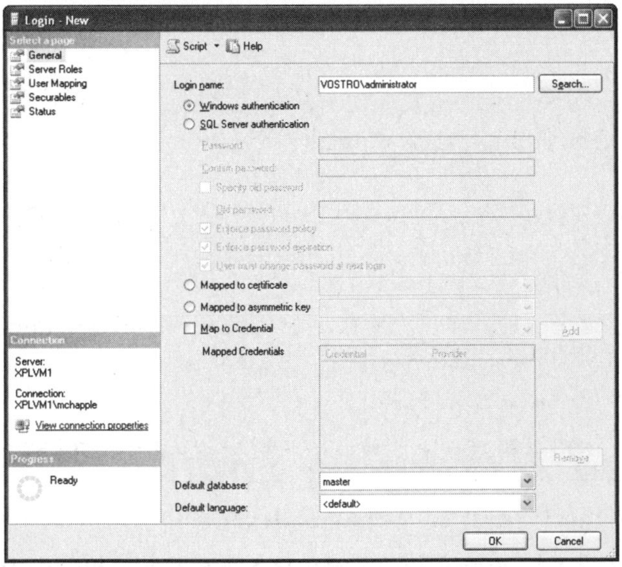

Figure 16-1:
Creating a new data-base login.

If you chose SQL Server authentication, simply provide a login name (such as jdoe). If you chose Windows authentication, provide it in the form DOMAIN\username (such as MYDOMAIN\jdoe). In addition to selecting Windows domain users, you may also create a login corresponding to a Windows domain group.

6. **Provide SQL Server authentication details, if applicable.**

   If you are creating a SQL Server authentication login, provide a password by typing it in the Password text box and the Confirmation text box. You may also choose whether you want to enforce the server's password complexity and expiration policies or force the user to change the password at the next login.

7. **Use the drop-down lists to change the login's default database and language, if you want.**

8. **Click the OK button to create the login.**

Removing database logins

If you want to remove an existing login (using either SQL Server authentication or Windows authentication), simply right-click it in the Logins folder of SSMS and choose Delete from the pop-up menu.

You cannot delete a login associated with an active server session. You must first disconnect the user before deleting the login.

Adding Database Users

Once you've created server logins, you must explicitly grant those logins access to databases by creating corresponding database users. Here's how you create a new database user:

1. **With SSMS open, connect to the server containing the database where you would like to add a user.**

2. **Expand the Databases folder.**

3. **Expand the folder of the databases where you would like to add a user.**

4. **Expand the Security folder of that database.**

5. **Right-click the Users folder and select New User from the pop-up menu.**

   SSMS displays the Database User - New window shown in Figure 16-2.

Database User - New

Select a page
- General
- Securables
- Extended Properties

Script ▾ Help

User name: `VOTRO\mchapple`

◉ Login name: `VOTRO\mchapple`
○ Certificate name:
○ Key name:
○ Without login

Default schema:

Schemas owned by this user:

Owned Schemas
☐ db_accessadmin
☐ db_backupoperator
☐ db_datareader
☐ db_datawriter
☐ db_ddladmin
☐ db_denydatareader

Database role membership:

Role Members
☐ db_accessadmin
☐ db_backupoperator
☐ db_datareader
☐ db_datawriter
☐ db_ddladmin
☐ db_denydatareader
☐ db_denydatawriter

Connection

Server:
VOSTRO

Connection:
sa

View connection properties

Progress

◌ Ready

OK   Cancel

Figure 16-2:
Creating a
new data-
base user.

Note that Login Name isn't the only user option on this page. SQL Server also allows you to create database users associated with digital certificates, asymmetric encryption keys, and no login. These advanced options are beyond the scope of this book.

6. **Provide the name of the login you wish to associate with the database user in the Login Name text box.**

   You may click the ellipses (. . .) button if you want to search for the login.

7. **Provide the name of the database user in the User Name check box.**

   You may choose anything you want. However, best practice dictates that you use the same name for both the username and the login name.

8. **Click the OK button to create the user.**

If you want, you may explicitly grant permissions to database users in the Securables page of the New Database User window. However, database roles offer a much more efficient way to manage user permissions. I discuss the creation and management of database roles in the next section.

Managing Rights with Roles

Managing individual user permissions on a large SQL Server deployment can be an absolute nightmare for database administrators. It's very difficult to track the large number of permissions associated with each user account, and the sheer complexity of this approach makes errors very likely.

SQL Server helps avoid these problems by providing server and database roles. You may define roles that are associated with a *type* of user, rather than an individual, and then assign that role the permissions required by that type of user. You may then associate each user with one or more roles necessary to complete the user's job function.

Understanding fixed server roles

SQL Server provides eight built-in server-level roles that define sets of user permissions that apply to the entire server. These fixed server roles appear in Table 16-1. These are the only possible options for server-wide roles; you can't create your own server roles.

Table 16-1	SQL Server 2008 Fixed Server Roles
Role Name	**Description**
Bulkadmin	Authorized to perform bulk insert operations
Dbcreator	Authorized to create, alter, drop or restore any database on the SQL Server instance
Diskadmin	Authorized to manage disk files
Processadmin	Authorized to end processes running on the SQL Server instance
Securityadmin	Authorized to grant, revoke and deny server and database permissions and reset passwords
Serveradmin	Authorized to shut down the server and modify server configuration options
Setupadmin	Authorized to add and removed linked server instances
Sysadmin	Authorized to perform any action on the SQL Server

You may grant fixed server roles only to server logins. Database users may not be members of a server role. Here's how to view and modify the membership of a fixed server role:

1. **With SSMS open, connect to the server instance for which you want to modify role membership.**

2. **Expand the Security folder.**

3. **Expand the Server Roles folder.**

4. **Right-click the role you want to modify and choose Properties from the pop-up menu.**

   SSMS displays the Server Role Properties window, shown in Figure 16-3. You may review the list of role members that appears within this window.

5. **Use the Add or Remove buttons to modify role members.**

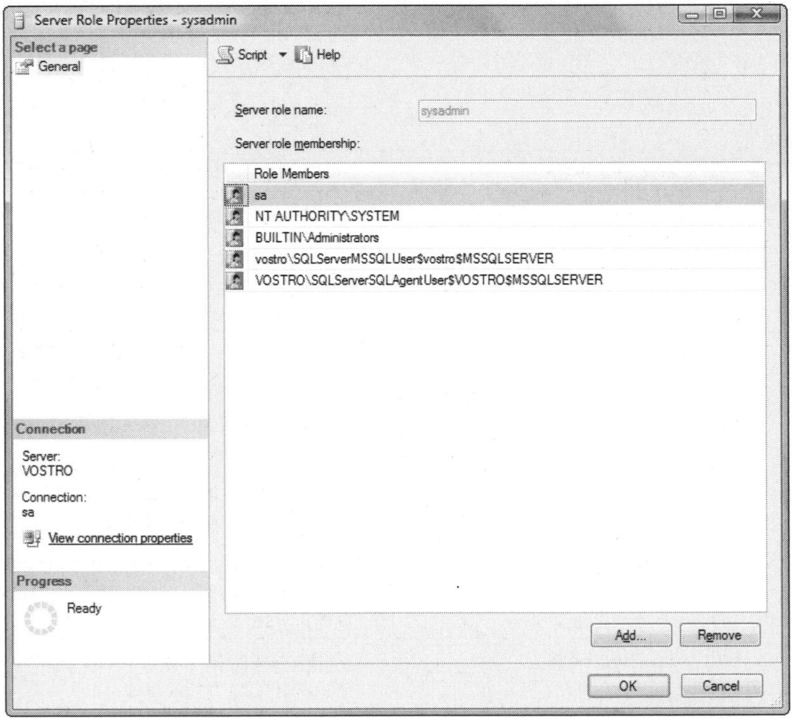

Figure 16-3:
Modifying
server role
member-
ship.

By default, any member of the Administrators group on the local Windows server is also a member of the sysadmin fixed server role. Generally speaking, you should practice separation of privileges and not grant this permission to system administrators. Rather, it should be reserved for database administrators. You may change this default behavior by removing the BUILTIN\ Administrators group from the sysadmin role.

Understanding fixed database roles

Just as SQL Server provides built-in fixed server roles to grant server-wide permissions, it also provides fixed database roles to grant users predetermined sets of permissions to individual databases. The SQL Server 2008 fixed database roles appear in Table 16-2.

Table 16-2	Fixed Database Roles
Role Name	*Description*
db_accessadmin	Authorized to add or remove database users corresponding to Windows users/groups and SQL Server logins
db_backupoperator	Authorized to back up the database
db_datareader	Authorized to read any data from all user tables
db_datawriter	Authorize to add, delete or modify data in any user table
db_ddladmin	Authorized to run any DDL command, modifying the structure of the database
db_denydatareader	Prohibited from reading data stored in any user table
db_denydatawriter	Prohibited from adding, deleting or modifying data from any user table
db_owner	Authorized to perform any database configuration activity, including dropping the database
db_securityadmin	Authorized to modify role membership and database permissions

You may grant database role membership to any database user by following these steps:

1. **With SSMS open, connect to the server instance that contains the database for which you want to modify role membership.**

2. **Expand the Databases folder.**

3. **Expand the folder corresponding to the database for which you want to modify role membership.**

4. **Expand the Security folder.**

5. **Expand the Roles folder.**

6. **Expand the Database Roles folder.**

7. **Right-click the role you want to modify and choose Properties from the pop-up menu.**

   SSMS displays the Database Role Properties window, shown in Figure 16-4. You may review the list of role members that appears within this window.

8. **Use the Add or Remove buttons to modify role members.**

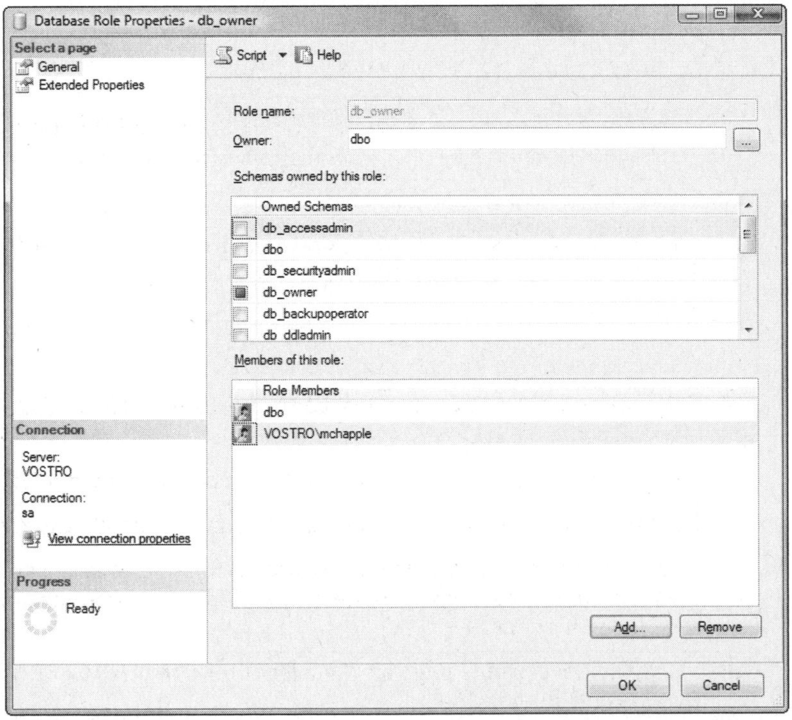

Figure 16-4: Modifying database role membership.

Creating database roles

In contrast to server roles, SQL Server allows you to create your own custom database roles to simplify database management. For example, if you're running a retail store, you might create database roles for cashiers, store managers, district managers, and executives. You could then grant different permissions to each one of these roles. Granting different permissions gives you tremendous flexibility in management. For example, if a user changes jobs within the organization, you simply need to change his or her role membership to correspond to the new job responsibilities. Similarly, if you replace an employee, you need only to remove the old employee's user account and create an account for the new employee with the same role membership.

The real power of roles becomes clear when you need to change the permissions associated with a role. Suppose, for example, that you create a new table that store managers must access. Rather than go through every user account to determine whether the individual is a store manager requiring access to that role, you simply add permissions for that table to the store manager role.

Here's the process for creating a new database role:

1. **With SSMS open, connect to the server instance that contains the database for which you want to modify role membership.**

2. **Expand the Databases folder.**

3. **Expand the folder corresponding to the database for which you want to modify role membership.**

4. **Expand the Security folder.**

5. **Expand the Roles folder.**

6. **Right-click the Database Roles folder and select New⇨Database Role from the pop-up menu.**

   SSMS displays the Database Role - New window, shown in Figure 16-5.

7. **Provide a descriptive name for the role in the Role Name text box.**

   The Owner text box allows you to specify the database user that will own the role. If you leave this text box blank, the account used to create the role will own it.

8. **Click the Securables page in the Select a Page portion of the New Database Role window.**

   SSMS displays the Securables page, shown in Figure 16-6.

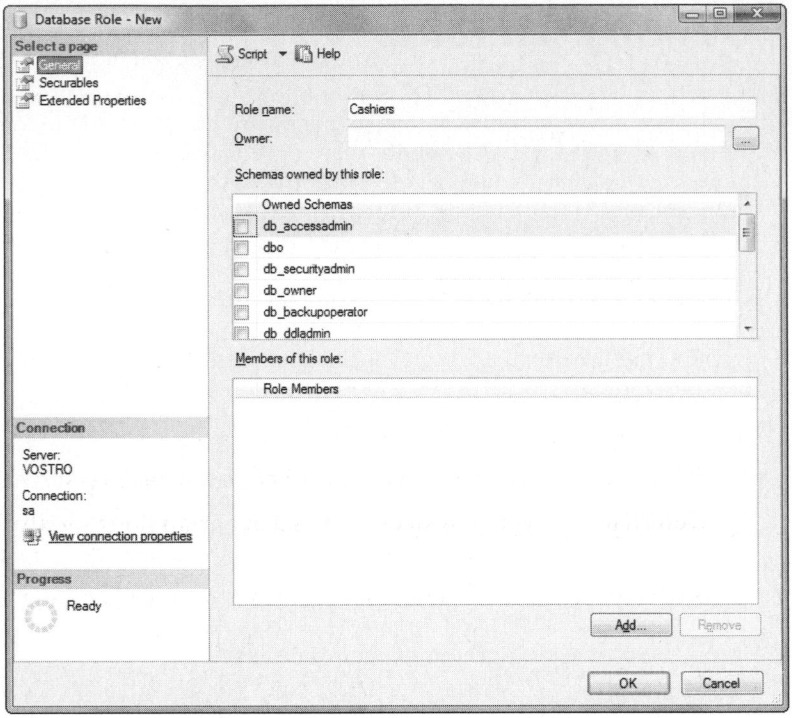

Figure 16-5:
Creating a new database role.

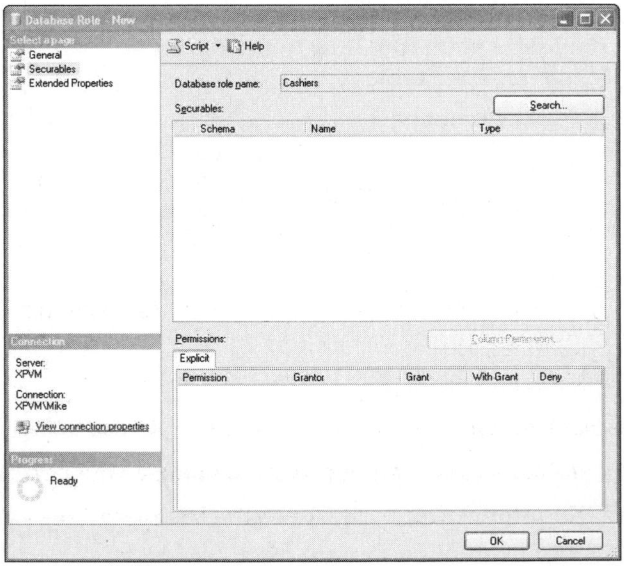

Figure 16-6:
Adding role permissions.

9. **Click the Search button.**

   SSMS displays the Add Objects dialog box, shown in Figure 16-7.

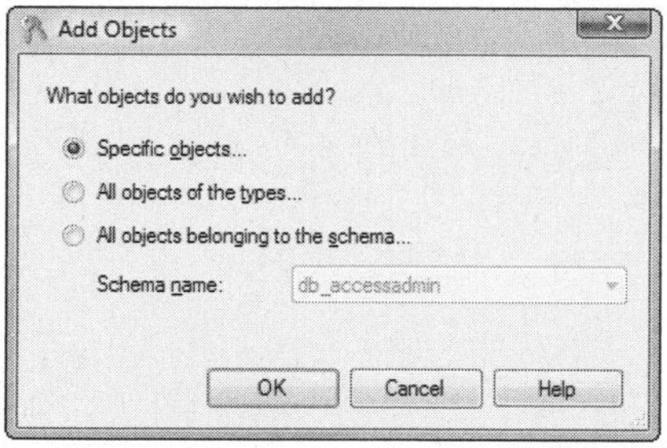

Figure 16-7:
The Add
Objects dia-
log box.

10. **Click the OK button to accept the Specific Objects option.**

    (Alternatively, you may decide to assign permissions for all objects of a certain type or all objects contained within a database schema.)

    SSMS displays the Select Object Types window, shown in Figure 16-8.

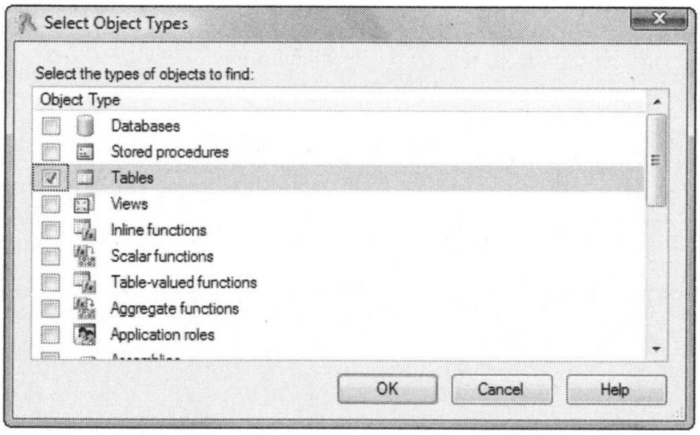

Figure 16-8:
Selecting
object
types.

11. **Select the type(s) of objects you want to grant the role permissions on and click OK to continue.**

12. **Click the Browse button.**

    SSMS displays the Browse for Objects window, shown in Figure 16-9.

13. **Select the database object(s) you want to change role permissions on.**

14. **Click the OK button twice to return to the Database Role - New window.**

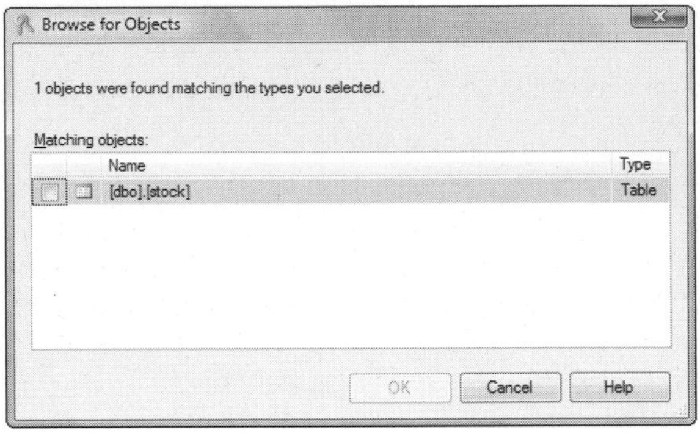

Browse for Objects

1 objects were found matching the types you selected.

Matching objects:

Name	Type
[dbo].[stock]	Table

OK   Cancel   Help

Figure 16-9:
Browsing
for database
objects.

15. **Highlight the first object in the Securables portion of the page and click the appropriate check boxes for the permissions you want to grant the role on that object.**

16. **Repeat Step 15 for each object in the Securables portion of the page.**

17. **Click OK to create the new role.**

During this process, you assigned permissions on database objects to the new role. The permissions you may choose from depend on the type of object you are accessing. For each of those permissions, you may grant the following types of access:

- ✔ **GRANT** allows role members to use the permission.

- ✔ **WITH GRANT** allows role members to grant others use of the permission.

- ✔ **DENY** explicitly forbids role members to use the permission.

Keep in mind that DENY permissions override GRANT permissions.

Assigning users to database roles

You may assign a user to one or more roles within a database by selecting the role in the Database role membership section of the user's Properties page. This page is shown in Figure 16-2, which appears earlier in this chapter.

Preserving Confidentiality with Encryption

Encryption technology allows you to prevent unauthorized access to information by people who bypass the normal security controls implemented by your database. For example, someone with access to your network might attempt to eavesdrop on network communications, or a person with physical access to your server might try to remove the hard drive and access it with data recovery tools.

Encryption blocks these attacks by making the data undecipherable to people who don't have access to the appropriate encryption key. SQL Server provides encryption mechanisms that allow you to protect your data while it's in transit (protection against network eavesdroppers) and while it's stored (protection against those accessing the physical disk). In this section, I explain how you can implement these protections.

Encrypting database connections

Encrypting database connections protects you against network eavesdroppers who might intercept the communications between a user and the database server.

To encrypt database connections, you must first ensure that your server administrator has configured an SSL certificate for the server. This process varies depending upon your server operating system and is beyond the scope of this book.

Here's how to encrypt database connections in SQL Server 2008:

1. **Start SQL Server Configuration Manager.**

2. **Expand the SQL Server Network Configuration folder.**

3. **Right-click the Protocols folder corresponding to the SQL Server instance you want to configure and select Properties from the pop-up menu.**

   SQL Server Configuration Manager displays the Protocol Properties window, shown in Figure 16-10.

4. **Use the drop-down box to change the Force Encryption value to Yes.**

   Selecting this option will require that all database users connect using encryption, thereby providing maximum protection for your database.

5. **Select the Certificate tab of the Protocol Properties window.**

6. **Use the Certificate drop-down menu to select the certificate installed by your server administrator.**

7. **Click the OK button to close the window.**

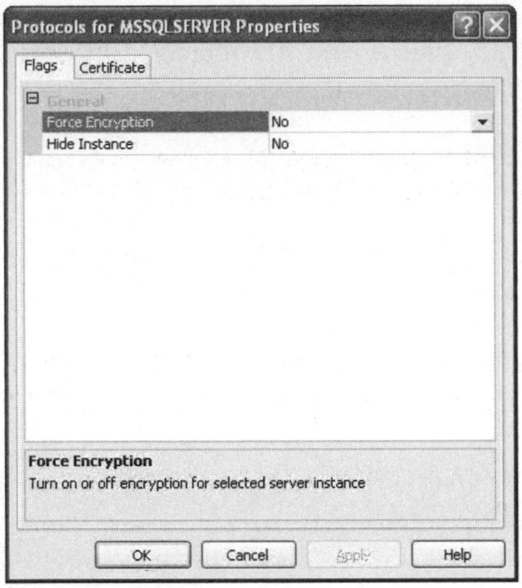

Figure 16-10:
Configuring
encryption
for SQL
Server
connections.

When you complete this process, the server will reject any requests for unencrypted communications. This feature will protect your database contents from eavesdropping while in transit between the client and server.

Encrypting stored data

SQL Server 2008 introduces Transparent Data Encryption (TDE), a new technology designed to allow the encryption of stored data. TDE provides real-time encryption and decryption of the data and log files that SQL Server stores on disk. TDE also ensures the encryption of database backups.

Creating a master encryption key and certificate

Before you can use TDE for the first time on a SQL Server instance, you need to perform two preliminary tasks: creating a master encryption key and creating a certificate based upon that key. SQL Server will use this key to protect the keys you use to encrypt individual databases.

To create a master encryption key, use the following Transact-SQL statements:

```
USE master;
CREATE MASTER KEY ENCRYPTION BY PASSWORD = 'pick_a_strong_
            password';
```

Replace the phrase `pick_a_strong_password` with the password of your choice. This password is literally the key to the security of your entire SQL Server database; be sure to treat it with care!

After you've created a master encryption key, you need to create a server certificate with the following Transact-SQL statement:

```
CREATE CERTIFICATE MyCert WITH SUBJECT = 'My Encryption
        Certificate';
```

You may replace the certificate name (`MyCert`) and the subject (`My Encryption Certificate`) with the name and subject of your choice.

Encrypting a database with Transparent Data Encryption

After you've created a server certificate, you can use it to configure Transparent Data Encryption for your database. First, you must create a database encryption key based upon your server certificate. Here's the Transact-SQL to create such a key:

```
USE sales;

CREATE DATABASE ENCRYPTION KEY
WITH ALGORITHM = AES_256
ENCRYPTION BY SERVER CERTIFICATE MyCert;
```

Replace `sales` with the name of the database you plan to encrypt. You may choose among several encryption algorithms supported by SQL Server 2008:

- ✔ `AES_256` uses the Advanced Encryption Standard (AES) with a 256-bit encryption key. This is the strongest encryption supported by SQL Server, but it also causes the greatest performance impact on the server.

- ✔ `AES_192` uses AES with a shorter, 192-bit encryption key.

- ✔ `AES_128` uses AES with the shortest possible (128-bit) encryption key. This is the default algorithm used by SQL Server 2008 unless you specify an alternative algorithm.

- ✔ `TRIPLE_DES_3KEY` uses three iterations of the Data Encryption Standard (DES) with three different keys. It has an effective key length of 112 bits.

After creating the encryption key, you may turn on encryption using the following Transact-SQL statement:

```
ALTER DATABASE Sales
SET ENCRYPTION ON;
```

SQL Server then begins a background process that encrypts the database. The time required to complete the initial database encryption will vary based upon the size of the database and the available server resources.

Backing up your master key and certificates

You must create backups of both your master encryption key and any server certificates used to encrypt data stored in your database. Without those backups, you will be unable to restore data to SQL Server in the event of a disaster. Be sure to create the backups and store them in a safe location.

Here's the Transact-SQL statement to back up your master encryption key:

```
BACKUP MASTER KEY TO FILE = 'filename'
  ENCRYPTION BY PASSWORD = 'choose_a_strong_password'
```

You can use the following command to back up a server certificate:

```
BACKUP CERTIFICATE MyCert TO FILE = 'cert_filename'
  WITH PRIVATE KEY ( FILE = 'key_filename',
  ENCRYPTION BY PASSWORD = 'choose_a_strong_password');
```

Restoring a master key or certificate

If you later need to restore a master key, you may use the following Transact-SQL command:

```
RESTORE MASTER KEY FROM FILE = 'filename'
  DECRYPTION BY PASSWORD = 'backup_password'
  ENCRYPTION BY PASSWORD = 'choose_a_strong_password'
```

The password specified in the first clause must be the same password specified in the ENCRYPTION BY PASSWORD clause of the BACKUP MASTER KEY command used to create the backup. SQL Server will use the password specified in the second clause to encrypt the new master key.

There is no comparable command to restore a certificate. Rather, you use the CREATE CERTIFICATE command and specify that the certificate be created from a file, as follows:

```
CREATE CERTIFICATE MyCert
FROM FILE = 'cert_filename'
WITH PRIVATE KEY (FILE = 'key_filename',
DECRYPTION BY PASSWORD = 'backup_password')
```

Auditing SQL Server Activity

SQL Server 2008 introduces a greatly enhanced auditing capability that allows you to meet regulatory compliance requirements. For example, if you're responsible for a database that stores credit card information, the Payment Card Industry Data Security Standard requires that you use automated auditing to log all individual user accesses to cardholder data. SQL Server's auditing facility allows you to meet these requirements.

Enabling and configuring auditing

Using SQL Server's auditing functionality involves two discrete steps: creating an audit object and creating either a server audit specification or a database audit specification. As you might imagine, server audit specifications allow you to track server-level events, such as logins. Database audit specifications, on the other hand, monitor database-specific activity, including data insertions, deletions, modifications, and accesses.

Creating an audit object

Before you begin auditing SQL Server activity, you must create a SQL Server audit object. This object identifies the location where SQL Server will store the audit trail, but does not identify the activities that will be audited. Here's how to create a new audit object:

1. **Open SQL Server Management Studio and connect to the database server you want to audit.**

2. **Click the plus (+) icon to the left of the Security folder to expand the folder.**

3. **Right-click the Audits folder and select New Audit from the pop-up menu.**

   You see the Create Audit page, shown in Figure 16-11.

4. **Provide a name for your audit object in the Audit name field.**

5. **Select an audit destination from the list.**

   SQL Server allows you to store your audit records in three different types of location:

   - To a file
   - To the Windows Application log
   - To the Windows Security log

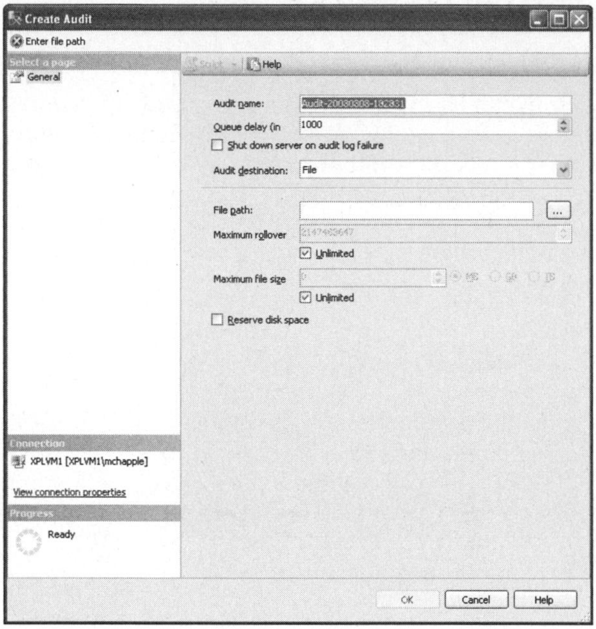

Figure 16-11:
Creating an
audit object.

6. **Click the OK button to create the audit object.**

Creating a server audit specification

Server audit specifications allow you to identify the specific activities you'd like SQL Server to audit. Here's how to create one:

1. **Open SQL Server Management Studio and connect to the database server you want to audit.**

2. **Click the plus (+) icon to the left of the Security folder to expand the folder.**

3. **Right-click the Server Audit Specifications folder and select New Server Audit Specification from the pop-up menu.**

   You see the Create Server Audit Specification page, shown in Figure 16-12.

4. **Provide a name for the specification in the Name field.**

5. **Select a Server Audit object from the list.**

6. **Provide details of the actions you want to audit by creating rows in the grid in the bottom half of the window.**

You may add new audit activities by using the Audit Action Type drop-down menu in a blank row of the grid. For example, you might select the SCHEMA_OBJECT_PERMISSION_CHANGE_GROUP to audit all object permission changes. Similarly, you may use the FAILED_LOGIN_GROUP to monitor failed login attempts.

7. **Click the OK button to create the specification and begin auditing.**

Creating a database audit specification

If you wish to audit database-specific activity, you may do so by creating a database audit specification. Here's the process:

1. **Open SQL Server Management Studio and connect to the database server you wish to audit.**

2. **Click on the plus (+) icon to the left of the Databases folder to expand the folder.**

3. **Expand the folder for the database you want to audit.**

4. **Expand the Security folder for that database.**

5. **Right-click Database Audit Specifications and select New Database Audit Specification from the pop-up menu.**

   You see the Create Database Audit Specification window, shown in Figure 16-13.

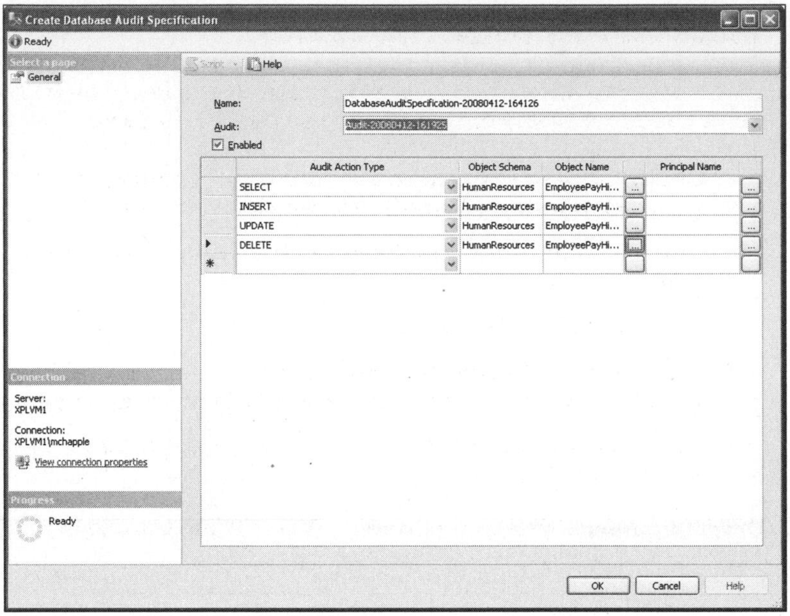

Figure 16-13:
Creating a
database
audit
specification.

6. **Provide a name for the specification in the Name field.**

7. **Select a Server Audit object from the list.**

8. **Use the Audit Action Type drop-down menu to select an action you want to audit in the first empty row of the grid.**

9. **Click the ellipses (. . .) icon in the Object Name field of that row to open the Select Objects window.**

10. **Click the Browse button.**

11. **Select the check boxes to the left of the object(s) you want to audit.**

12. **Click the OK button to close the Browse for Objects window.**

13. **Click the OK button to close the Select Objects window.**

   You may repeat Steps 8–13 as many times as you want to audit different actions in the same database audit specification.

14. **Click the ellipses (. . .) icon in the Principal Name field of that row to open the Select Objects window.**

   Follow the same process used in Steps 10–13 to select the principal(s) you wish to audit.

15. **Click the OK button to create the specification and begin auditing.**

Reviewing audit records

SQL Server provides a built-in log file viewer that allows you to peruse SQL Server audit records. Here's how you can open the viewer:

1. **Open SQL Server Management Studio and connect to the database server containing the audit records you want to view.**

2. **Click the plus (+) icon to the left of the Security folder to expand the folder.**

3. **Expand the Audits folder.**

4. **Right-click the Server Audit object used to log the audit events you want to view and choose View Audit Logs from the pop-up menu.**

   The records in Log File Viewer open, as shown in Figure 16-14.

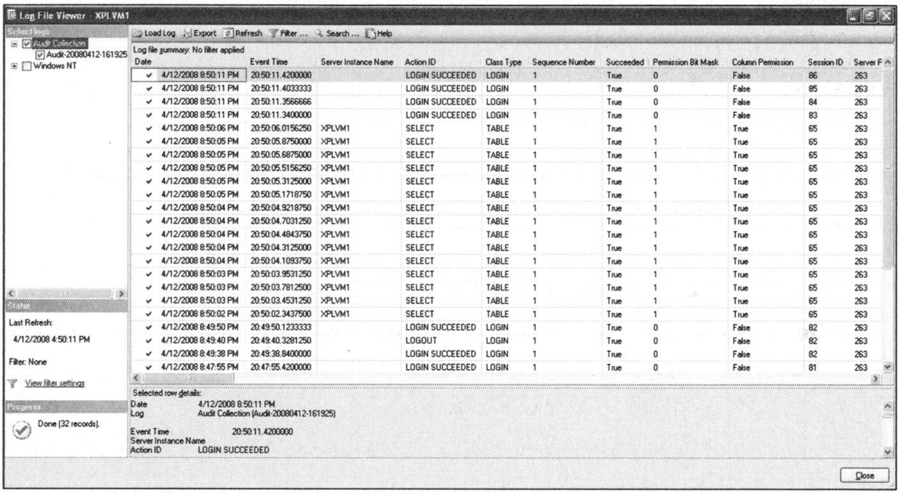

Figure 16-14: Reviewing Audit Records with Log File Viewer.

Chapter 17

Preserving the Integrity of Your Transactions

In This Chapter

▶ Using the ACID model to describe transaction benefits

▶ Creating, committing, and rolling back transactions in SQL Server 2008

▶ Testing Transact-SQL statements using transactions

▶ Handling error conditions within transactions using `TRY . . .CATCH`

*U*ntil this point in the book, I've presented each Transact-SQL statement as an isolated event. When I've used more than one statement, they've been a series of independent statements. Sometimes, however, this isn't the behavior you want. In many cases, you'll want a series of SQL statements to occur as an "all or nothing" event. Transactions are the answer to this dilemma. They allow you to bundle independent Transact-SQL statements into a linked bundle.

For example, consider the process used to transfer money between two different bank accounts. You might view the transfer of $50 from account X to account Y as two separate steps:

1. Deduct $50 from account X.

2. Add $50 to account Y.

However, the bank certainly doesn't want these two steps to occur independently, for several reasons:

✔ If the deduction of funds from account X doesn't succeed (perhaps the balance is less than $50), the bank doesn't want $50 credited to account Y.

✔ If the addition of funds to account Y doesn't succeed (perhaps account Y doesn't exist or is closed), the bank doesn't want $50 deducted from account X.

Combining these two statements into a single transaction allows the bank to ensure that they happen in the desired "all or nothing" fashion.

In this chapter, you find out how to use the ACID model to preserve transaction integrity and to work with transactions in SQL Server 2008.

Preserving Transaction Integrity with the ACID Model

Database professionals use the ACID model to describe the four essential features of a database transaction. That is, a database transaction should be

- ✔ Atomic
- ✔ Consistent
- ✔ Isolated
- ✔ Durable

In the remainder of this section, I describe each one of these transaction characteristics.

Atomicity

The atomicity requirement of the ACID model formalizes the "all or nothing" principle I describe in the introduction to this chapter. Atomicity requires that, in order for a transaction to succeed, all the components of that transaction must succeed. If a single component of the transaction fails, all the transaction components must be rolled back (undone).

In addition to scenarios in which Transact-SQL statements may dictate that the transaction be rolled back, atomicity requires that the database be resilient in the face of hardware and software failures. If a database server crashes in the middle of a transaction, the database should not contain any changes made as intermediate steps in that transaction when it restarts.

To put this idea in the context of the banking example I use in the introduction to this chapter, suppose that the database server crashes after Step 1 executes but before Step 2 takes place. When the database restarts, account X should not show the $50 deduction because the second half of the transaction (crediting the funds to account Y) did not take place.

Consistency

The consistency principle requires that all data written to the database is consistent with business rules. In Chapter 6, I discuss how you can use constraints and relationships to enforce business rules in your database. The consistency principle ensures that the database always honors those requirements.

In the world of transactions, consistency requires that the database be compliant with all those rules when the transaction completes. You can view a transaction as bringing the database from one consistent state (the state prior to the transaction) to another consistent state (the state after the transaction).

If the Transact-SQL statements contained within the transaction would bring the database into an inconsistent state, the entire transaction must be rolled back so that the database remains in its original, consistent state.

Isolation

The isolation principle states that each database transaction must be executed independently of other database transactions. For example, suppose you had the following two transactions:

Transaction 1

1. Check to see whether account X has a balance >= $50.
2. Deduct $50 from account X.
3. Add $50 to account Y.

Transaction 2

1. Check to see whether account X has a balance >= $50.
2. Deduct $50 from account X.
3. Add $50 to account Z.

As you can see, I've added a step to this example that verifies the balance of account X before deducting funds. If you execute these transactions sequentially (that is, execute transaction 1, wait until it completes, and then execute transaction 2 or vice versa), it's obvious that there isn't any problem.

However, suppose that you execute these two transactions simultaneously? If they are not isolated from each other, the sequence of events shown in Figure 17-1 might occur.

Transaction 1

1. Check account X balance

2. Deduct $50 from account X

3. Add $50 to account Y

Transaction 2

1. Check account X balance

2. Deduct $50 from account X

3. Add $50 to account Y

Figure 17-1:
Improper
transaction
sequencing.

In that sequence of events, trouble occurs if the opening balance of account X is $75. Both transactions first check the balance and see that it's over $50. Then they go and carry out their tasks, leaving account X with a negative balance.

Fortunately, databases prevent this scenario by enforcing isolation — transactions must execute independently. In this case, all three statements of Transaction 1 must complete before Transaction 2 may begin.

Durability

Durability ensures that after a transaction commits, it is permanently recorded in the database. If a hardware or software failure occurs, administrators may use database backups and transaction logs to restore the database to its state prior to the failure.

Creating SQL Server Transactions

Creating a SQL Server transaction in Transact-SQL is straightforward. Simply write the series of T-SQL statements that you'd like to bundle in a transaction and wrap them in BEGIN TRANSACTION and COMMIT TRANSACTION statements, as follows:

```
BEGIN TRANSACTION

<Transact-SQL Statements>
COMMIT TRANSACTION
```

SQL Server is now responsible for executing all the statements between the BEGIN TRANSACTION and COMMIT TRANSACTION statements in an atomic, consistent, isolated, and durable fashion.

COMMIT or ROLLBACK?

In addition to adding protection against a database failure, you may programmatically rollback transactions because of an error condition. For example, consider the following transaction, designed to record the transfer of 100 oranges from a Tampa warehouse to a New York warehouse:

```
DECLARE @tampa INT

BEGIN TRANSACTION

UPDATE stock
SET inventory = inventory + 100
WHERE item = 'Oranges'
AND warehouse = 'New York'

UPDATE stock
SET inventory = inventory - 100
WHERE item = 'Oranges'
AND warehouse = 'Tampa'

SELECT @tampa = inventory
FROM stock
WHERE item = 'Oranges'
AND warehouse = 'Tampa'

IF (@tampa < 0)
          BEGIN
              PRINT 'Insufficient Inventory'
              ROLLBACK TRANSACTION
          END
ELSE
          BEGIN
              PRINT 'Transfer Successful'
              COMMIT TRANSACTION
          END
```

Note that this transaction includes several steps:

1. Increase the inventory of oranges in New York by 100.

2. Decrease the inventory of oranges in Tampa by 100.

3. Check the inventory of oranges in Tampa to see whether it is greater than zero. If the transaction resulted in a negative inventory, print an insufficient inventory error message and roll back the transaction. If the inventory in Tampa is zero or greater, print a message that the transfer was successful and commit the transfer to the database.

You may have noticed that there's an easier way to accomplish this task: I could have simply checked the Tampa inventory level before changing either warehouse's inventory. I used this somewhat roundabout approach to provide a simple scenario of programmatically making the decision of whether to commit or roll back a transaction.

Testing Transact-SQL statements with transactions

Transactions are a great way to test Transact-SQL statements. If you're trying to determine whether a transaction will execute properly, wrap it in a set of BEGIN TRANSACTION...ROLLBACK TRANSACTION statements.

Suppose, for example, that you wanted to evaluate the effect of a 20 percent increase in the wholesale price of products in your store with a current wholesale price under 50 cents. You might first want to see what the table would look like after the price increase without actually making changes to your database. You can test the increase by using this Transact-SQL code:

```
SELECT item, warehouse, wholesale_price
FROM stock;


BEGIN TRANSACTION

UPDATE stock
SET wholesale_price = wholesale_price * 1.2
WHERE wholesale_price < 0.5;

SELECT item, warehouse, wholesale_price
FROM stock;

ROLLBACK TRANSACTION

SELECT item, warehouse, wholesale_price
FROM stock;
```

Before I show you the results, take a moment to walk through this series of statements. Note that the first thing I do is show the prices in the stock table, outside the transaction. This provides a "before" look at the table's contents.

Next, I begin the transaction with the BEGIN TRANSACTION statement. Inside the transaction, I change the prices and then check the price table again.

Finally, I cancel my work by rolling back the transaction with the ROLLBACK TRANSACTION statement and then display the final state of the table.

Here are the results:

```
item              warehouse         wholesale_price
---------------   ---------------   ----------------------
Apples            Seattle           0.13
Limes             Seattle           0.33
Oranges           New York          0.55
Oranges           Tampa             0.52

(4 row(s) affected)

(2 row(s) affected)

item              warehouse         wholesale_price
---------------   ---------------   ----------------------
Apples            Seattle           0.156
Limes             Seattle           0.396
Oranges           New York          0.55
Oranges           Tampa             0.52

(4 row(s) affected)

item              warehouse         wholesale_price
---------------   ---------------   ----------------------
Apples            Seattle           0.13
Limes             Seattle           0.33
Oranges           New York          0.55
Oranges           Tampa             0.52

(4 row(s) affected)
```

The results demonstrate the usefulness of rolling back transactions as a testing tool. The first table in the output is the status of the stock table before I make any modification. It concludes with the statement (4 row(s) affected).

Next, you see the simple statement (2 row(s) affected). This is your indication that the UPDATE statement processed successfully and changed the price of the two items in the table with wholesale prices under 50 cents.

The evidence of this appears in the following table output. Note that the prices of apples and oranges in Seattle are 20 percent higher in that table. This output is from the second SELECT statement.

Recall that I followed the second SELECT statement with a ROLLBACK TRANSACTION command. This command undoes the effect of all SQL statements that occurred after the BEGIN TRANSACTION statement, including the price update.

Finally, the last set of output is from the SELECT statement that appeared after the ROLLBACK TRANSACTION statement. This output is outside the loop of our transaction and shows that the final table state is the same as the initial table state. My test transaction had no effect on the integrity of the table.

SQL Server also supports the use of named savepoints to partially roll back a transaction to an intermediate step. You might find this feature useful for performance reasons when dealing with large, complex transactions. The use of savepoints is beyond the scope of this book. For more information, see *SQL Server Books Online*.

Changing the Transaction Isolation Level

Early in this chapter, I describe how the ACID model requires databases to enforce strict isolation between transactions. Well, as with any rule, there are exceptions to the strict enforcement of transaction isolation. You may, when the situation warrants, change the way SQL Server isolates transactions from one another.

SQL Sever provides five different isolation levels that define different techniques for handling isolation. I describe them in the next five subsections.

READ UNCOMMITTED

READ UNCOMMITTED is the lowest possible isolation level in SQL Server. When you set this mode, you allow the reading of data that a transaction has written, but not committed, to the database. Reading at this level may result in three potentially unpleasant situations:

✔ **Dirty reads** occur when a transaction reads data written by another uncommitted transaction that is later rolled back.

✔ **Phantom reads** occur when a transaction inserts or deletes a row from a range of values accessed by another transaction. The other transaction, if it reads the values before and after the update, may see "phantom" rows that appear or disappear.

✔ **Nonrepeatable reads** occur when a transaction reads the same data twice. If another transaction writes the same data between the two read statements, the original transaction may retrieve two different values for the same data element at different points in the transaction.

To set the transaction isolation level to READ UNCOMMITTED, execute the following Transact-SQL statement within SSMS:

```
SET TRANSACTION ISOLATION LEVEL READ UNCOMMITTED
```

READ COMMITTED

READ COMMITTED is the default isolation level used by SQL Server 2008. It implements traditional database isolation and ensures that Transact-SQL statements cannot read data written to a database by an uncommitted transaction. The statement will instead see the state of the database table before the transaction executed.

The READ COMMITTED level solves the problems associated with dirty reads but still suffers from nonrepeatable reads and phantom reads.

If you need to restore the transaction isolation level to the READ COMMITTED state, execute this statement within SSMS:

```
SET TRANSACTION ISOLATION LEVEL READ COMMITTED
```

REPEATABLE READ

If you need to prevent nonrepeatable reads, SQL Server offers the REPEATABLE READ isolation level. It enhances READ COMMITTED mode by adding the requirement that a transaction may not modify data already read by a second transaction until the second transaction completes or rolls back.

To set the transaction isolation level to REPEATABLE READ, use the following Transact-SQL statement within SSMS:

```
SET TRANSACTION ISOLATION LEVEL REPEATABLE READ
```

SERIALIZABLE

SERIALIZABLE transaction isolation prevents phantom reads through the use of range locks. These locks prevent other transactions from inserting or deleting records within a range accessed by a second transaction until the second transaction completes.

To set the transaction isolation level to SERIALIZABLE, use the following Transact-SQL statement within SSMS:

```
SET TRANSACTION ISOLATION LEVEL SERIALIZABLE
```

SNAPSHOT

SNAPSHOT isolation offers an interesting twist: It essentially takes a picture of the data at the beginning of a transaction and allows the transaction to access that snapshot until it completes.

To set the transaction isolation level to SNAPSHOT, use the following Transact-SQL statement within SSMS:

```
SET TRANSACTION ISOLATION LEVEL SNAPSHOT
```

In case you're having trouble keeping SQL Server transaction isolation levels straight, Table 17-1 offers a convenient summary of their benefits.

Table 17-1	SQL Server 2008 Isolation Issues		
Isolation Level	*Dirty Reads?*	*Nonrepeatable Reads?*	*Phantom Reads?*
READ UNCOMMITTED	X	X	X
READ COMMITTED		X	X
REPEATABLE READ			X
SERIALIZABLE			
SNAPSHOT			

Handling Errors

Error handling is another essential component of Transact-SQL development. SQL Server contains robust mechanisms to detect error conditions and, by default, aborts a Transact-SQL statement that would cause an error. However, you may want to handle errors more gracefully by specifically instructing SQL Server how it should react to an error. You can use error handling in conjunction with transactions to accommodate error situations with an explicitly defined response.

Transact-SQL uses the "try. . .catch" exception handling model familiar to many software developers. Simply put, you write a T-SQL statement that you want SQL Server to "try" and then provide instructions on how it should "catch" an error if one occurs. The syntax for implementing "try. . .catch" error handling is as follows:

```
BEGIN TRY
        <T-SQL to "try">
END TRY

BEGIN CATCH
        <T-SQL to execute in the event of an error>
END CATCH
```

Here's a more concrete example. Suppose someone attempted to execute the following statement:

```
INSERT INTO stock(item, warehouse, inventory, wholesale_
        price)
VALUES('Apples', 'Seattle', 100, 0.15)
```

If the stock table already contained a record with the same item and warehouse (the table's primary key), SQL Server would report this error and terminate the statement's execution with this error:

```
Msg 2627, Level 14, State 1, Line 1
Violation of PRIMARY KEY constraint 'PK_stock'. Cannot
        insert duplicate key in object 'dbo.stock'.
The statement has been terminated.
```

If the SQL statement is part of a larger application, this type of error might cause a program crash. Additionally, it doesn't provide you with the ability to handle the error in a manner of your own choosing. Suppose, for example, that you wanted the program to print a friendly error message and notify the supervisor of the error by e-mail. You might use the following "try. . .catch" statement:

```
BEGIN TRY
        INSERT INTO stock(item, warehouse, inventory,
        wholesale_price)
        VALUES('Apples', 'Seattle', 100, 0.15)
END TRY
BEGIN CATCH
        PRINT 'Error: ' + ERROR_MESSAGE();
        EXEC msdb.dbo.sp_send_dbmail
        @profile_name = 'Inventory Mail',
        @recipients = 'supervisor@foo.com',
        @body = 'An error occurred creating the Seattle
         Apples inventory record.',
        @subject = 'Inventory Duplication Error' ;
END CATCH
```

Executing this statement produces the following result:

```
Error: Violation of PRIMARY KEY constraint 'PK_stock'.
        Cannot insert duplicate key in object 'dbo.
        stock'.
Mail queued.
```

Isn't that a much friendlier response? More important, the execution of the calling program may continue normally.

When writing Transact-SQL statements that may produce error conditions, you should always enclose them in a "try. . .catch" statement that gracefully handles the error. This is especially important if you're accessing SQL Server programmatically.

Chapter 18

Preparing for Disaster

*W*hether we like it or not, bad things happen. When I was a new system administrator, an old pro in my office summed this reality up well by offering me this advice: "Don't think of disaster recovery as preparing for *if* a disaster happens; think of it as preparing for *when* a disaster happens." Sure, your data center might not be swept away by floodwaters or destroyed by a fire or earthquake. I can, however, guarantee that you will suffer some sort of disaster at some point in the future.

The most common type of disaster you need to prepare for is a system failure caused by faulty hardware, software, or user error. Hard drive failure, for example, is one of the most common problems occurring on production systems. Despite the march of technology, hard drives still rely upon mechanical, fast-moving parts that are prone to failure. Disaster recovery technologies such as RAID arrays and clustering help minimize the impact of such a failure on your environment, but no set of countermeasures can totally eliminate the risk.

Fortunately, SQL Server 2008 includes advanced disaster recovery functionality designed to help you protect your organization's data from the effects of such events. In this chapter, I discuss the use of these technologies to back up and restore your business data.

Backing Up Your Data

The general concept of a backup is simple and probably something you're familiar with from other aspects of computing. Backups involve the creation of a copy of your data that's stored in a separate location for use the in the event of a critical failure. If such a failure occurs, administrators restore that backup, bringing the system back to its state at the time the backup occurred.

Backing up databases

The *full database backup* is the most basic type of backup offered by SQL Server. Full backups create a file that contains a copy of every single scrap of data used by a database for any type of object (for example, tables, stored procedures, user-defined functions, triggers). If you create a full backup, you can use that file at a later date to restore your entire database to any SQL Server instance.

Here's how to create a full database backup:

1. **With SSMS open, connect to the server containing the database you want to back up.**

2. **Expand the Databases folder.**

3. **Right-click the database you want to back up and choose Tasks⇨Back Up from the pop-up menu.**

   SQL Server presents the Back Up Database window, shown in Figure 18-1.

4. **Verify that the database specified in the drop-down menu is the database that you want to back up.**

5. **Verify that the Backup type is set to Full.**

6. **Provide a name and description for your database backup in the appropriate text boxes.**

7. **Choose whether you want to create the backup on disk or tape by selecting the appropriate radio button.**

   In this example, I assume that you're backing up your data to disk.

8. **Click the Remove button to clear the default destination file location.**

   You may, of course, leave this default location, but most people prefer to specify the exact location for backup storage.

9. **Click the Add button.**

   SQL Server presents the Select Backup Destination window, shown in Figure 18-2.

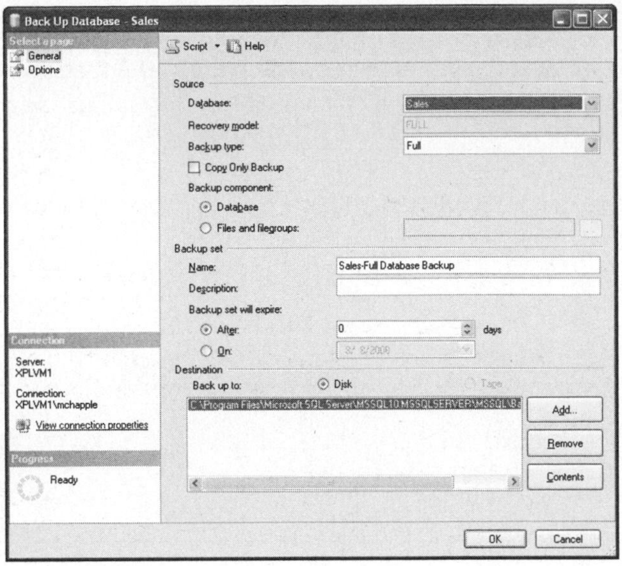

Figure 18-1:
Backing
up a SQL
Server
database.

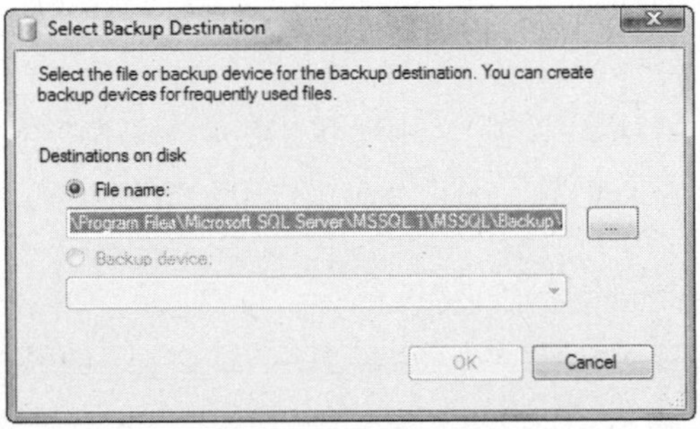

Figure 18-2:
Selecting a
backup
destination.

10. **Provide the appropriate filename/path in the File name textbox and click OK.**

One of the purposes of a backup is to protect you from hard drive failure. Be sure to store your backup on a physical hard drive that's separate from where your data files are located. Ideally, you should store your backups on tape and then store those tapes in a different building.

TIP

One easy way to keep your backups secure is to write them to a location on disk that's backed up by your enterprise backup software. Doing so spares you, as a DBA, from the burden of managing backup tapes and lets you take advantage of the backup infrastructure used and managed by the rest of your organization. It's always nice to transfer your work to someone else!

11. Click the Options page in the Select a Page pane of the Back Up Database window.

The Options page appears, as shown in Figure 18-3.

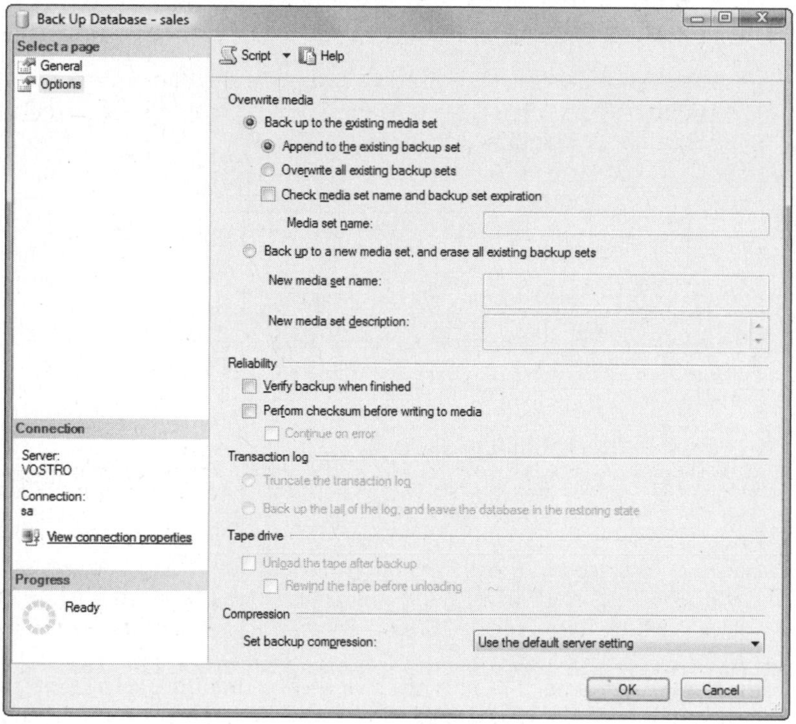

Figure 18-3:
The
Back Up
Database
Options
page.

![Back Up Database - sales window showing the Options page with sections for Overwrite media, Reliability, Transaction log, Tape drive, and Compression]

12. Verify that the Overwrite Media options match your preferences.

These options are extremely important if you're backing up your database to a file that already exists. By default, SQL Server will append your backup to the end of that file. If you want to conserve space by discarding older backups, you need to select the Overwrite All Existing Backup Sets option.

Other options on this page allow you more advanced control over your backup sets. You may choose to use expiration dates to determine over-write behavior and tell SQL Server how to handle older backup sets.

13. **Select the Verify Backup when Finished check box.**

   When you select this box, SQL Server automatically tests the validity of your backup when it completes. You should almost always enable this option to ensure the integrity of your backups. The only case in which you might not want to perform this verification is when time doesn't permit the full verification on the primary server. In such a case, you should test your backup by other means, such as by restoring it on a test/development SQL Server.

14. **Click the OK button to begin your backup.**

   The length of time required to complete the backup will vary depending upon the size of your database. When it completes, SQL Server displays the dialog box shown in Figure 18-4.

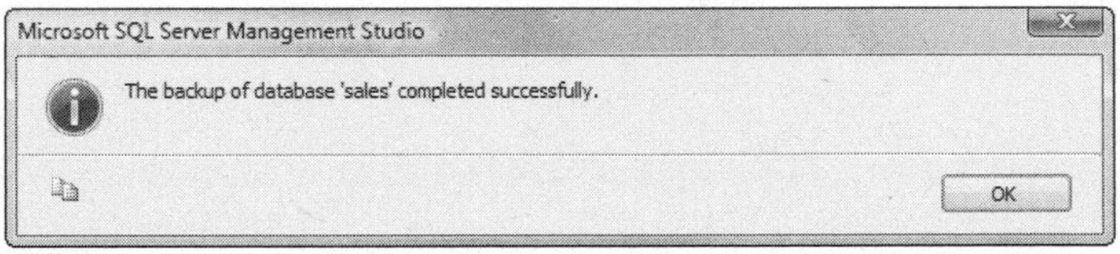

Figure 18-4:
The Backup Complete dialog box.

Microsoft SQL Server Management Studio

The backup of database 'sales' completed successfully.

OK

Saving time with differential backups

For small databases, you may be able to perform full backups on a regular basis, but larger databases may not provide that luxury. Large production databases may not be able to frequently suffer the performance hit that occurs during a backup. That's where *differential backups* come into play.

In a large database, chances are that a very small percentage of data actually changes in any given day. Therefore, when you perform a full backup, you're likely spending a lot of time copying the same data, day after day. Differential backups eliminate this inefficiency by backing up only data that has been added or changed since the last full backup. When it comes time to restore your database, you need to first restore the full backup and then restore the most recent differential backup.

Many organizations use a simple approach to database backups: Perform a full backup on the weekend and then perform a differential backup daily on other days. This common approach works well.

Performing a differential backup follows almost exactly the same process as creating a full backup, as described in the previous section. The only difference is that you should select the Differential backup type in the Back Up Database window, as shown in Figure 18-5.

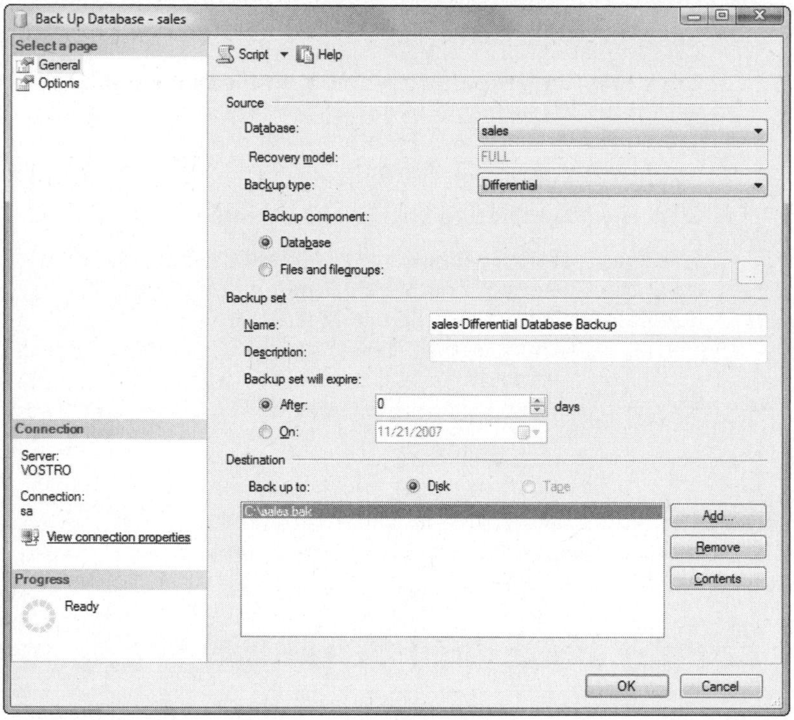

Figure 18-5:
Creating a
differential
backup.

If you've worked in disaster recovery before, you may be familiar with the concept of an incremental backup. In this approach, each incremental backup contains only changes made since the last full *or incremental* backup. Restoring backups created with this approach requires the full backup and all incremental backups. SQL Server 2008 does *not* support incremental backups.

Saving space with backup compression

A new feature in SQL Server 2008 allows you to compress your backups to save storage space. Compression uses mathematical algorithms to reduce the size of database files, in a fashion similar to that used to create compressed ZIP folders in Windows.

Using backup compression requires setting the Compress Backup option within SQL Server. You may do this by setting the server-wide compression default using the following process:

1. **With SSMS open, right-click the server you want to configure and select Properties from the pop-up menu.**

2. **In the left pane under Select a Page, select Database Settings.**

3. **Click the Compress Backup check box, as shown in Figure 18-6.**

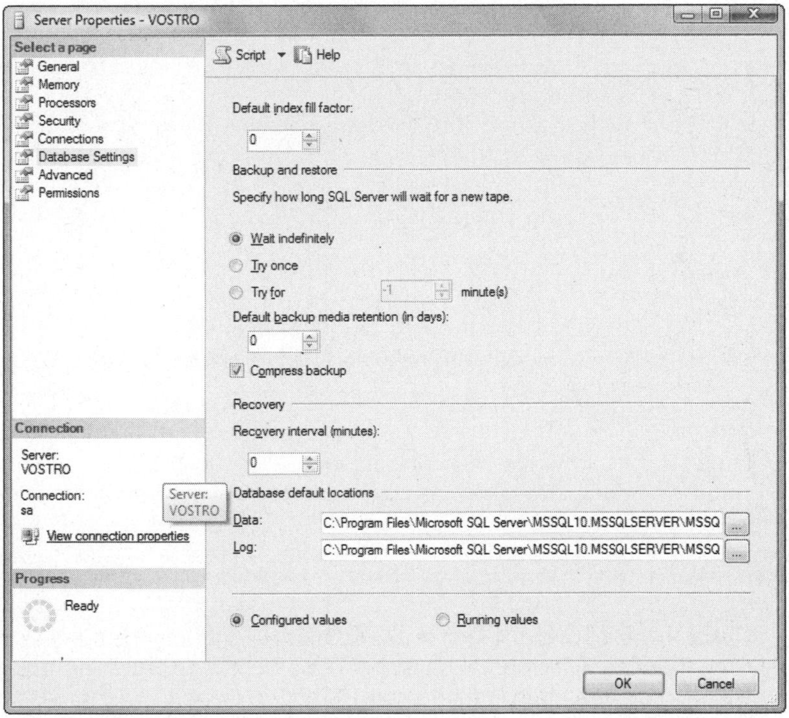

Figure 18-6:
Configuring
backup
compres-
sion.

You may override the server default on a per-backup setting by selecting either the Compress Backup or Do Not Compress Backup option on the Database Back Up Options page (shown previously in Figure 18-3).

Before creating a backup, be sure to consider the cost/benefit trade-off of using this option. Compressed backups take up less space on your disk. Additionally, they often take less time to complete because the majority of backup time is spent writing data to disk, and compression reduces the amount of this data dramatically. The trade-off is that backup compression consumes more CPU cycles than uncompressed backups, reducing the performance of your server during the backup creation process.

Full support for backup compression exists in SQL Server 2008 Enterprise Edition only. Other editions may *restore* compressed backups, but Microsoft restricted the ability to *create* backups to Enterprise Edition installations of SQL Server. SQL Server 2005 and earlier installations cannot create or restore compressed backups.

If you'd like to see how much of an effect compression has on the size of your backups, issue the following Transact-SQL command:

```
SELECT name, backup_size/compressed_backup_size AS 'ratio'
FROM msdb..backupset;
```

SQL Server will respond with the name of each backup on your system and the file's compression ratio. For example, the following result shows two backup sets for the same database. The first is uncompressed, and the second uses backup compression:

```
name                           ratio
------------------------       --------------------
scan-Full Database Backup      1.000000000000000000
scan-Full Database Backup      4.876425871709171865

(2 row(s) affected)
```

The compression ratio of approximately 5 shown here indicates that the compressed backup is saving approximately 80 percent of the disk space used by the uncompressed backup.

Backing up the transaction log

SQL Server maintains a log file called the *transaction log* that includes a record of any modifications made to the database. The transaction log plays an important role in disaster recovery efforts because you can use it to restore data modified after the most recent backup.

The contents (and usefulness!) of the transaction log vary based upon the recovery model you select. Specifically, transaction log backups are not available under the simple recovery model. I discuss this in more detail in the next section.

If you have a database failure and need to restore from disk, you need to first restore a full backup. You may then restore the most recent differential

Truncating and shrinking the transaction log

The transaction log can take up a significant amount of space for an active SQL Server database. There are two actions SQL Server performs to manage the amount of space consumed by the log: *log truncation* and *log shrinking.*

Normally, log truncation happens automatically. If you're using the simple recovery model, SQL Server truncates the log every time you reach a transaction checkpoint. If you're using the full or bulk-logged recovery model, SQL Server truncates the transaction log after each log backup, assuming that a checkpoint occurred since the last backup. (For details on the situations that may prevent this automatic truncation, see the SQL Server Books Online article "Factors That Can Delay Log Truncation.")

Truncation simply removes entries from the transaction log, making space available for other log entries. It doesn't affect the physical size of the transaction log file on disk. In Chapter 12, I discuss how you may need to manage database file sizes manually. The same is true for transaction logs.

If you want to reduce the amount of physical disk space consumed by the transaction log file, you must manually shrink the file. You may do this within SQL Server Management Studio by right-clicking the database and choosing Tasks⇨Shrink⇨Files from the pop-up menu.

backup, if any exist. Finally, you can restore the database to the most current state possible by applying *all* of the transaction log backups created since the most recent full or differential backup.

A transaction log backup scenario

A common backup scenario for large databases is performing full backups every Sunday, differential backups every day at midnight, and transaction log backups on an hourly basis. In this case, if a database failure occurs at 2:30 a.m. on Tuesday, you would apply backups in the following order:

- ✔ Sunday's full backup restores the database to its state on Sunday morning.

- ✔ Applying Wednesday's differential backup restores any modifications made between Sunday's full backup and Wednesday's differential backup. This restores the database to its current state as of midnight Wednesday.

- ✔ Applying Wednesday's 1 a.m. transaction log backup restores the database to its state as of 1 a.m. Wednesday.

- ✔ Applying Wednesday's 2 a.m. transaction log backup restores the database to its state as of 2 a.m. Wednesday.

In this scenario, any modifications made to the database during the 30-minute period between 2:00 a.m. and 2:30 a.m. on Wednesday are irretrievably lost.

Creating a transaction log backup

You may create a transaction log backup using the process described earlier for creating a full or differential backup. The only difference is that you should select the Transaction Log backup type on the Back Up Database screen. You also have two new options on the Back Up Database Options page, as shown in Figure 18-7.

The first option (which is selected by default) is Truncate the Transaction Log. This process, described in the "Truncating and shrinking the transaction log" sidebar, ensures the efficient use of transaction log disk space. The tail-log backup is used if you want to capture all entries not yet backed up. For example, in the scenario I describe in the previous section, if the database failure was not fatal, you may be able to create a tail-log backup to capture those transactions occurring between 2:00 a.m. and 2:30 a.m.

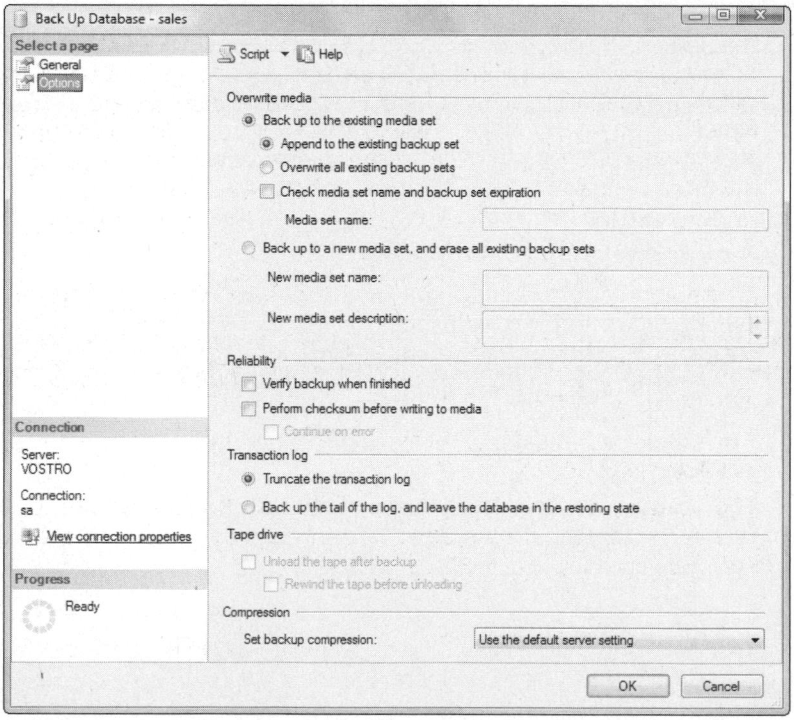

Figure 18-7: Transaction log backup options.

Specifying Disaster Recovery Requirements with Recovery Models

SQL Server recovery models allow you to easily define the way you would like to balance the robustness of your disaster recovery approach with the amount of server resources consumed in those efforts.

Choosing a recovery model

SQL Server offers three different choices of recovery model. They differ in the approach used to manage transaction log files. The models supported by SQL Server 2008 are the full recovery model, the simple recovery model, and the bulk-logged recovery model. I discuss each of these models in the upcoming sections.

The full recovery model

The full recovery model maintains the entire transaction log until the transactions in the log are backed up. Using this model, you can restore a database to any particular point in time by using the transaction log backups. For example, you can choose to restore a backup to a very specific time (such as 2:36 p.m. Tuesday) regardless of the time the transaction log backups occurred. SQL Server accomplishes this by reading timestamps on transaction log entries to determine whether they occurred before or after your specified point in time.

If you choose the full recovery model, you should always schedule transaction log backups. Failure to do so not only negates the benefit of using the full recovery model but also can cause the transaction logs to consume large amounts of disk space.

The simple recovery model

The simple recovery model keeps the transaction log entries for only an extremely short period of time. This renders the transaction log useless for disaster recovery purposes.

Choosing the simple recovery model minimizes SQL Server's use of transaction log space, but also inhibits your ability to recover recent changes in the event of a database failure.

The bulk-logged recovery model

The bulk-logged recovery model is a variant of the full recovery model that treats bulk transactions (such as bulk imports) differently. Rather than record the details of each transaction that occurs within a bulk transaction, it records the end result of those imports using a technique called minimal logging. This model is highly efficient because it reduces the drastic impact that the logging of bulk transactions can have on server performance.

If you use the bulk-logged recovery model and a bulk transaction occurs within the scope of a particular log file, you will be able to restore the changes made in that log file, but you won't be able to take advantage of the point-in-time restore option available under the full recovery model.

Because you can't use the point-in-time option with the bulk-logged model, Microsoft's best practices dictate that you the bulk-logged recovery model only for short periods of time. If you plan to perform bulk transactions, change your database to the bulk-logged recovery model immediately before the bulk operations and then return to the full recovery model immediately afterward.

Changing recovery models

If you'd like to change the recovery model used by your database, follow these steps:

1. **With SSMS open and connected to the server containing the database, expand the Databases folder.**

2. **Right-click the database you want to modify and select Properties from the pop-up menu.**

3. **Click the Options page in the Database Properties window.**

4. **Select the appropriate recovery model (Full, Simple or Bulk-logged) from the Recovery model drop-down box, as shown in Figure 18-8.**

5. **Click OK to apply the change to your database.**

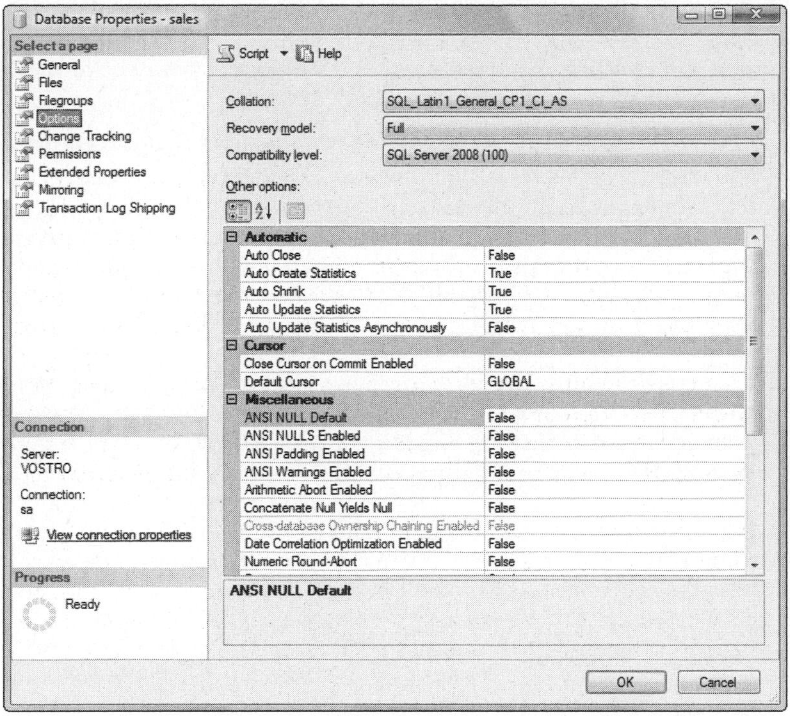

Figure 18-8:
Changing
a database
recovery
model.

Restoring Your Data after a Disaster

Restoring a full backup requires access to the backup file(s) you created earlier. You may restore the backup on the same SQL Server instance or on any other SQL Server.

It's important to remember that you have some constraints on which database backup(s) you may restore:

✔ You may restore a full backup of any database from any time period.

✔ You may restore a differential backup if you also restore the full backup created most recently before that differential backup.

✔ You may restore transaction log backups only if you're using the full or bulk-logged recovery model.

✔ You may restore your database to an arbitrary date and time only if you're restoring transaction log backups.

Here's the process for restoring a backup that was created using disk file(s):

1. **Open SQL Server Management Studio and connect to the instance for which you want to restore the database.**

2. **Right-click the Databases folder and select Restore Database from the pop-up menu.**

   SSMS presents the Restore Database window, as shown in Figure 18-9.

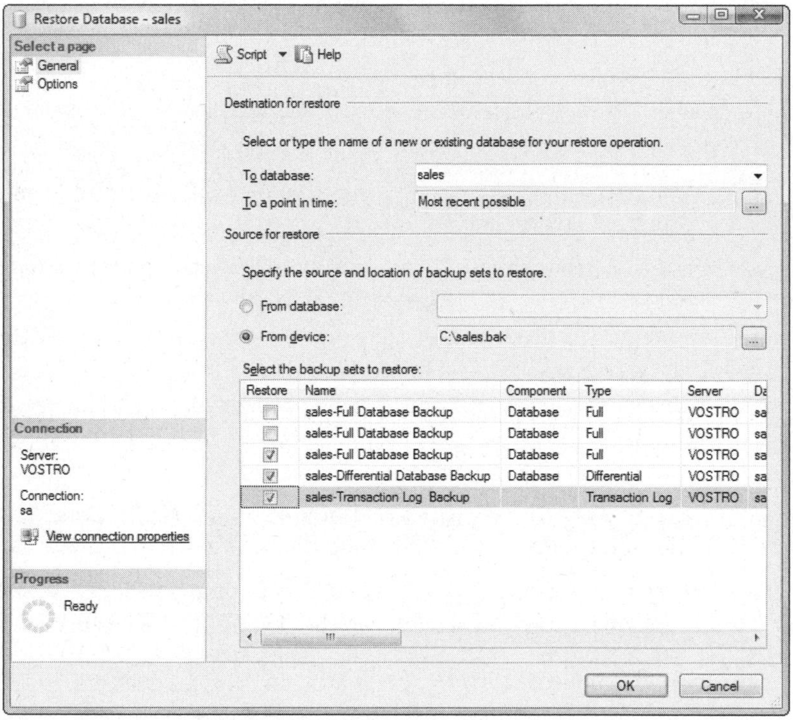

Figure 18-9:
Restoring a
database.

3. **Select the From Device radio button in the Source for Restore section of the Restore Database window.**

4. **Click the ellipses (. . .) button to open the Specify Backup window, shown in Figure 18-10.**

5. **Click the Add button and select the file(s) you want to restore. When finished, click the OK button to close the Specify Backup window.**

6. **Select the boxes next to the backup sets you want to restore.**

   Review the list of backups contained within the files you specified in the Select Backup Sets to Restore section of the Restore Database window.

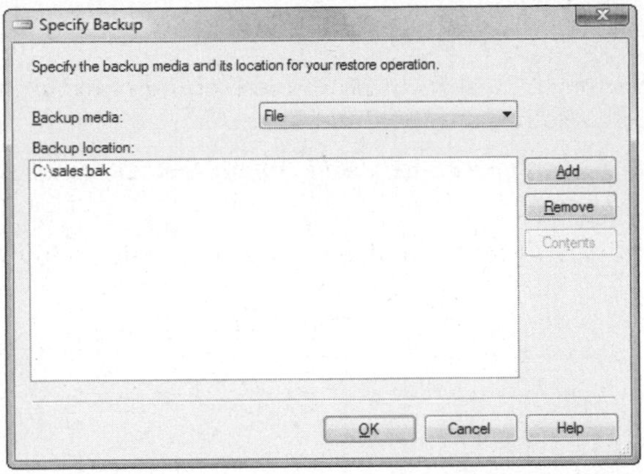

Figure 18-10:
Selecting
backup files.

You may select any valid combination of full, differential, and transaction log backups.

7. **Use the drop-down arrow to select the database that you want to restore the backup set to in the To Database field.**

   You may restore your backup to an existing database or type the name of a new database in the text box.

   Note that if you already have a database with the same name on the target server that you want to overwrite, you need to also select the Overwrite the Existing Database check box on the Options page.

8. **If you want to restore your database to a specific point in time, click the ellipses (. . .) button to the right of the To a Point in Time text box.**

   This action brings up the Point in Time Restore dialog box, shown in Figure 18-11. Select the A Specific Date and Time option and then use the drop-down boxes to enter the date and time you want to restore to. When finished, click OK to close the Point in Time Restore dialog box.

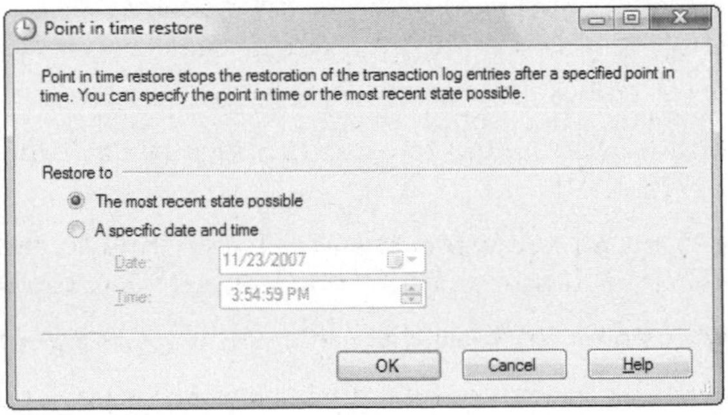

Figure 18-11:
The Point
in Time
Restore
dialog box.

9. **Click OK to restore the backup set.**

Using Database Snapshots

Database snapshots allow you to take a moment-in-time picture of a database for later reference. They provide you with the ability to "freeze" your database by creating a read-only copy. You can then later issue read-only queries against that data or even use a snapshot to revert your database to an earlier state.

Snapshots can play an important role in your disaster recovery strategy. They're also useful when you have a special need to maintain a frozen copy of your data (such as in response to legal issues). Snapshots are also useful for historical reporting purposes.

Snapshots are a feature of SQL Server Enterprise Edition only and were first introduced in SQL Server 2005.

SQL Server manages snapshots intelligently using a concept known as *sparse files* to conserve both time and space. When you create a database snapshot, SQL Server simply creates an empty file that consumes very little disk space. SQL Server then manages these sparse files by using a *copy-on-write* approach. Whenever the first change is made to a data page in the original source database, SQL Server first copies the pre-change page to the database snapshot and then writes the change to the source database. When a user later requests data from the snapshot, SQL Server first checks to see whether each page exists in the snapshot. If it does not, SQL Server knows that the page was unchanged from the original source database and retrieves the unchanged page from the source. This prevents the redundant storage of unchanged pages in both the source and snapshot databases.

Creating a database snapshot

In contrast to most of the technologies I describe in this book, you can't create a database snapshot using the graphic interface of SQL Server Management Studio. You'll need to break out your Transact-SQL skills for this one.

To create a database snapshot, simply write a `CREATE DATABASE` statement as you would for the original database, with two differences:

- ✔ Add the clause `AS SNAPSHOT OF <source_database>` to your statement.
- ✔ Specify the logical filenames for every file in your snapshot database.

For example, if I wanted to create a snapshot of the sales database, I would issue the following Transact-SQL command:

```
CREATE DATABASE sales_snapshot_friday ON
( NAME = 'sales', FILENAME =
   'C:\DATA\sales_snapshot_friday.ss')
AS SNAPSHOT OF sales
```

You may name your data file anything you want. However, as a matter of best practice, you should use the .ss file extension to alert others to the fact that the file contains a SQL Server snapshot. Also, you may have many snapshots of the same database from different points in time, so I recommend naming your snapshot something that conveys both the name of the source database and the time that the snapshot was taken.

Accessing a database snapshot

Accessing a database snapshot is straightforward: You simply reference the snapshot name just as you would any other database. For example, to retrieve the contents of the stock table from the snapshot, issue the following Transact-SQL statements:

```
USE sales_snapshot_friday;
```

```
SELECT * FROM stock;
```

Accessing a snapshot from within SQL Server Management Studio is slightly different. Rather than expand the Databases folder, expand the Database Snapshots folder to locate your snapshot.

Reverting to a database snapshot

In the event of a serious user error, you may want to revert your database to the state it was in when you took a database snapshot. SQL Server makes this possible, but I must share a few words of caution first:

✓ You may revert a database to a snapshot only when it's the only existing snapshot of that database. If other snapshots exist, you must drop them first, using the following Transact-SQL statement:

```
DROP DATABASE <snapshot_name>
```

For example, if I wished to remove the Friday snapshot from my database, I would issue the following command:

```
DROP DATABASE sales_snapshot_Friday
```

Database snapshots basically stick around forever and can consume large amounts of disk space. You should always keep tabs on the number of snapshots that exist for each one of your databases and drop them when you no longer need them around to meet business requirements.

✔ Reverting to a snapshot automatically drops any full-text catalogs you created on the database.

✔ Reverting a database to a snapshot won't work if the database becomes corrupted. It won't work because of the use of sparse files: The corrupted data may not even exist in the snapshot file. Therefore, although snapshots play a role in a disaster recovery scenario, they are not a panacea and should be used only in conjunction with normal backups and restores.

With those words of caution under your belt, if you still want to revert a database to a snapshot, use the following Transact-SQL command:

```
RESTORE DATABASE <source_database_name>
FROM DATABASE_SNAPSHOT = '<snapshot_name>'
```

For example, suppose that on Friday morning, a user accidentally issued this query against my sales database:

```
UPDATE stock set inventory =  0
```

This wiped out all of the organization's inventory records. I could revert my sales database to the snapshot I took on Friday, using the following command:

```
RESTORE DATABASE sales
FROM DATABASE_SNAPSHOT 'sales_snapshot_Friday'
```

Chapter 19

Staying Alive: High Availability in SQL Server 2008

. . . .

In This Chapter

▶ Using database mirroring to create redundant databases

▶ Using log shipping to synchronize databases

. . . .

Many organizations depend upon their databases for the very livelihood of their businesses. For example, an e-commerce store would cease to operate without the database that drives its product catalog and ordering process. Similarly, a bank would be unable to process any customer transactions without access to live financial data.

In enterprises like these, time is literally money. You can directly measure the financial cost of database downtime in terms of lost revenue. There are also additional intangible factors, such as reputation and customer goodwill, that play a definite role. Would you want to do your banking with a financial institution that has unreliable databases?

For these reasons, SQL Server provides a number of high-availability solutions designed to reduce the amount of downtime suffered by your organization. Database mirroring allows you to maintain a completely redundant database environment that serves as a hot or warm standby in the event of a primary server failure. Log shipping lets you transfer the transaction log from a primary database to secondary database(s) on a regular basis, providing a way to both keep a backup server ready and waiting and to provide users with a secondary data source for queries where time is not of the essence.

Creating Redundancy with Database Mirroring

When you establish a database mirroring relationship, you define a partnership between two servers. The result of this partnership is that one server will always act as the primary server, processing all transactions and providing updates to the other (secondary) server. The secondary server stays in standby mode, applying changes received from the primary server to ensure that it maintains a current copy of the primary server's data. In the event that the primary server fails, the secondary server is ready for an automatic or manual failover. At that time, it takes on the role of the primary server and processes all transactions for the mirrored database with minimal impact on database availability.

Database mirroring is available only in the Standard and Enterprise editions of SQL Server. Additionally, you may implement database mirroring only on databases that use the full recovery model. If you're not sure which recovery model is in use on your database, see Chapter 18.

Database mirroring provides three important benefits to your enterprise:

✔ **Mirroring increases the availability of your enterprise database architecture.**

By implementing mirroring, you gain the ability to automatically or manually fail over to a standby server in the event of a database failure. Depending upon your operating mode (I discuss operating modes later in this section), you may have little or no downtime with zero data loss when your primary server fails.

✔ **Mirroring provides you with an efficient way to patch your servers.**

Mirroring allows you to employ the concept of a *rolling upgrade* when you want to apply service packs to your SQL Servers. For more information on this topic, see the MSDN article "How to: Install a Service Pack on a System with Minimal Downtime for Mirrored Databases," available at http://msdn.microsoft.com/en-us/library/bb497962.aspx.

✔ **Mirroring provides an automated way to correct minor errors.**

If a database server experiences a read error and is part of a cluster, it will attempt to retrieve the offending page from its mirroring partner and use that page to resolve the local read error. This feature is available only with SQL Server 2008 Enterprise Edition.

Choosing an operating mode

SQL Server offers two database mirroring operating modes: high-safety mode, which is designed to prevent data loss at the expense of performance, and high-performance mode, which provides less assurance of data protection but offers less of a performance hit.

High-safety mode

Mirror partners running in high-safety mode (also known as synchronous operation) require the confirmed commitment of transactions on both partners before returning an acknowledgement to the client. This confirmation guarantees that both mirror partners retain consistent copies of the database at all times, but it increases the transaction latency by requiring the wait for synchronization.

High-safety mode also supports the use of automatic failover, when implemented with a *witness server*. The witness server does not contain a copy of the database but bears responsibility for monitoring the status of the primary and mirror server to determine whether a failover is required.

High-performance mode

The alternative, high-performance mode, eliminates the synchronization latency by allowing transactions to commit on the principal server before the mirror server synchronizes. Doing so introduces the possibility of data loss in the event of a primary server failure. High-performance mode does not support automatic failover.

Configuring mirroring

Configuring SQL Server mirroring requires several preparatory steps before you create the mirror relationship. In this section, I explain the process of creating a SQL Server database mirror. First, you must ensure that you meet the prerequisites for mirroring:

- The mirroring partners must be running the same edition (either Standard or Enterprise) of SQL Server.
- The mirroring partners (and witness, if applicable) must be running the same version of SQL Server.

Creating logins on the mirror server

SQL Server doesn't allow you to mirror either the *master* or *msdb* databases. Therefore, you must ensure that accounts exist for database users on both

SQL Server instances. If both instances run under the same domain account, SQL Server handles this automatically. If not, you must manually create the accounts. I describe how to create accounts in Chapter 16.

Restoring data to the mirror server

Next, you need to load the database onto the mirror server. To do this, restore a backup from your primary server on the secondary server. You should follow the process I explain in Chapter 18, with one modification. On the Options page of the Restore Database window, select the RESTORE WITH NORECOVERY option, as shown in Figure 19-1. You must restore a full backup and any transaction log backups required to make the two databases consistent.

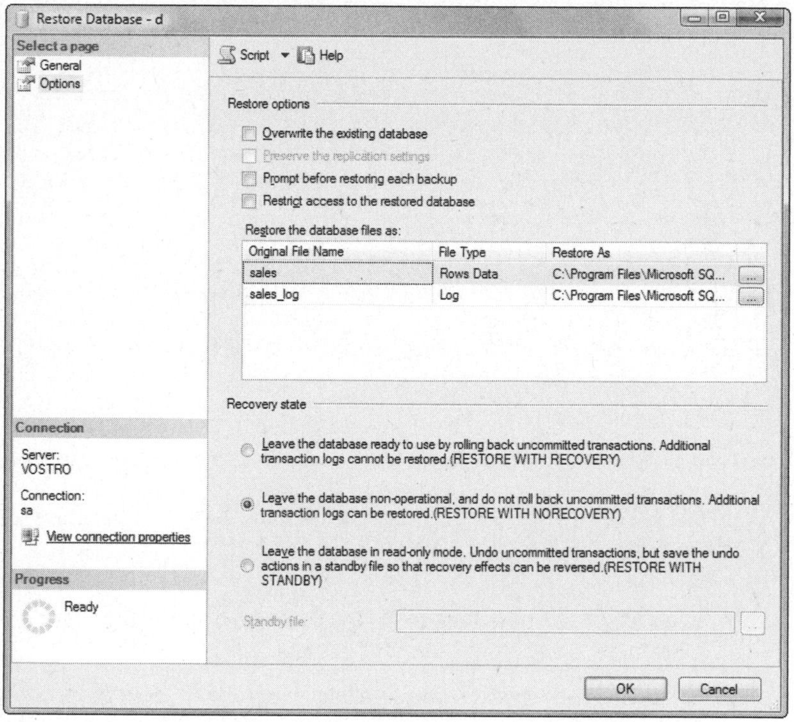

Figure 19-1: Restoring a database using the WITH NO RECOVERY option.

Configuring the mirror partnership

After you've restored data to the mirror server, you may configure the mirroring partnership by following these steps:

1. **Open SSMS and connect to the SQL Server instance hosting the primary copy of the database.**

2. **Expand the Databases folder.**

3. **Right-click the database you want to mirror and choose Tasks⇨Mirror from the pop-up menu.**

   This brings up the Mirroring page of the Database Properties window, as shown in Figure 19-2.

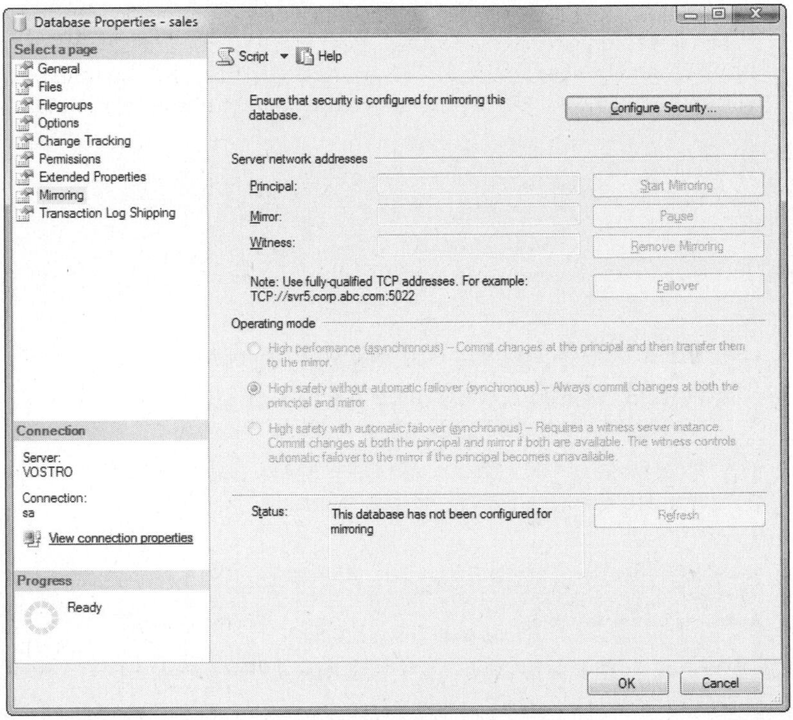

Figure 19-2: Database mirroring properties.

4. **Click the Configure Security button to bring up the Configure Database Mirroring Security Wizard.**

5. **Click the Next button to advance to the first page of the wizard.**

6. **If you want to include a witness server in the mirroring relationship, answer Yes to the question on the next screen and click Next to continue.**

   Remember, a witness server is required if you intend to run in synchronous high-safety mode with automatic failover. This screen is shown in Figure 19-3.

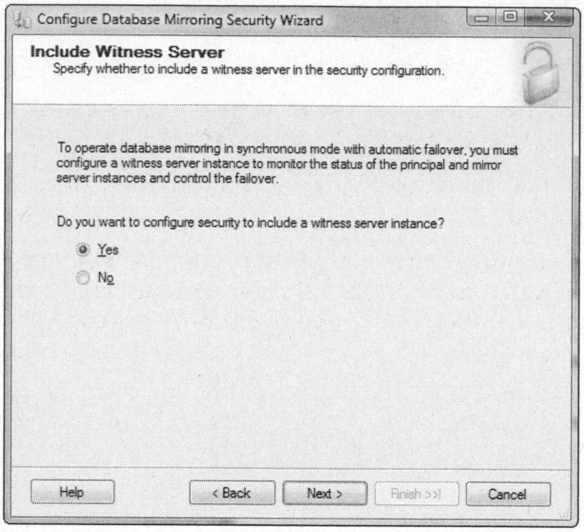

Figure 19-3:
Including
a witness
server.

7. **Click Next to confirm that you want to configure all servers.**

8. **Provide details for the principal server on the next screen, as shown in Figure 19-4, and then click Next to continue.**

   You need to provide an endpoint name and listener port if you want to change the SQL Server default settings.

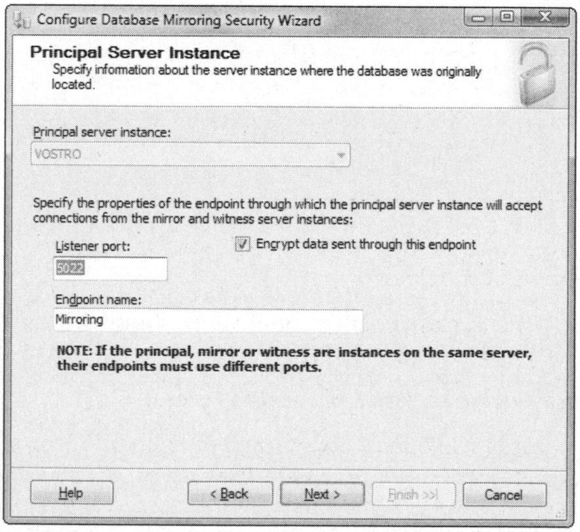

Figure 19-4:
Configure
the princi-
pal server
instance.

9. **Click the Connect button to connect to the mirror server instance.**

   SQL Server prompts you for credentials.

10. **Provide details for the mirror server if you want to change the default settings; then, click the Next button to continue.**

11. **Provide details for the witness server, if applicable, and click the Next button to continue.**

12. **If the service accounts for any of the servers involved are different accounts within the same domain, provide the details in the Service Accounts window; otherwise, leave the text boxes empty, as shown in Figure 19-5.**

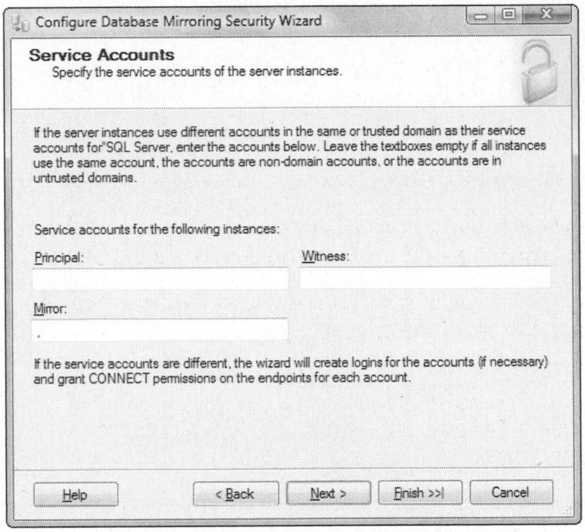

Figure 19-5:
Server
account
specification.

13. **Click the Next button to continue.**

14. **Review the mirroring details in the confirmation screen and click Finish to complete the wizard.**

   SQL Server displays a status screen while it configures the mirroring endpoints, as shown in Figure 19-6.

15. **Click the Close button to close the status screen.**

   SQL Server presents the dialog box shown in Figure 19-7, asking you whether you'd like to start mirroring immediately. (In this example, I'm running all three SQL Server instances on the same server. That's why you see the shared server name "vostro" in the dialog box.)

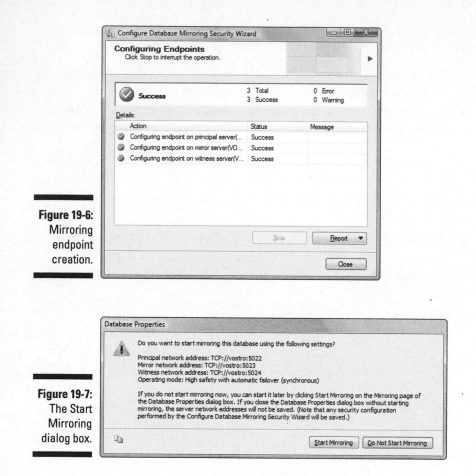

Figure 19-6:
Mirroring
endpoint
creation.

Figure 19-7:
The Start
Mirroring
dialog box.

16. **Click the Start Mirroring button to initiate database mirroring.**

Monitoring Database Mirroring

SQL Server provides a Database Mirroring Monitor to help you monitor the status of your mirroring relationships. Here's how to start the monitor:

1. **With SSMS open, expand the Databases folder on either the primary or mirror server.**

2. **Right-click the name of the mirrored database and choose Tasks➪ Launch Database Mirroring Monitor from the pop-up menu.**

Figure 19-8 shows the Database Mirroring Monitor. The monitor displays the status of each server instance participating in database mirroring:

- ✔ **Unknown:** The monitor is not connected to either of the mirroring partners.

- ✔ **Synchronized:** The primary server and mirror server are synchronized. In high-safety mode, this indicates that a failover can occur without any data loss.

- ✔ **Synchronizing:** The contents of the two instances are not yet synchronized and failover may not occur.

- ✔ **Suspended:** The principal database is online, but the mirror server is not receiving logs.

- ✔ **Disconnected:** The server cannot connect to its mirroring partner.

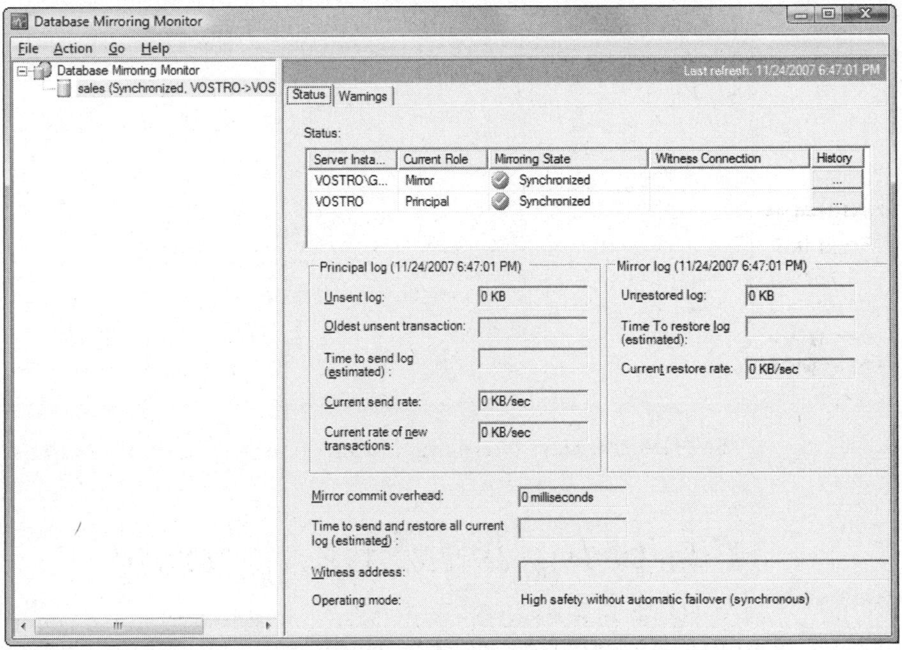

Figure 19-8:
The
Database
Mirroring
Monitor.

Failing over a mirrored database

If you're using high-safety mode with a witness server, SQL Server will automatically fail over when the following conditions are met:

✔ The primary and mirror databases are in the synchronized state.

✔ The mirror and witness are able to communicate with each other.

✔ Neither the mirror nor the witness can communicate with the primary server for 10 seconds.

You may also manually failover to a mirror database as follows:

1. **With SSMS open, connect to the primary server instance.**

2. **Expand the Databases folder.**

3. **Right-click the database to be failed over and choose Tasks⇨Mirror from the pop-up menu.**

   SQL Server opens the Database Properties window to the Mirroring page, as shown in Figure 19-9.

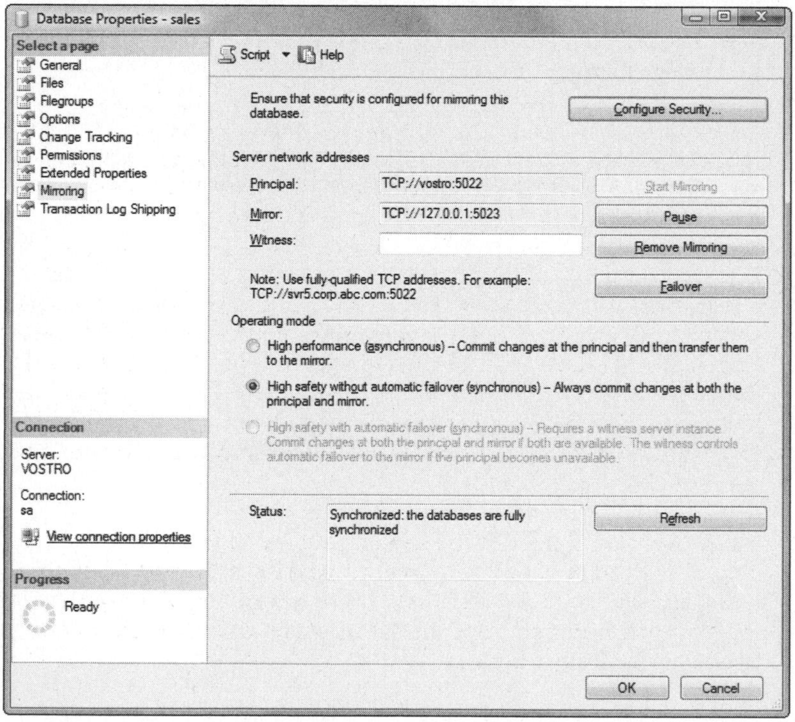

Figure 19-9:
Mirroring
properties.

4. **Click the Failover button.**

5. **Click the Yes button to commence the failover.**

Synchronizing Databases with Log Shipping

SQL Server's other major mechanism for high availability databases is log shipping. This technology allows you to keep databases synchronized through the use of the transaction log. In a log shipping relationship, the primary server automatically transfers backups of the synchronized database's transaction logs to one or more secondary SQL Server instances.

There are three stages in the log shipping process:

1. The primary server creates a transaction log backup using a SQL Server Agent job. (I discuss SQL Server Agent in Chapter 13.)

2. The secondary server(s) retrieve the transaction log backup from the primary server using a SQL Server Agent job.

3. The secondary server(s) apply the transaction log backup to their databases using a different SQL Server Agent job.

All servers participating in log shipping must be running SQL Server Standard Edition, Workgroup Edition, or Enterprise Edition. The primary server must also be running either the full recovery model or the bulk-logged recovery model. For more on recovery models, see Chapter 18.

You may combine database mirroring and log shipping if dictated by your business needs. Both technologies have the same goal: creating a redundant server that receives transaction updates as the primary database changes. However, there are important differences between the two. A primary server may only have one mirror partner. The same server may have multiple log shipping partners. However, a secondary server created with log shipping can't participate in an automatic failover relationship, whereas a mirrored server in high-safety mode can.

Many organizations that require more than one redundant server implement a combination of database mirroring and log shipping. The mirror server is the "primary" backup server and takes advantage of automatic failover. The log shipping recipients are the "secondary" backup servers and may also be used for read-only queries.

Configuring log shipping

Configuring log shipping is similar to the process used to configure database mirroring. After you identify the primary server and secondary server(s) that will participate in log shipping, follow these steps to configure log shipping:

1. **Create a new database on the secondary server(s) by restoring backups, including transaction log backups, using the WITH NORECOVERY option.**

   If you're not sure how to do this, see the "Restoring data to the mirror server" section, earlier in this chapter. The process is identical.

2. **Create a network file sharing location where you will store transaction log backups.**

   This may be a location on the primary server, or it may be a shared folder on another server. It must be accessible to all servers that will participate in the log shipping relationship. The SQL Server service account for the primary server must have both read and write permission to this share so that it may write transaction log backups to the share. The SQL Server Agent service account on the secondary server(s) must have read permission to retrieve the transaction log backups.

3. **Open SSMS and connect to the SQL Server instance hosting the primary copy of the database.**

4. **Expand the Databases folder.**

5. **Right-click the database you want to mirror and choose Tasks⇨Ship Transaction Logs from the pop-up menu.**

   This brings up the Transaction Log Shipping properties page, as shown in Figure 19-10.

6. **Select the Enable This as a Primary Database in a Log Shipping Configuration check box.**

7. **Click the Backup Settings button.**

   You see the Transaction Log Backup Settings window, shown in Figure 19-11.

8. **Enter the network share path you created in Step 2 in the network path text box.**

9. **If the network share is located on the primary server, enter the local path in the second text box. Otherwise, leave this field blank.**

   You should also review the other settings in this window. You may either accept the default values or modify them to meet your requirements.

10. **Click OK to close the Transaction Log Backup Settings window.**

11. **Click the Add button in the Secondary Databases section of the Transaction Log Shipping properties page.**

    SQL Server displays the Secondary Database Settings window, shown in Figure 19-12.

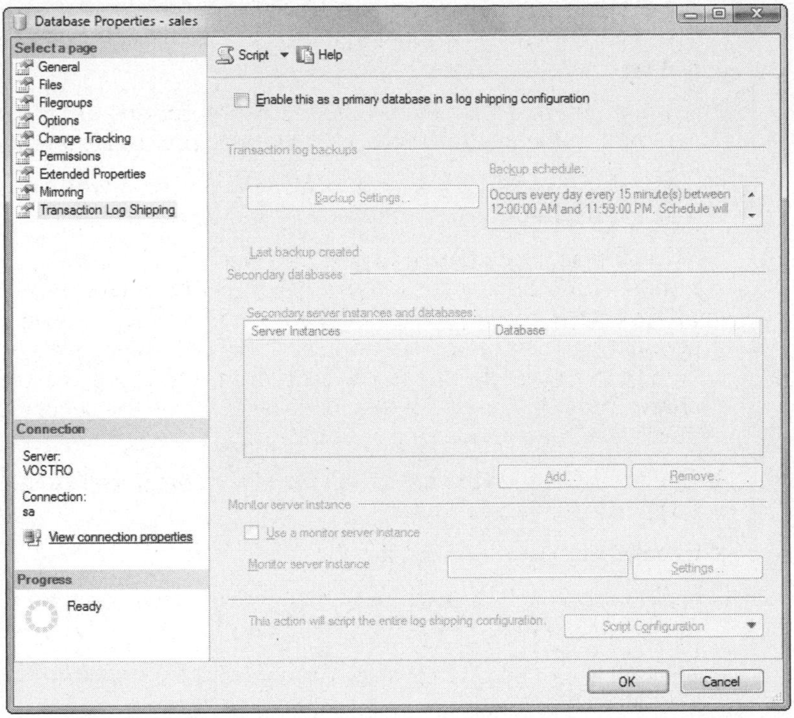

Figure 19-10:
Transaction
Log
Shipping
properties.

12. **Click the Connect button and provide connection details for the first secondary server you want to include in the log shipping relationship.**

    Note that the Initialize Secondary Database page on this screen allows you to automatically create and restore the necessary backups to initialize the database. You may explore this option if you want, but I prefer to create and restore the backups manually to maintain control over the process. That's why I have you restore your own backups in Step 1.

13. **Verify that the Secondary Database drop-down box contains the name of the database you created in Step 1.**

14. **Click the Copy Files tab.**

15. **Provide a destination folder for the copied files in the text box on this page.**

    You may choose any path you want. For performance reasons, you should normally choose a local path on the secondary server.

16. **Review the settings on the Restore Transaction Log tab and make any changes to the default values you deem necessary.**

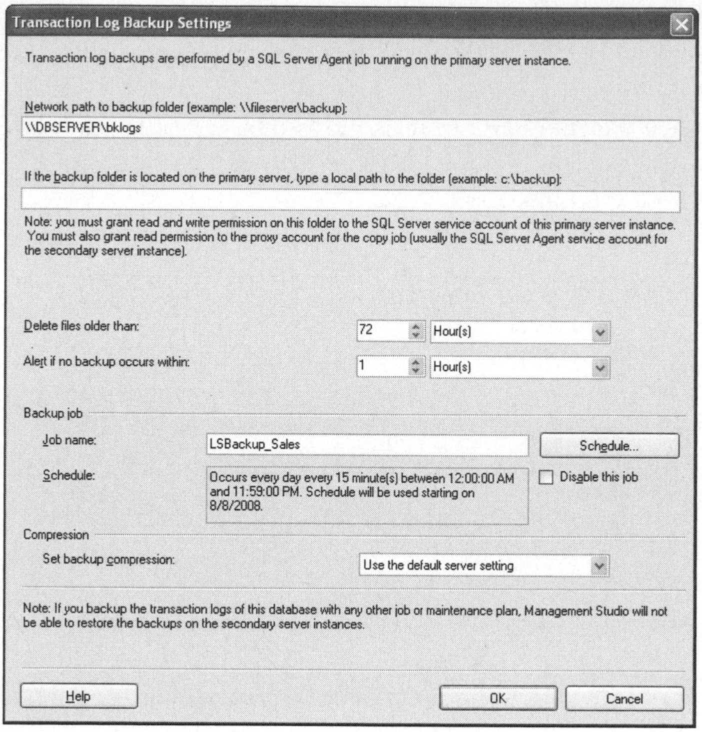

Transaction Log Backup Settings

Transaction log backups are performed by a SQL Server Agent job running on the primary server instance.

Network path to backup folder (example: \\fileserver\backup):

\\DBSERVER\bklogs

If the backup folder is located on the primary server, type a local path to the folder (example: c:\backup):

Note: you must grant read and write permission on this folder to the SQL Server service account of this primary server instance. You must also grant read permission to the proxy account for the copy job (usually the SQL Server Agent service account for the secondary server instance).

Delete files older than: 72 Hour(s)

Alert if no backup occurs within: 1 Hour(s)

Backup job

Job name: LSBackup_Sales   Schedule...

Schedule: Occurs every day every 15 minute(s) between 12:00:00 AM and 11:59:00 PM. Schedule will be used starting on 8/8/2008.   □ Disable this job

Compression

Set backup compression: Use the default server setting

Note: If you backup the transaction logs of this database with any other job or maintenance plan, Management Studio will not be able to restore the backups on the secondary server instances.

Help   OK   Cancel

Figure 19-11: Transaction Log Backup settings.

Secondary Database Settings

Secondary server instance: VOSTRO\GAMMA   Connect...

Secondary database: sales

Select an existing database or enter the name to create a new database.

Initialize Secondary Database | Copy Files | Restore Transaction Log

You must restore a full backup of the primary database into secondary database before it can be a log shipping destination.

Do you want the Management Studio to restore a backup into the secondary database?

○ Yes, generate a full backup of the primary database and restore it into the secondary database (and create the secondary database if it doesn't exist)   Restore Options...

○ Yes, restore an existing backup of the primary database into the secondary database (and create the secondary database if it doesn't exist)

Specify a network path to the backup file that is accessible by the secondary server instance.

Backup file:

Restore Options...

● No, the secondary database is initialized.

Help   OK   Cancel

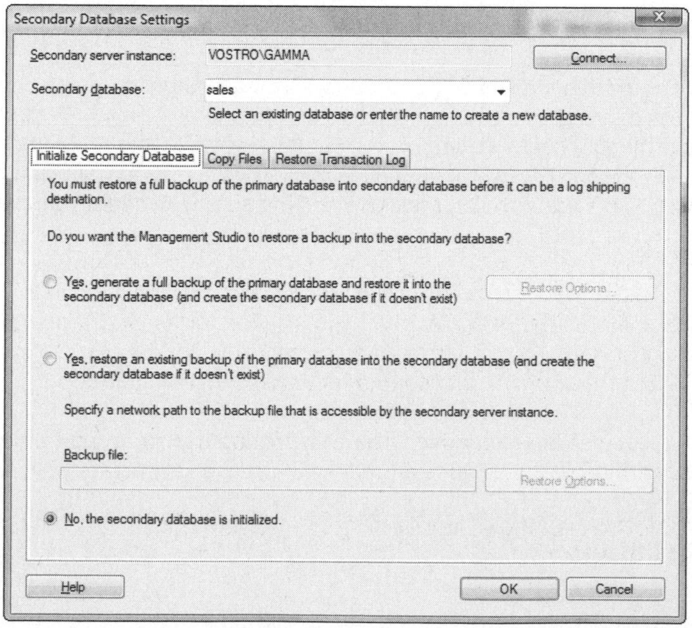

Figure 19-12: Secondary Database settings.

17. **Click the OK button to continue.**

18. **Repeat Steps 11–17 if you want to configure any additional secondary servers.**

19. **Click the OK button to close the Database Properties window.**

    SQL Server displays the status window shown in Figure 19-13 while it enables log shipping.

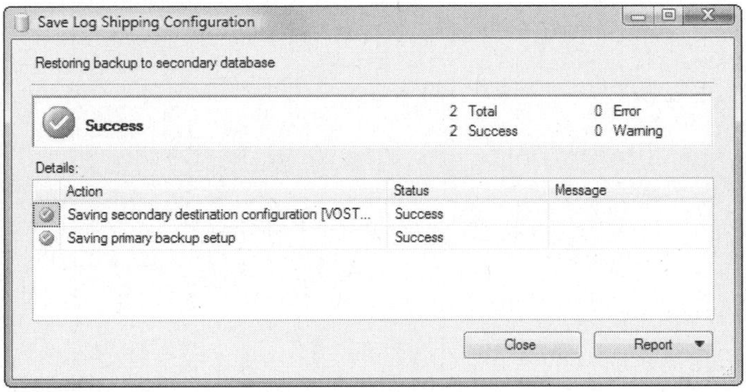

Figure 19-13: The Log Shipping Configuration status window.

Save Log Shipping Configuration		

Restoring backup to secondary database

Success	2 Total	0 Error
	2 Success	0 Warning

Details:

Action	Status	Message
Saving secondary destination configuration [VOST...	Success	
Saving primary backup setup	Success	

Close   Report ▼

20. **Click the Close button to close the status window.**

Failing over to a log shipping secondary instance

If your primary database fails, you may manually failover to a secondary database synchronized with log shipping. In contrast to database mirroring, there is no automatic failover option for log shipping secondary servers.

Before failing over, ensure that the secondary server has applied as many recent transaction log backups as possible. If the primary server is still accessible, you should perform a manual transaction log backup and apply it to the secondary server. This ensures that the secondary server includes transactions occurring after the last scheduled transaction log backup.

When you are ready to failover, issue the following command on the secondary server:

```
RESTORE DATABASE <secondary_database_name>
WITH RECOVERY
```

For example, to restore the sales database, you would execute this Transact-SQL statement:

```
RESTORE DATABASE sales
WITH RECOVERY
```

You then need to manually reconfigure any database clients to use the secondary server instead of the primary server.

Chapter 20

Implementing Policy-Based Management with the Declarative Management Framework

*T*he Declarative Management Framework (DMF) is one of the most exciting new features in SQL Server 2008. DMF allows administrators to create and apply policies that regulate the configuration and operation of SQL Server(s) in an enterprise.

For example, suppose that your business has a security policy that requires the use of SQL Server's password expiration functionality. You may use DMF to create a policy that requires this feature on all SQL Servers in your organization. You may then use that policy to perform the following actions (which I cover in this chapter):

✔ Verify whether a server complies with the policy (that is, password expiration is turned on).

✔ Apply the policy to a server manually, changing the server's configuration to make it compliant with the policy.

✔ Prevent changes to the server that would violate the policy.

✔ Record log entries when the server fails to comply with the policy.

Coming to Terms with DMF

Before you can manage servers with DMF, you should understand a few DMF-specific terms. These can be somewhat confusing but they're essential to understanding how DMF works. Be sure to take a few moments to review these terms before proceeding:

- **Targets:** Entities that you may manage by DMF. They may be broad in scope, such as an entire SQL Server instance, or narrow, such as an individual database, table, or login.

- **Management facets:** Collections of related properties of a management target. Some examples of management facets include logins, filegroups, servers, and stored procedures.

- **Conditions:** Collections of one or more clauses that specify properties of a management facet. Each management facet has many properties that may be specified in conditions. For example, the logins management facet may have conditions related to the login name, creation date, and password complexity enforcement, among others.

- **Policies:** Specify the condition that you expect a target to comply with and way you'd like to enforce that policy (the *evaluation mode*). Each policy contains one (and only one) condition.

Here's an example to tie this all together. Earlier, I used an example of enforcing password expiration requirements. If you decide to enforce that requirement on a SQL Server instance called MyDatabase, you use the following configuration:

- The target of your policy is the SQL Server instance: MyDatabase.

- The relevant management facet is Logins, which contains properties related to SQL Server logins.

- You then create a condition based upon the Logins management facet containing a single clause requiring that the `@Password ExpirationEnabled` field has a value of `True`.

- Finally, you create a policy that enforces your condition against the MyDatabase target.

Creating DMF Policies

SQL Server 2008 includes a number of predefined policies created by Microsoft for your convenience. For example, some of the policies included with SQL Server are the following:

✔ **SQL Server Password Expiration Best Practice:** Verifies that the SQL Server requires password expiration for every login.

✔ **SQL Server Password Policy Best Practice:** Ensures every login requires a password.

✔ **Database Auto Shrink Best Practice:** Verifies that auto shrink is disabled for all online user databases.

✔ **Data and Log File Location Best Practice:** Checks whether the data and log files are stored on separate drives for any database that is 5GB or larger.

In many cases, you can make use of these built-in DMF policies and avoid creating your own policies or conditions. However, if you want to experience the true power of DMF, you'll want to create your own customized policies and conditions that implement your organization's specific business requirements. If you simply want to execute predefined policies, you can skip ahead to the "Verifying policy compliance" section of this chapter.

In the remainder of this section, I show you how to create a custom DMF policy that enforces a specific business requirement: that all nonsystem stored procedures have names that begin with the prefix "sp_" and end with a non-numeric character.

Creating a condition

I mentioned earlier that SQL Server includes a number of predefined best practice DMF policies. In addition, it includes a wide range of conditions that you may use or modify for your own purposes. SQL Server does not, however, ship with a predefined condition that requires compliance with the stored procedure naming convention of the previous section, so I have to create a new one. Here's how:

1. **With SSMS open, expand the Management folder.**

2. **Expand the Conditions folder.**

   Take some time to explore the predefined conditions that appear in this folder. There are many useful items here, such as:

   • Auto Close Disabled

   • Database is 5GB or Larger

   • File is 1GB or Larger

• Not Enterprise Edition

• Recovery Model Full

• Windows Authentication Mode

Figure 20-1 shows some of the conditions included in this folder by default.

3. **Right-click the Conditions folder and select New Condition from the pop-up menu.**

SQL Server displays the blank Create New Condition window, as shown in Figure 20-2.

4. **Provide a name for the condition in the appropriate text box.**

You have plenty of space here, so try to choose a very descriptive name that will help you understand the condition later when you incorporate it into a policy. For example, I'm calling my condition "Stored Procedure Follows Naming Convention."

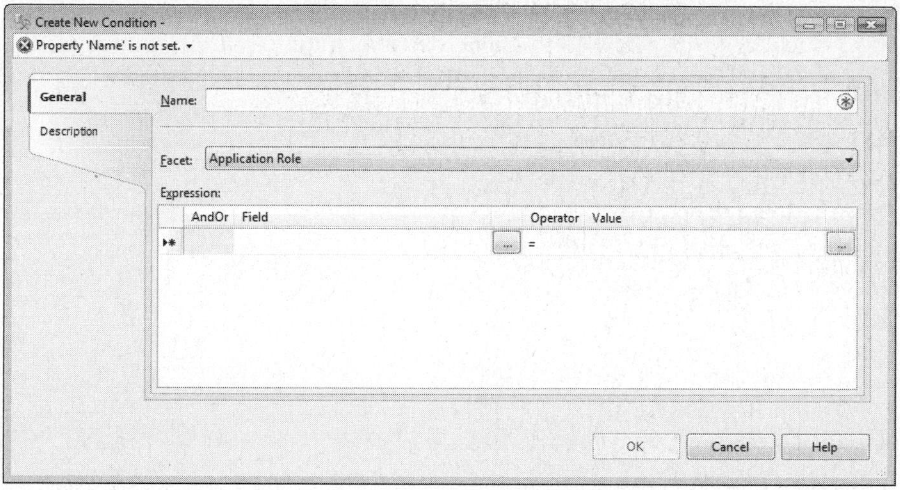

Figure 20-2:
Creating a
new DMF
condition.

5. **Select the appropriate management facet from the drop-down menu.**

   In my example, I'm creating a DMF condition for use with stored procedures, so I choose that management facet.

6. **Provide the field, operator and value for the first clause in your
   condition.**

   As I mentioned earlier, each condition may consist of one or more
   clauses. Each clause is a single, testable statement about a property of
   the management facet. For example, I want to ensure that all stored procedures begin with the three characters "sp_". I can verify this by testing the @Name field using the LIKE operator against the clause 'sp_%'.
   If you're not familiar with the use of the LIKE operator, see Chapter 7.

7. **Create additional clauses, as necessary, joining them with the AND or
   OR operator.**

   Many conditions may require multiple tests. For example, I checked
   only whether the stored procedure name begins with the "sp_" prefix. I
   still need to check whether it ends with a non-numeric character. I can
   do this by verifying that @Name is NOT LIKE '%[0-9]'. Finally, I want
   this condition to apply only to nonsystem stored procedures, so I must
   create a third clause that verifies that the @IsSystemObject field is
   False.

   In this example, I wanted to create three clauses, each of which is joined
   with the AND condition. If you need to create very complex queries, you
   may need to perform more complex comparisons. For example, you
   could perform the same check by testing whether the stored procedure name follows the naming convention OR the @IsSystemObject

property is false. To create this type of condition, you must first group the two @Name clauses by selecting them both. You do so by clicking each one while holding down the Shift key. You may then right-click them and select Group Clauses from the pop-up menu. Grouping the clauses allows you to join them together in an OR statement with the @ IsSystemObject clause.

The resulting condition window appears, as shown in Figure 20-3.

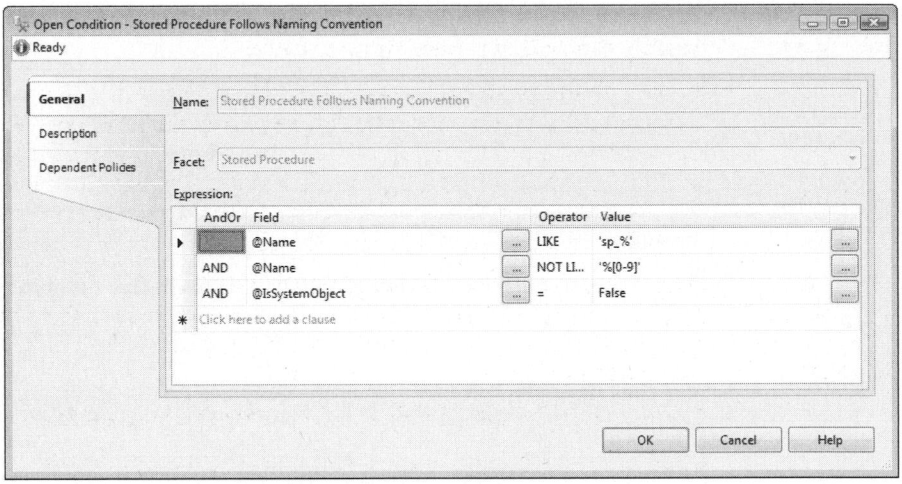

Figure 20-3: Stored procedure naming convention condition.

8. **Click the OK button to create the condition.**

The new condition then appears in the list of available DMF conditions.

Creating a policy

After you've created the condition that you would like to enforce, you may create a DMF policy object that enforces that condition against DMF target(s). Here's how to create a new DMF policy:

1. **With SSMS open, expand the Management folder.**

2. **Expand the Policies folder.**

Take some time to explore the predefined policies that appear in this folder.

3. **Right-click the Policies folder and select New Policy from the pop-up menu.**

4. **Provide a name for your policy by typing it into the Name text box.**

   I call my example policy "Stored Procedure Naming Convention."

5. **From the drop-down menu, choose the condition you want to enforce.**

   You'll find the conditions sorted by the management facet they affect. I found my "Stored Procedure Follows Naming Convention" condition under the Stored Procedure facet.

6. **Modify the policy targets, if necessary.**

   You may modify any of the target characteristics that appear in blue. For example, when I chose the "Stored Procedure Follows Naming Convention" condition, SQL Server allowed me to specify conditions to limit the types of stored procedures or databases that the policy includes. You may modify these conditions by clicking the down arrow icon next to the blue text.

   You may use conditions here to apply policies selectively. For example, rather than apply a policy to "Every" database, you could create a new condition that applies the policy to only those databases with a name of "MyDatabase."

7. **Choose the evaluation mode from the drop-down menu.**

   SQL Server 2008 offers four DMF policy evaluation modes:

   - **On Demand:** Does not perform any automated policy enforcement. It allows you to manually run the policy at your discretion.

   - **On Schedule:** Allows you to specify a schedule for policy execution. In this mode, SQL Server creates log entries each time the policy runs and detects noncompliant targets. These policies run using SQL Server Agent jobs. For more information on SQL Server Agent, see Chapter 13.

   - **On Change – Log Only:** Creates a log entry immediately whenever the database changes in a fashion that causes it to violate the policy.

   - **On Change – Prevent:** Checks the policy before allowing any changes to the database, blocking those that would violate the policy.

   For now, I use the On Demand evaluation mode. I discuss the other evaluation modes in the "Automated Policy Enforcement" section, later in this chapter.

Note that the Create New Policy window contains an Enabled checkbox. This checkbox does not apply to policies using the On Demand evaluation mode. For other evaluation modes, you must select this box, or SQL Server will not enforce the policy.

8. **Click the OK button to create the policy.**

Figure 20-4 shows the completed Create New Policy window. After you click OK, SQL Server creates the policy, and you may view it in the SSMS Policies folder.

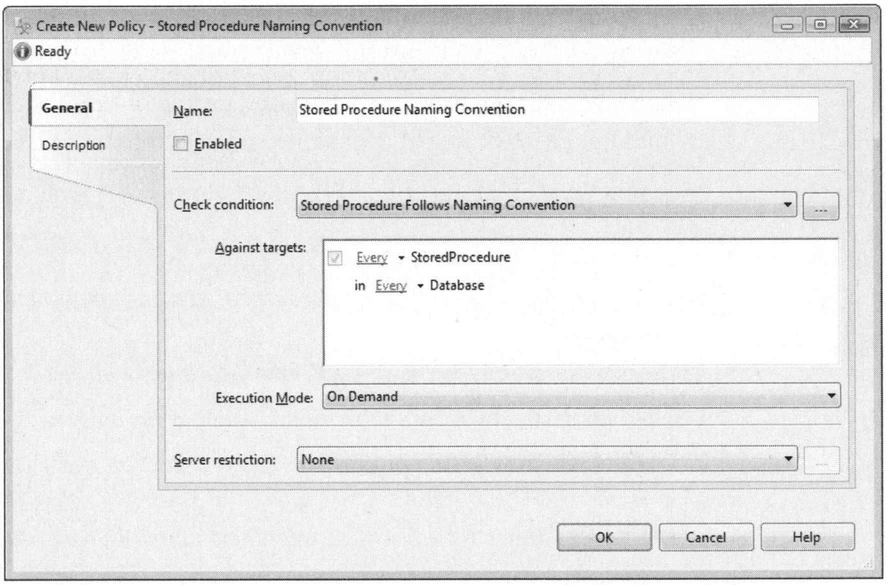

Figure 20-4:
Creating a
new DMF
policy.

SQL Server stores DMF policies and conditions in the msdb database. If you don't back up this database, you won't be able to restore DMF policies after a system failure. For more information on backing up databases, see Chapter 18.

Using On Demand Evaluation Mode

On Demand evaluation mode allows you to manually test targets for policy compliance and manually apply settings required by a policy to DMF targets. This mode does not apply to any DMF policies automatically and is a good way to get started with DMF.

Verifying policy compliance

The most basic DMF task you can perform is verifying whether DMF target(s) comply with a specific policy. Here's how you can perform that check:

1. **With SSMS open, expand the Management folder.**

2. **Expand the Policies folder.**

3. **Scroll through the list of policies and locate the policy you want to test. Right-click it and select Test Policy from the pop-up menu.**

4. **Review the results.**

   Depending upon the type of policy you verify and the number of targets, policy verification may take an extended period of time. When the check is complete, you may review the results. As shown in Figure 20-5, the results window uses a red "X" symbol to denote targets that failed the policy and a green checkmark to identify targets that passed the policy check.

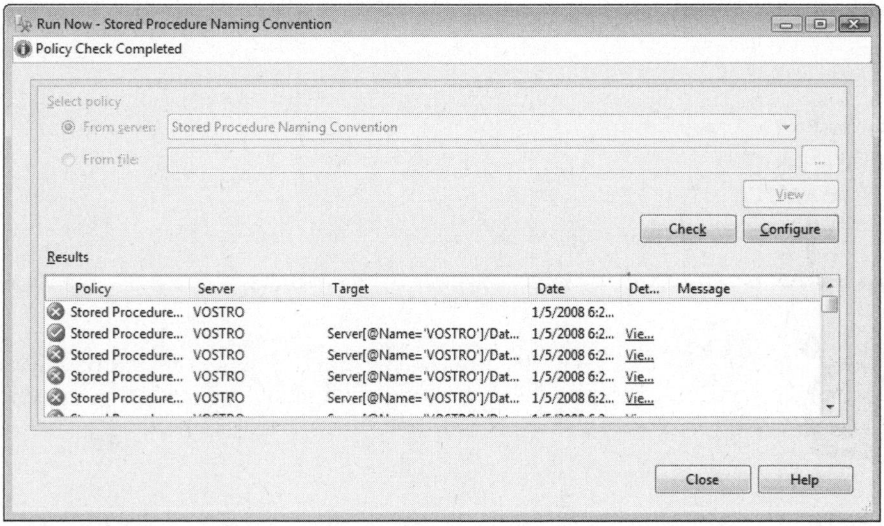

Figure 20-5: Testing compliance with a DMF policy.

5. **Investigate detailed results by clicking the View link in the Details column.**

   SQL Server allows you to view the details of the condition checked by the policy for a particular target by clicking the View link. An example appears in Figure 20-6. The Results Detailed View window includes a line for each clause in the condition specified by the policy and uses the red "X"/green checkmark notation to indicate which clause(s) the target failed.

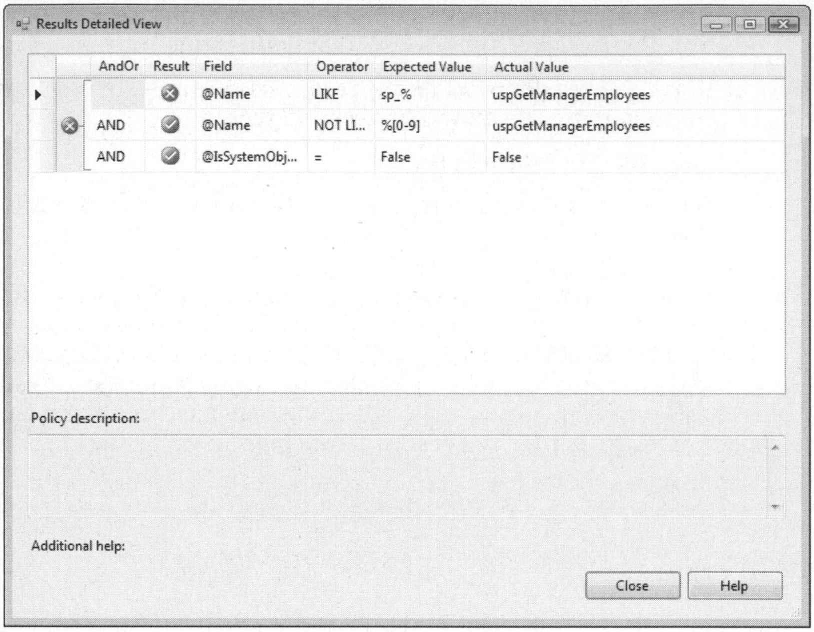

	AndOr	Result	Field	Operator	Expected Value	Actual Value
▶		✕	@Name	LIKE	sp_%	uspGetManagerEmployees
✕	AND	✓	@Name	NOT LI...	%[0-9]	uspGetManagerEmployees
	AND	✓	@IsSystemObj...	=	False	False

Policy description:

Additional help:

Close   Help

Figure 20-6:
Viewing
detailed
policy
compliance
results.

6. **Click the Close buttons on the Results Detailed View and Run Now windows to return to SSMS.**

Enforcing a policy manually

DMF also allows you to reconfigure a target to comply with a DMF policy.

Not all conditions may be enforced using this mechanism. For example, SQL Server would not be able to reconfigure targets to comply with the stored procedure naming convention policy I created earlier in this chapter. The reason for this is simple: Although SQL Server would know that a given stored procedure name doesn't meet my standards, it wouldn't know how to rename it to meet those standards without potentially breaking queries and applications that depend on that stored procedure.

Here's how to configure a target to comply with a DMF policy:

1. **With SSMS open, expand the Management folder.**

2. **Expand the Policies folder.**

3. **Scroll through the list of policies and locate the policy you want to test. Right-click it and choose Test Policy from the pop-up menu.**

4. **When the results window appears, click the row representing the non-compliant target you want to reconfigure.**

5. **Click the Configure button.**

   SQL Server attempts to reconfigure the target to comply with the DMF policy.

The process described in this section forces compliance with a DMF policy, but it is only a one-time change. It reconfigures the target to comply with the policy, but does nothing to prevent future configuration changes from bringing the target out of compliance or alert you to such changes. If you want to have this type of proactive notification, you must use one of the automated policy enforcement techniques described in the next section.

Automated Policy Enforcement

You may choose to have SQL Server automatically enforce your policy by using an evaluation mode other than the On Demand mode I used earlier in this chapter. Here's how SQL Server enforces DMF policies using other evaluation modes:

✔ SQL Server creates SQL Server Agent jobs for On Schedule evaluation mode policies. Each time the SQL Server Agent job executes, it verifies that the targets satisfy the condition and reports noncompliant targets by creating a log entry.

✔ SQL Server monitors event notifications to identify any events that conflict with On Change – Log Only policies and records them in the log.

✔ SQL Server uses DDL triggers to enforce On Change – Prevent policies, blocking actions that would bring a target out of compliance.

You may activate automated policy enforcement by changing a policy's evaluation mode. Simply double-click the policy in SSMS to bring up the Open Policy window and choose the appropriate mode from the Evaluation Mode drop-down menu.

When you choose an automated policy evaluation mode, you must also ensure that you enabled the policy by either selecting the Enabled box on the policy's General tab or by right-clicking it in the SSMS Policy folder and choosing Enable from the pop-up menu.

Viewing Policies Affecting a Target

SQL Server allows you to view all the polices that affect a target in a consolidated report using SSMS. To view this report, right-click the target in SSMS and choose Policies⇨View from the pop-up menu. An example of the View Policies report appears in Figure 20-7.

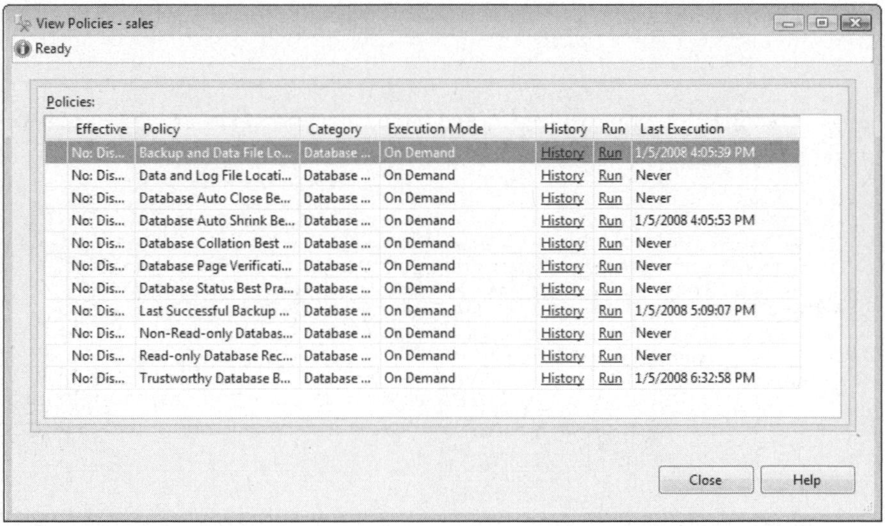

Figure 20-7: View policies report.

Part VII
The Part of Tens

The 5th Wave   By Rich Tennant

"Yes, I know how to query information from the program, but what if I just want to leak it instead?"

In this part . . .

A Part of Tens is a standard component of most
kinds of *For Dummies* books. In the first list of ten, I
describe ways you can keep your database operating in an
efficient fashion. In the second list of ten, I give you tips
for properly designing new SQL Server databases.

Ten Ways to Keep Your SQL Server 2008 Databases Humming

● ●

In This Chapter

▶ Monitoring your SQL Server database performance and logs

▶ Protecting your data through backups and database integrity checks

▶ Using the Database Engine Tuning Advisor

▶ Saving disk space by controlling the transaction log size

▶ Automating administrative alerts

▶ Managing large SQL Server enterprise deployments with multiserver administration

▶ Simplifying user rights administration with database roles and account reviews

● ●

Administering a SQL Server 2008 database can certainly be a full-time job! Throughout this book, I share some tips that will help you reduce the amount of time you spend on database administration and improve the effectiveness of your efforts. In this chapter, I summarize the top ten things you can do to improve your SQL Server database performance and preserve your sanity!

Monitor Query Performance

When it comes to SQL Server 2008 performance tuning, one size definitely does *not* fit all. You should monitor your database performance to watch for bottlenecks and tune the database to the specific queries that your users commonly perform. SQL Server 2008 provides two tools to help you with this monitoring:

> ✔ **SQL Trace:** Allows you to monitor the performance of individual queries running on a SQL Server database.

✔ **SQL Server Profiler:** Provides a user-friendly graphical interface to SQL Trace functionality.

For more detail, see the discussion of SQL Server Profiler and SQL Trace in Chapter 14.

Back Up Your Data Routinely

Something *will* go wrong with your SQL Server database at some point. This isn't a question of "if", but "when." Therefore, you should routinely perform database backups to ensure that your data is available in the event of a disaster or technical failure.

For more information on backing up and restoring SQL Server 2008 databases, see Chapter 18.

Verify Database Integrity Often

As with any complex information systems, databases may become corrupt over time. You can help prevent database corruption by using SQL Server's built-in integrity verification and repair functionality. The following DBCC commands help you perform this routine maintenance:

✔ DBCC CHECKDB verifies the integrity of your entire database structure.

✔ DBCC CHECKALLOC verifies the integrity of the database's disk structure.

✔ DBCC CHECKTABLE verifies the integrity of an individual table or view.

✔ DBCC CHECKCATALOG validates the consistency of the database catalog.

I offer a detailed discussion of database integrity verification and the DBCC commands in Chapter 12.

Tune the Physical Structure of Your Databases

The Database Engine Tuning Advisor allows you to analyze the performance of your database against various workload scenarios. DETA makes specific recommendations for improving the index structure of your database and provides you with the Transact-SQL statements you need to execute to implement the recommendations.

For more information on the Database Engine Tuning Advisor, see Chapter 14.

Conserve Transaction Log Disk Space

Transaction logs provide an important piece of the disaster recovery puzzle (see Chapter 18 for more about transaction logs), allowing you to restore a database to its exact state prior to a failure. However, if left unmanaged, they can consume quite a bit of valuable disk space. You can perform two tasks to help you manage your database transaction logs:

- **Log truncation:** Frees up space in the transaction log file for potential reuse.
- **Log shrinking:** Frees up space reserved for the transaction log file for reuse by other files.

I discuss transaction log management, including log truncation and shrinking, in Chapter 18.

Monitor Database Logs

During troubleshooting and routine maintenance, you may want to know about events that occurred in your SQL Server database. SQL Server records important database performance and error information in two locations for your review:

- The SQL Server Error Log contains specific database system events recorded by SQL Server. SQL Server stores this file on disk as a plain-text file.
- The Windows Application Log contains information recorded by SQL Server to the standard Windows logging facility. You may view the Windows Application Log using Event Viewer.

SQL Server offers a consolidated log viewer, SQL Server Management Studio Log Viewer, that allows you to monitor both logs in a single view. You can find more information on database monitoring and other troubleshooting tasks in Chapter 14.

Automate Administrative Alerts

SQL Server is a complex system and has many individual components that you'll want to track. You certainly don't want to check each of those manually on a daily basis, only to find nothing of interest.

To help alleviate this monotony, SQL Server provides an automated administrative alert facility. You may configure SQL Server to automatically notify you via pager, e-mail, or network message when specific events or performance conditions occur.

I provide a full discussion of automating SQL Server 2008 administrative tasks in Chapter 13.

Manage Multiple Servers

If you work in a large enterprise, you may have many SQL Server databases and servers running within a single environment. When you grow beyond one or two servers, administrative chores can become a nightmare. Fortunately, SQL Server offers a multiserver administration facility that allows you to manage multiple servers and schedule information flows within a data warehouse.

Administration of enterprise database deployments is beyond the scope of this book. For more information, see *Microsoft SQL Server 2008 Bible* (Wiley).

Simplify User Rights Administration with Roles

SQL Server roles allow you to create job-based permissions for groups of database users and then apply those permissions uniformly to all users performing similar functions. Doing so reduces the administrative burden of managing individual user permissions and helps ensure that you won't lose track of the permissions assigned to an individual over time.

A full discussion of database user rights administration with roles appears in Chapter 16.

Perform Security Reviews

In addition to using role-based user administration to simplify SQL Server user management, you should perform periodic account reviews to ensure that users retain only the level of access necessary to perform their job functions. The frequency of these reviews will depend upon your organization's security requirements, but they should always consist of several core tasks:

- Verify that each user account was authorized through your organization's access-approval process.

- Verify with each user's account sponsor (typically a manager or supervisor) that each user has a continued need for such access.

- Verify that each user is assigned only to role(s) required for the performance of his or her assigned job duties.

You can find more information on database users, roles, and objects in Chapter 16.

Chapter 22

Ten Database Design Tips

*P*utting a little time and energy into properly designing your databases can pay big dividends down the road when your database is in production. Well-designed databases perform better, providing users with more efficient and more reliable service.

In this section, I provide ten short database design tips that will help you design your databases well.

Plan Ahead

Planning your database before you implement it is one of the most important steps in ensuring a good database design. You'll benefit greatly by sitting down with the eventual end users of the database and designing it to meet their business requirements. Take the time to determine the appropriate fields for your database and group them into logical tables. You'll find that designing your database correctly from the start is much easier than correcting those issues after you've deployed your database.

I provide a detailed discussion of effectively planning a database design in Chapter 4.

Draw Before You Click

Database professionals have long relied upon the power of visualization to convey important design characteristics to others. Entity relationship (ER) diagrams provide a convenient, standardized mechanism to record database design decisions in an easy-to-read format. ER diagrams capture both the contents and structure of database tables as well as the relationships between those tables.

I discuss Entity relationship diagrams in depth in Chapter 4.

Choose Primary Keys Carefully

Primary keys play a critical role in the design of database tables; they uniquely identify individual rows, allowing you to differentiate records. If you choose a poor primary key, you may wind up running into problems when the need arises to have duplicate records with the same key. In some cases, you may not be able to find a natural primary key that suits your needs and you may wish to use an artificially generated identifier that's used only for the purpose of guaranteeing uniqueness.

I cover this topic in more detail in Chapter 4.

Select Data Types with Space Efficiency in Mind

When designing tables, you may be tempted to choose large data types "just in case" you have entries that require the extra space down the road. This type of decision making can become extremely costly as your database grows in size.

For example, consider the decision to use an `int` data type to store a four-digit product ID. Each record will consume four bytes for the product ID field. On the other hand, if you use the `smallint` data type instead, you cut that requirement in half, using only two bytes for this field in each record. Now, two bytes might not sound like much, but if the table contains 10 million records, that's a total of around 20MB of storage saved by that minor change to a single field.

I discuss the various SQL Server data types and their space requirements in Chapter 4.

Make Sure Your Fields Are Single Purpose

When designing tables, make sure you develop columns that have a clearly defined single purpose. You want to store only one type of data in each column.

Why is this important? Allow me to share an example from practical experience. I recently came across a database that stored data from credit card transactions. One table contained a field that combined several different pieces of credit card data, including the card number, expiration date, and three-digit security code. New regulations set forth by the credit card industry required that they no longer store the three-digit security code in the database. The design that combined three different pieces of data into a single column made this removal very difficult. Rather than be able to simply deleting the security code column, we had to deconstruct the column and rewrite all the software that interacted with the database to work with the new design.

Remember the Meaning of NULL

NULL means "unknown." It does not mean "none" or "zero," and it requires special checks to determine whether it exists (such as the IS NULL query clause). When adding data to a database, keep this in mind and ensure that you're using the NULL value properly.

I provide a more detailed discussion of NULL values in Chapter 4.

Normalize when Possible

Database normalization principles consolidate the collective wisdom of years of database design into some straightforward rules that help you design databases well. Making your database designs consistent with the first, second, and third normal forms ensures that you take advantage of this community knowledge. However, you won't always be able to fully comply with this advice because business requirements or operational efficiencies may require you to deviate from best practice. When you must deviate from the normal forms, do so with your eyes wide open, understanding the compromise you make and the rationale behind that decision.

I discuss the three most common normal forms in Chapter 4.

Manage Your Relationships

Databases naturally contain a good deal of related information (that's why we call them "relational" databases!). SQL Server allows you to keep track of those relationships automatically, using foreign keys to define relationships between tables at a high level. After you define those relationships, SQL Server can ensure that the database enforces referential integrity, requiring that any changes to the database preserve those high-level relationships between tables.

I discuss this topic in greater detail in Chapter 6.

Use Descriptive Names

Life is much easier if you use descriptive names for your database fields. Use a few extra letters, if necessary, to provide intuitive names. Anyone navigating your database will have a much easier time understanding the purpose of a column called "Item Unit Cost" than one called "D_IUC."

Although you should always try to use descriptive column names, it's also important to avoid including data in the name. For example, you wouldn't want to have a column in a vehicle dealership inventory table called "Car Color." In that case, the word "car" is actually data. What if, in the future, the dealership adds trucks to its inventory? Would you then need to create a new "Truck Color" column or rename the existing "Car Color" column? You'd be much better off calling this column "Color" and using a separate "Vehicle Type" column to track whether each record relates to a car or truck, if necessary.

Document Your Design

Many novice database designers are tempted to perform design work "in their heads," insisting that they'll remember the design down the road or that the design is simple enough to be intuitive. Those thought patterns are fallacies and have haunted many a database administrator.

Whether you're inheriting a database designed by someone else or trying to interpret a design that you implemented years ago, you'll find it incredibly difficult to untangle the mysterious web of an undocumented database. For this reason, be considerate to both yourself and your successors by taking the time to document your design with descriptions of database tables, views, stored procedures, and other critical elements. Keep that documentation in a location where those needing it will be sure to locate it.

Index

• *U* •

Notes

Notes

Notes

BUSINESS, CAREERS & PERSONAL FINANCE

Fundraising For Dummies
0-7645-9847-3

Investing For Dummies
0-7645-2431-3

Also available:
- Business Plans Kit For Dummies
  0-7645-9794-9
- Economics For Dummies
  0-7645-5726-2
- Grant Writing For Dummies
  0-7645-8416-2
- Home Buying For Dummies
  0-7645-5331-3
- Managing For Dummies
  0-7645-1771-6
- Marketing For Dummies
  0-7645-5600-2

- Personal Finance For Dummies
  0-7645-2590-5*
- Resumes For Dummies
  0-7645-5471-9
- Selling For Dummies
  0-7645-5363-1
- Six Sigma For Dummies
  0-7645-6798-5
- Small Business Kit For Dummies
  0-7645-5984-2
- Starting an eBay Business For Dummies
  0-7645-6924-4
- Your Dream Career For Dummies
  0-7645-9795-7

HOME & BUSINESS COMPUTER BASICS

Laptops For Dummies
0-470-05432-8

Windows Vista For Dummies
0-471-75421-8

Also available:
- Cleaning Windows Vista For Dummies
  0-471-78293-9
- Excel 2007 For Dummies
  0-470-03737-7
- Mac OS X Tiger For Dummies
  0-7645-7675-5
- MacBook For Dummies
  0-470-04859-X
- Macs For Dummies
  0-470-04849-2
- Office 2007 For Dummies
  0-470-00923-3

- Outlook 2007 For Dummies
  0-470-03830-6
- PCs For Dummies
  0-7645-8958-X
- Salesforce.com For Dummies
  0-470-04893-X
- Upgrading & Fixing Laptops For Dummies
  0-7645-8959-8
- Word 2007 For Dummies
  0-470-03658-3
- Quicken 2007 For Dummies
  0-470-04600-7

FOOD, HOME, GARDEN, HOBBIES, MUSIC & PETS

Chess For Dummies
0-7645-8404-9

Guitar For Dummies
0-7645-9904-6

Also available:
- Candy Making For Dummies
  0-7645-9734-5
- Card Games For Dummies
  0-7645-9910-0
- Crocheting For Dummies
  0-7645-4151-X
- Dog Training For Dummies
  0-7645-8418-9
- Healthy Carb Cookbook For Dummies
  0-7645-8476-6
- Home Maintenance For Dummies
  0-7645-5215-5

- Horses For Dummies
  0-7645-9797-3
- Jewelry Making & Beading For Dummies
  0-7645-2571-9
- Orchids For Dummies
  0-7645-6759-4
- Puppies For Dummies
  0-7645-5255-4
- Rock Guitar For Dummies
  0-7645-5356-9
- Sewing For Dummies
  0-7645-6847-7
- Singing For Dummies
  0-7645-2475-5

INTERNET & DIGITAL MEDIA

eBay For Dummies
0-470-04529-9

iPod & iTunes For Dummies
0-470-04894-8

Also available:
- Blogging For Dummies
  0-471-77084-1
- Digital Photography For Dummies
  0-7645-9802-3
- Digital Photography All-in-One Desk Reference For Dummies
  0-470-03743-1
- Digital SLR Cameras and Photography For Dummies
  0-7645-9803-1
- eBay Business All-in-One Desk Reference For Dummies
  0-7645-8438-3
- HDTV For Dummies
  0-470-09673-X

- Home Entertainment PCs For Dummies
  0-470-05523-5
- MySpace For Dummies
  0-470-09529-6
- Search Engine Optimization For Dummies
  0-471-97998-8
- Skype For Dummies
  0-470-04891-3
- The Internet For Dummies
  0-7645-8996-2
- Wiring Your Digital Home For Dummies
  0-471-91830-X

* Separate Canadian edition also available
† Separate U.K. edition also available

Available wherever books are sold. For more information or to order direct: U.S. customers visit www.dummies.com or call 1-877-762-2974.
U.K. customers visit www.wileyeurope.com or call 0800 243407. Canadian customers visit www.wiley.ca or call 1-800-567-4797.

WILEY

SPORTS, FITNESS, PARENTING, RELIGION & SPIRITUALITY

0-471-76871-5

0-7645-7841-3

Also available:

- Catholicism For Dummies
0-7645-5391-7
- Exercise Balls For Dummies
0-7645-5623-1
- Fitness For Dummies
0-7645-7851-0
- Football For Dummies
0-7645-3936-1
- Judaism For Dummies
0-7645-5299-6
- Potty Training For Dummies
0-7645-5417-4
- Buddhism For Dummies
0-7645-5359-3

- Pregnancy For Dummies
0-7645-4483-7 †
- Ten Minute Tone-Ups For Dummies
0-7645-7207-5
- NASCAR For Dummies
0-7645-7681-X
- Religion For Dummies
0-7645-5264-3
- Soccer For Dummies
0-7645-5229-5
- Women in the Bible For Dummies
0-7645-8475-8

TRAVEL

0-7645-7749-2

0-7645-6945-7

Also available:

- Alaska For Dummies
0-7645-7746-8
- Cruise Vacations For Dummies
0-7645-6941-4
- England For Dummies
0-7645-4276-1
- Europe For Dummies
0-7645-7529-5
- Germany For Dummies
0-7645-7823-5
- Hawaii For Dummies
0-7645-7402-7

- Italy For Dummies
0-7645-7386-1
- Las Vegas For Dummies
0-7645-7382-9
- London For Dummies
0-7645-4277-X
- Paris For Dummies
0-7645-7630-5
- RV Vacations For Dummies
0-7645-4442-X
- Walt Disney World & Orlando
For Dummies
0-7645-9660-8

GRAPHICS, DESIGN & WEB DEVELOPMENT

0-7645-8815-X

0-7645-9571-7

Also available:

- 3D Game Animation For Dummies
0-7645-8789-7
- AutoCAD 2006 For Dummies
0-7645-8925-3
- Building a Web Site For Dummies
0-7645-7144-3
- Creating Web Pages For Dummies
0-470-08030-2
- Creating Web Pages All-in-One Desk
Reference For Dummies
0-7645-4345-8
- Dreamweaver 8 For Dummies
0-7645-9649-7

- InDesign CS2 For Dummies
0-7645-9572-5
- Macromedia Flash 8 For Dummies
0-7645-9691-8
- Photoshop CS2 and Digital
Photography For Dummies
0-7645-9580-6
- Photoshop Elements 4 For Dummies
0-471-77483-9
- Syndicating Web Sites with RSS Feed
For Dummies
0-7645-8848-6
- Yahoo! SiteBuilder For Dummies
0-7645-9800-7

NETWORKING, SECURITY, PROGRAMMING & DATABASES

0-7645-7728-X

0-471-74940-0

Also available:

- Access 2007 For Dummies
0-470-04612-0
- ASP.NET 2 For Dummies
0-7645-7907-X
- C# 2005 For Dummies
0-7645-9704-3
- Hacking For Dummies
0-470-05235-X
- Hacking Wireless Networks
For Dummies
0-7645-9730-2
- Java For Dummies
0-470-08716-1

- Microsoft SQL Server 2005 For Dumm
0-7645-7755-7
- Networking All-in-One Desk Referen
For Dummies
0-7645-9939-9
- Preventing Identity Theft For Dummie
0-7645-7336-5
- Telecom For Dummies
0-471-77085-X
- Visual Studio 2005 All-in-One Desk
Reference For Dummies
0-7645-9775-2
- XML For Dummies
0-7645-8845-1

EALTH & SELF-HELP

0-7645-8450-2

0-7645-4149-8

Also available:
- Bipolar Disorder For Dummies
  0-7645-8451-0
- Chemotherapy and Radiation For Dummies
  0-7645-7832-4
- Controlling Cholesterol For Dummies
  0-7645-5440-9
- Diabetes For Dummies
  0-7645-6820-5* †
- Divorce For Dummies
  0-7645-8417-0 †

- Fibromyalgia For Dummies
  0-7645-5441-7
- Low-Calorie Dieting For Dummies
  0-7645-9905-4
- Meditation For Dummies
  0-471-77774-9
- Osteoporosis For Dummies
  0-7645-7621-6
- Overcoming Anxiety For Dummies
  0-7645-5447-6
- Reiki For Dummies
  0-7645-9907-0
- Stress Management For Dummies
  0-7645-5144-2

DUCATION, HISTORY, REFERENCE & TEST PREPARATION

0-7645-8381-6

0-7645-9554-7

Also available:
- The ACT For Dummies
  0-7645-9652-7
- Algebra For Dummies
  0-7645-5325-9
- Algebra Workbook For Dummies
  0-7645-8467-7
- Astronomy For Dummies
  0-7645-8465-0
- Calculus For Dummies
  0-7645-2498-4
- Chemistry For Dummies
  0-7645-5430-1
- Forensics For Dummies
  0-7645-5580-4

- Freemasons For Dummies
  0-7645-9796-5
- French For Dummies
  0-7645-5193-0
- Geometry For Dummies
  0-7645-5324-0
- Organic Chemistry I For Dummies
  0-7645-6902-3
- The SAT I For Dummies
  0-7645-7193-1
- Spanish For Dummies
  0-7645-5194-9
- Statistics For Dummies
  0-7645-5423-9

Get smart @ dummies.com®

- **Find a full list of Dummies titles**
- **Look into loads of FREE on-site articles**
- **Sign up for FREE eTips e-mailed to you weekly**
- **See what other products carry the Dummies name**
- **Shop directly from the Dummies bookstore**
- **Enter to win new prizes every month!**